Autobiographical Traditions in Egodocuments

Autobiographical Traditions in Egodocuments

Icelandic Literacy Practices

Sigurður Gylfi Magnússon

BLOOMSBURY ACADEMIC
LONDON • NEW YORK • OXFORD • NEW DELHI • SYDNEY

BLOOMSBURY ACADEMIC
Bloomsbury Publishing Plc, 50 Bedford Square, London, WC1B 3DP, UK
Bloomsbury Publishing Inc, 1385 Broadway, New York, NY 10018, USA
Bloomsbury Publishing Ireland, 29 Earlsfort Terrace, Dublin 2, D02 AY28, Ireland

BLOOMSBURY, BLOOMSBURY ACADEMIC and the Diana logo are trademarks of
Bloomsbury Publishing Plc

First published in Great Britain 2024
This edition published in 2025

Copyright © Sigurður Gylfi Magnússon, 2024

Sigurður Gylfi Magnússon has asserted his right under the Copyright, Designs and Patents Act, 1988, to be identified as Author of this work.

Cover image: EIE 077 1-1 (Front cover) © Einar Einarsson
MAÓ 429 (Back cover) © Magnús Ólafsson
Reykjavík Museum of Photography and Reykjavík City Museum

All rights reserved. No part of this publication may be: i) reproduced or transmitted in any form, electronic or mechanical, including photocopying, recording or by means of any information storage or retrieval system without prior permission in writing from the publishers; or ii) used or reproduced in any way for the training, development or operation of artificial intelligence (AI) technologies, including generative AI technologies. The rights holders expressly reserve this publication from the text and data mining exception as per Article 4(3) of the Digital Single Market Directive (EU) 2019/790.

Bloomsbury Publishing Plc does not have any control over, or responsibility for, any third-party websites referred to or in this book. All internet addresses given in this book were correct at the time of going to press. The author and publisher regret any inconvenience caused if addresses have changed or sites have ceased to exist, but can accept no responsibility for any such changes.

Every effort has been made to trace the copyright holders and obtain permission to reproduce the copyright material. Please do get in touch with any enquiries or any information relating to such material or the rights holder. We would be pleased to rectify any omissions in subsequent editions of this publication should they be drawn to our attention.

A catalogue record for this book is available from the British Library.

A catalog record for this book is available from the Library of Congress.

ISBN: HB: 978-1-3504-1317-7
PB: 978-1-3504-1316-0
ePDF: 978-1-3504-1318-4
eBook: 978-1-3504-1319-1

Typeset by Deanta Global Publishing Services, Chennai, India

For product safety related questions contact productsafety@bloomsbury.com.

To find out more about our authors and books visit www.bloomsbury.com and sign up for our newsletters.

Contents

List of illustrations — vi
Acknowledgments — vii

Part I Introduction

Culture and History — 3

Part II Historiography and Theoretical Framework

1. The Biographical Tradition and the Icelandic School of Microhistory — 25
2. Egodocuments in the Twentieth Century — 44
3. The Autobiographical Expression — 66
4. The Formation of the *Self* — 88

Part III The Autobiography and Life

5. Icelandic Egodocuments — 113
6. Egodocuments and the Environment — 132
7. The Autobiography and the Life Course — 158

Part IV Conclusion

Face 2 Face with the General Public — 181

Notes — 195
Select Bibliography — 233
Index — 246

Illustrations

This book contains twenty-four photographs taken of Icelanders' homes in 1930–45 by bank employee Sigurður Guttormsson of the Westman Islands. The photos appear throughout the book, with no captions, but this list is from his archive and indicates where in the country each photograph comes from. The photographic archive, in the keeping of the National Archives, totals about 230 images, and part of it is used in this book with the permission of the Archives. One needs to have in mind that Sigurður was not a professional photographer so many of them are in rather poor quality.

1	Grímsey	1
2	Úlfstaðir, Landeyjum	6
3	Keldumýrar á Síðu	20
4	Reykir, Ölfusi	23
5	Miðgrund, Skagafirði	31
6	In Raufarhöfn	42
7	In Hvammstangi	54
8	Grímsstaðir, Eyrabakka	64
9	Vallakot, Grímsey	68
10	Hólakot, Borgarfirði	77
11	A farm in Fljótshlíð	86
12	Bræðraborg, Seyðisfirði	93
13	Blómsturvellir, Eyrabakka	108
14	In Glerárþorp, Akureyri	111
15	In Skagafjörður	123
16	Glaumbær, Skagafjörður	130
17	Keflavík, Hegranes	136
18	Ormarsstaðir, Fellum	156
19	In Raufarhöfn	164
20	In Djúpavogi	177
21	In Grímsey	179
22	Öxl, Snæfellsnes	184
23	Snjóholt, Eiðaþinghá	191
24	Litli-Gjábakki, Vestmannaeyjar	192

Acknowledgments

This book has been a long time in the making. I have been working with the ideas discussed here for more than a quarter of a century. Egodocuments have certainly informed my entire approach to history; I have made use of these historical sources in a range of studies of eighteenth-, nineteenth-, and twentieth-century societies. Hence, parts of my arguments have been published in journal articles and books, as well as discussed in seminars, in many conferences across Europe and the United States, and in private conversations with friends and colleagues. All this academic conversation has had a formative influence on my ideas and thinking. Some of the material which is discussed in my earlier books and articles has been reworked into this book. I am grateful to journals and publishing houses for their permission to use some of the text in this book for arguing specific points; passages which have previously been published are indicated in the book.

I have opted to publish here twenty-four photographs taken of Icelanders' homes in 1930–45 by bank employee Sigurður Guttormsson of the Westman Islands. He spent his summer holidays travelling around Iceland with his family and photographed poor people's homes, in order to demonstrate to his fellow-countrymen that the glossy image of Iceland projected by the élite on ceremonious occasions was a distortion of reality. The photos appear throughout the book, with no captions: they are self-explanatory and come from various regions of Iceland (see List of Illustrations). The idea is in this manner to give the reader an insight into the society which the autobiographers cited in the book knew and belonged to. The photographic archive, in the keeping of the National Archives, totals about 230 images. Sigurður presented his photographs to the Icelandic Confederation of Labour, whose archives are housed at the National Archives. I am grateful to Njörður Sigurðsson of the National Archives for his collaboration in copying the photographs.

I also wish to point out that in the main text of the book I give the Icelandic titles of the autobiographies, and other sources, followed by an English translation in brackets. I do this so that the reader will get a sense of the Icelandic language and its cadences, and gain insight into the content of the works. At the end of the book is a Select Bibliography, which omits Icelandic publications, focusing instead on studies published in other languages about Iceland, as well as publications relating to historiographical development and addressing historical methods such as microhistory.

The extraordinary generosity of many colleagues around the world who have been in touch with me, first through the Reykjavík Academy and the Center for Microhistorical Research, the National Museum of Iceland, and later the University of Iceland, has affected the development of my thinking a great deal. I wish to thank my friends and colleagues of many years' standing: Davíð Ólafsson, associate professor of cultural studies at the Faculty of Icelandic and Comparative Cultural Studies, University of Iceland; Guðrún Valgerður Stefánsdóttir, professor in disability studies, School of Education, Faculty of Education and Diversity at the University of Iceland; and my former doctoral students Dr. Sólveig Ólafsdóttir and Dr. Anna Heiða Baldursdóttir, as well as many other students of mine, who have enriched my scholarly projects in so many ways. I have been working on this book in recent years both as a professor of history at the Department of History, University of Iceland, and as a visiting scholar at the University of California, Santa Barbara, California, 2016–17. I also want to thank Professor Hans Renders, at the Biography Institute at the University of Groningen, and his wife Lisa Kuitert, professor of book history at the University of Amsterdam for reading my manuscript and giving useful comments. The same goes to Dr. David Veltman at the University of Groningen who has also commented on my work throughout the years. I spent a wonderful time in Groningen in the fall of 2022 with all of them. I am grateful for all the support I have received from colleagues on both sides of the Atlantic in the development of this book.

I would also like to express my gratitude to my specialist in the English language—Anna Yates—who helped with the text, editing parts of the book, reworking, and translating some of the text. It has been extremely valuable for me to have access to her expertise and have the opportunity for interaction with her—a specialist who has shown my work, in this book and others published in recent years, both interest and understanding; Anna Yates is certainly in a class of her own.

I hereby acknowledge that the project was partly funded by the Icelandic Research Fund—IRF 184976-051 (in Icelandic: *Rannsóknasjóður*)—a Grant of Excellence for the project "My Favourite Things: Material Culture Archives, Cultural Heritage and Meaning," where I am the principal investigator (PI). Also, the book was partly funded by another project which enjoyed support by the Icelandic Research Fund—IRF 1393101—"Bíbí in Berlin: Disability Studies and

Microhistory – A New Academic Approach." Guðrún Valgerður and I are the principal investigators in this latter project. I am grateful for the fund's support for these two important projects.

We would like to thank my contact person at Bloomsbury, senior publisher of history, Rhodri Mogford and his staff, for all their help and guidance. It has been a stimulating and satisfying intellectual experience to work with him and the diverse set of people mentioned above. I also wish to thank my wife, Tinna Laufey Ásgeirsdóttir, professor of economics at the University of Iceland, and my son Pétur Bjarni, for their endless patience and support for all my scholarly toils. I am sure it has often been a strain on the nerves! I dedicate this book to the memory of my parents, Magnús Helgason (1916–2000) and Katrín Sigurðardóttir (1921–2021), for all their love and support throughout the years.

Part I

Introduction

Figure 1 Grímsey.

Culture and History

The Sources and the Book

What is an egodocument? Before answering this question, one might say that studying egodocuments provides evidence of the cultural values and practices of people who were growing up at any given time.[1] It is important to note that I make a distinction between "life writing" and "egodocuments." The former is marked by its publication process and by its focus on categories such as biographies, and in a way, it is a wider concept covering a diverse quality of written material, which contains personal expressions in any shape or form, published or unpublished. Egodocuments as sources are more confined to published autobiographies, semi-autobiographies, conversational books, diaries, collections of letters, and auto-fictions.[2] In this book, the focus will be on all the usual egodocuments in Iceland and elsewhere which historians have used in one form or another throughout the years; however, autobiographical material will take center stage.

The fruits of the Icelandic egodocument tradition are to be found in published autobiographies (where the author is also the protagonist), semi-autobiographies or memoirs (where the author is not the protagonist), and conversational books (where the cooperation between the author and the protagonist is marked in the text with questions and answers). A database which I created around twenty years ago with my student, the late Monika Magnúsdóttir, shows that from the latter half of the nineteenth century until 2004, 1,089 books were published in Iceland that can be categorized as egodocuments. The bulk of them were written by men, or approximately 85 percent. All the protagonists of the books that are under consideration here—which is 75 percent of the database—were born in the second half of the nineteenth or the beginning of the twentieth century.[3] I will discuss later some demographic categories related to the database.

To this list of research material can be added a huge body of other egodocuments—diaries, letters, and other personal testimony, much of it unpublished and hidden away in archives—that have formed part of Icelandic popular culture for many centuries.⁴ In these documents, one is more likely to hear the voices of women, especially in collections of letters and in the database created by the National Museum of Iceland, kept in its ethnological collection. This is a large body of material that has been built up systematically over the last sixty-five years in the form of questionnaires sent out to hundreds of informants throughout the country by the National Museum of Iceland. This material covers all conceivable aspects of everyday life and is accessible in digital form using a dedicated search facility. All these texts—the life-writing tradition and egodocuments—bear witness to lively literary activity and provide a rich source for the historian interested in investigating the relationship between personal writing and people's real-life experience.⁵

I shall also make use of a study of discussion in newspapers and periodicals during the period in question, which covers all print media—a total of nearly seventy different publications. These span the whole period, but most of them were published between 1875 and 1920. Some were published over a seventy-year period, while others lasted only a few years. To give some indication of the size of the sample used here, sixty-nine newspapers and magazines were published in Iceland between 1848 and 1898, according to an article in one of the leading Icelandic newspapers at the end of the nineteenth century.⁶ At that time, forty-eight had ceased publication, while twenty-one survived into the twentieth century. One new publication was established every year between 1848 and 1890, but from 1890 to 1898, three to four started up on average every year. So, toward the end of the nineteenth century, we see the beginning of a new era in the publishing business, a growth which has continued to the present day. This source material should give a reasonably good indication of how the public debate was carried out in the country and what it focused on in the nineteenth and early twentieth centuries. At the end of the nineteenth century, the population of Iceland was only 78,000.

All these sources have hitherto received precious little scholarly analysis and without doubt contain a wealth of information that will allow scholars to build up a much clearer picture of people's personal experience of life than has previously been possible, especially with regard to women.

This book is conceived as a colloquy about (a) egodocuments and all their strengths and weaknesses seen in an international and historiographical light; (b) the opportunities offered by this diverse flora of sources in historic research, especially all autobiographical writing; and finally (c) egodocuments as part of the material culture of the time, that is, the role of the book or the text (the written word) within individual households and how it affected the development of popular culture in the country. In this context, I have chosen to address the cultural background from which Icelandic egodocuments spring—*inter alia* the ancient Nordic culture and its ongoing influence persisting into the present— and the impact a source such as an autobiography had on people's daily lives.[7] In particular, I shall explore how egodocuments may be applied in approaching women's viewpoints in the past; many egodocuments allow little space for women. How is it possible to counteract the influence that males apparently had on such sources? My answer is to take the simple action of examining egodocuments and their development in Iceland through gender glasses, thus pinpointing their weaknesses and strengths in this regard. But the global perspective will never be far away in the arguments adduced in this book.

The reader will soon notice that I do not hesitate to step forward myself into the debate. This is because, in the first place, I have decades of experience using egodocuments in one form or another; and second, I have also created documents of this nature in my own life, thus gaining insight into how valuable a phenomenon such documents can be, not only for the person who creates them, but also in scholarship and other fields of human life.[8] For example, I have kept a diary since 1996 in seventy-five books, around 20,000 pages.[9] In this book, I wish to focus on the importance of the act of creation, that is, how these documents came to be, and their significance for the one who penned them. As soon as they let go of them, the documents are likely to acquire an entirely new life.

Society, Work, and Demography

After years of poverty and stagnation, Icelandic society underwent huge changes in the eighteenth, nineteenth, and twentieth centuries.[10] Some of these changes had their roots in contemporary political upheavals, both elsewhere in Europe and at home in Iceland around the struggle for independence. Without doubt more important, however, were the new social and cultural opportunities that were opening up to people for the first time in the country's history. The propertied classes' fear of any kind of social disruption was hardly a particularly Icelandic phenomenon; it existed in equal measure throughout Europe and in America. The political changes of the nineteenth century threatened the entire social and economic fabric of the Western world and promised to undermine the power of the moneyed classes in Iceland and elsewhere.

The most obvious characteristic of Icelandic society in the seventeenth, eighteenth, and nineteenth centuries was the sparse and scattered nature of

Figure 2 Úlfstaðir, Landeyjum.

its settlement. The local farming districts and their culture reigned supreme, dwarfing in influence the little pockets of urban settlements that started to coalesce during the period. The land was poor and its inhabitants were entirely dependent on the vagaries of the weather.[11] For much of the country, the eighteenth century was a time of difficult farming conditions, with things only starting to improve around 1820. The new conditions that appeared in most areas of human life in the nineteenth century laid the foundations for the even greater changes that were to occur in Iceland in the following century.[12]

The Island and the People Who Lived There

Iceland is an island of about 103,000 square kilometers located in the North Atlantic Ocean. It was colonized in the ninth century, mostly by farmers of Norwegian extraction, as part of the Viking migrations. By the eleventh century, the population had reached 70,000, around a third of that of Norway at the time.[13] Iceland was incorporated into the kingdom of Norway in the latter half of the thirteenth century, and subsequently, in 1383, it followed Norway when the country merged with Denmark. From then, up until the twentieth century, Icelanders were subjects of the Danish crown. Despite this, the people retained a distinct culture shaped by their harsh and isolated island environment. Notably, Icelanders spoke their own language, which by the later Middle Ages was incomprehensible to speakers of the continental Scandinavian languages: Icelandic remained close to the Old Norse brought by the original settlers, while

Norwegian, Danish, and Swedish diverged considerably under the influence of other European tongues.[14]

Iceland's isolation was somewhat alleviated in the eighteenth and nineteenth centuries.[15] The country became a focus of interest for a sizable group of educated European aristocrats interested in the folk cultures of remote European societies.[16] In his study of nineteenth-century political developments in Iceland, the historian Guðmundur Hálfdanarson tries to explain the attraction the place exerted over these foreign travelers, and what they might expect to see once they got there:

> Drawn to this northern country by their hunger for exploring the exotic, the upper class travellers certainly got what they were looking for. The landscape of the desolate island was unlike any they had experienced; scars of an unceasing struggle between the natural elements abounded and made large parts of the country a wasteland. Extensive tracts of lava, where only moss seemed to grow, black sand-deserts, hills eroded of all soil, and snow-capped mountains, served as constant reminders of the ever-present ice and fire. Furthermore, the harsh climatic conditions set their distinctive mark on the cultural landscape. Long winters and cool summers, strong winds and incessant rains rendered commercial grain growing impossible in Iceland and severely restricted all arboreal vegetation. Thus, the countryside lacked the familiar and comforting sight of fields or trees, further emphasizing the country's desolation.[17]

The country was almost entirely rural, with farmsteads scattered usually with long distances between them throughout the lower-lying areas. Isolation was the norm rather than the exception. Communication was extremely difficult due to the complete absence of roads and the frequent obstacles presented by glaciers and fast-flowing rivers. Each farm was, in this sense, an island of its own, often with minimal contact with the outside world, especially during the long, cold, dark months of winter. In addition, the frequency and unpredictability of earthquakes and volcanic eruptions, which repeatedly led to the destruction of grazing land and ensuing famine, made all life in Iceland uncertain and problematic. It is against this background of a constant challenge to survive everyday conditions, that we have to consider the individual participants whose lives are described in this book.

During the eighteenth and nineteenth centuries, Europe underwent a period of significant population growth—significant in various respects and with repercussions that were felt at all levels of society. This increase in population has been cited as one of the major causes of the chain of events that led to the Industrial Revolution and the introduction of capitalist modes of agriculture, as well as being the impetus for the emigration from European countries to the New World.[18] These changes occurred in Iceland in much the same way as elsewhere in Europe and the emigrations of the nineteenth and early twentieth centuries formed the material for great societal changes in Iceland.

The eighteenth century was a time of immense hardship: in the first decades of the century the population fell below 50,000 and did not increase beyond this figure until the second decade of the nineteenth century.[19] During the century, the country suffered repeated catastrophes in the form of epidemics, earthquakes, and eruptions. During the eruptions, much of the farming land was poisoned by layers of volcanic ash that led to virulent cattle diseases, leading in turn to famines in which a substantial part of the population starved, with mortality particularly high among the most productive members of society. By the last quarter of the eighteenth century, the country was unable to support more than a little over 40,000 people. Between 1787 and the end of the century, the population recovered rapidly and remained stable until 1830. This number of people, however, was barely sufficient to maintain normal life in the country and in many places it became difficult to effect even the most essential tasks.[20] For most Icelanders, life remained very hard for the first two decades of the nineteenth century. Thereafter, things began to improve somewhat and the population increased steadily as agriculture, fisheries, and trade began to develop.

A balance was restored in the nineteenth century as the age of marriage fell, the birth rate increased, and more children survived into adulthood. But as time went on resources became increasingly stretched; young people found it more difficult to obtain land to set up on their own and support a family and the age of marriage rose again, to about thirty for both sexes, consigning ever more Icelanders to a lifetime of bound service. A further factor in these developments was that for much of the nineteenth century climatic conditions in Iceland were tolerable and at times relatively good. There was little disruption to farming from natural disasters. Infant mortality fell sharply in the second half of the nineteenth century, largely as a result of improved diet and, probably, new ideas about breastfeeding and child rearing.[21] As a result there was a considerable increase in the population in the second half of the nineteenth century, a development that had a wide range of consequences for society.

One such consequence was the increased importance of fishing as a source of employment and income in the nineteenth century. The growth of fisheries put great pressure on the existing form of society, with the preeminence of farming communities and rural households forming the backbone of the nation. This old system presented few openings for people interested in making their living in any other way. By law, every person had to have a fixed place of abode and, if not an independent farmer, to have a place within the system of tied service. As viable farming land was limited, rural society was hard pressed to accommodate the increase in population. Existing farms were divided into smaller units and new farms were set up on marginal upland. The shortage of land led to an increase in the size of households.

Farmworkers who, under normal conditions, would have eventually established themselves as independent farmers, were constrained to remain in service. Fewer and fewer got the chance to set up on their own and live independently. The structure of society was thus put into a state of flux and for many the solution lay in the urban areas that were beginning to develop along the coasts of the country, or away from Iceland altogether. It was under these conditions that emigration to North America began around 1870. It is not unreasonable to suppose that one of its main motives was an attempt by ordinary people to break free of the stranglehold of those who controlled society, the landowning farmers. People who found their options severely limited in the rural areas of Iceland chose to move out and settle either on the coast or try their luck even farther away in the New World—in the land of the free and the brave, the United States and Canada.[22]

Despite the degree of tension and upheaval within rural society in the second half of the nineteenth century, ordinary people remained fettered within the system of tied service.[23] Only a small proportion of farmers owned the land they lived on; the rest were tenants who worked the land armed only with the sweat of their brow and without any but the most rudimentary tools and equipment. Most were sheep farmers and running a farm was a labor-intensive business, with production based on hand power alone. There were several heavy months each year during which work went on more or less day and night. In between, the use of manpower was patchy, making production levels throughout society very low. The working year was divided broadly between three different areas: (1) work on the land, that is, cultivation, haymaking, and other matters related to the upkeep of buildings and meadows; (2) animal husbandry and the accumulation of various kinds of supplies for the household; and (3) processing of dairy produce and wool. These jobs were distributed fairly evenly across the year, with one taking over from another without large breaks and often overlapping. This pattern was repeated year after year.[24]

This mode of production depended on the availability of a large and cheap labor force. Working people were obliged to contract themselves to a farm for one year at a time. This system of bonded service put severe constraints on people's freedom and extended to between 35 and 40 percent of the entire population of Iceland through most of the nineteenth century. Its primary function appears to have been to supply farmers with a ready source of cheap labor; in addition, it prevented poor and unlanded people from establishing families, since permission to marry was dependent on control of enough land to be self-sufficient. In its favor, it also served to provide a safety net for the poor, designed to ensure that everyone was able to keep a secure roof over their head and to prevent them from falling into destitution in times of hardship. However, the laws on bonded service were frequently applied with great inflexibility and severity. One significant effect was that the age of marriage remained very high in Iceland and a large percentage of each generation never managed to achieve the point where it could change its social status, especially as we move further into the nineteenth century.

At the heart of Icelandic society during this period lay agriculture, which was almost the only source of income and sustenance for the vast majority of the people. Farming in Iceland revolved entirely around livestock and the production of fodder for winter feed. The majority of farms were small and relatively unproductive. The size of farms differed considerably and was determined by the number of cattle the land could support. The number of farms had not changed for centuries, at around 4,000 "assessed farms," many of which were subdivided into independent or dependent farms. At the beginning of the nineteenth century, only 10 percent of farms were operated by the person who owned the land. This changed during the latter part of the nineteenth and the beginning of the twentieth century, when the church and state started to sell off their landholdings on reasonable terms in an attempt to bolster the underpinning of the peasant society and to prevent the constant drift of workers from one county to another. A further motive behind this move was to encourage farmers to break new lands and improve their farms. By around 1910, the number of those owning their own farms had reached 37.5 percent; by 1930 it stood at 58.8 percent.[25]

The Local Community

Independent farms formed the core of the commune (*hreppur*). Each commune contained at least twenty farms. The total number of farming units in Iceland in the eighteenth and nineteenth centuries was around 6,000, encompassing farms of all types—assessed farms (*lögbýli*), independent farms (*heimajörð*), and dependent farms (*hjáleigur*). The distinction between these types depended on their different duties to the commune. Social historian Gísli Ágúst Gunnlaugsson points out that the number of dependent farmers, cottars, and tenant farmers stood at around 2,200 at the start of the eighteenth century, in addition to independent farmers, but that this figure rose as the nineteenth century progressed. To give an indication of the extent of this expansion in the farming community during the nineteenth century, we can compare the number of households in the period in question. In 1703, Iceland had 8,191 households; by 1861, this number had risen to 9,607, the increase almost entirely the result of the growing number of dependent farms, cottages, and tenant farms. Dependent farms were always part of an independent farm, but with a separate farmhouse and operated by a separate family.[26] The farmers of assessed farms were responsible for paying the tithe for both independent and dependent farms and had to arrange the proportion of the tithe each farmer had to bear. The actual types of work carried out on the two types of farm were more or less identical: the difference lay in the size of the farms, a difference which undoubtedly "had far-reaching consequences in a country where a large proportion of the population was constantly struggling on the margins of subsistence."[27]

The central function of the commune in Icelandic rural society was to administer poor relief and determine if and where individual paupers qualified for it. By law, the provision of poor relief was the duty of a person's home commune, that is, the one where they were born. In practice, this requirement often proved highly problematic. In many cases, families and individuals who became destitute were forcibly removed from distant parts of the country back to their home commune. Individuals could, however, earn the right to poor relief in a commune other than their own after living in it for ten consecutive years. As a result, people on the edge of poverty were often forced to move when they approached ten years' residence in a commune because the local authorities were anxious to avoid any liability for new calls on their poor relief.

Poor relief and its administration were one of the most hotly debated issues of the nineteenth century. The law had remained unchanged from 1280 until 1834, when some statutory limitations were introduced on the transportation of paupers, for example, the enforced movement of pregnant women to their commune of origin was made illegal. But these reforms did nothing to change the fundamental principles of the law, that is, that those who needed poor relief should be forcibly removed to their home commune, and that those who received it were not allowed to marry until it had been repaid. Parliament tinkered with these laws throughout the nineteenth century, but it was not until the start of the twentieth century that any wholesale reform was undertaken. However much sympathy politicians might express for the plight of those thrown back on the commune, the effect of the law remained essentially the same. It was not until 1917 that major changes were introduced, and not until 1934 that those on relief were given the right to vote. Huge amounts of ink were spilt over the issue in newspapers and magazines.[28] In essence, the local authorities encouraged the independent farmers to evict their tenants if there appeared any likelihood that they might pose a burden on local resources.

There was a further aspect to the problem. Farms differed greatly in size and, because of the type of farming practiced in Iceland, they tended to be spread over large areas. Pasturing demanded space, which was one of the main reasons that village communities never developed in Iceland in the same way as in most other parts of rural Europe. When population pressure increased, as it did markedly in the nineteenth century, the tendency was to divide up the available land and establish new farms in marginal and less productive areas, especially on higher land closer to the interior. When temperatures dropped, as in the 1850s and early 1880s, the consequences could be catastrophic: farmers in these newly established areas and those living on small dependent farms found themselves unable to support themselves and their families and were driven from their land. Many were forced to apply for relief to the local commune and their families split up. As a result, the local authorities were encouraged to regulate even more closely the activities of the poorer sections of society.

Poor relief was seen as a great burden on society and the authorities often took draconian measures to expel poor families, often with large numbers of children, from their commune. It should be borne in mind that, when people became recipients of poor relief, they lost all right to participate in society as free members until they had paid back what they had received. In addition, as many autobiographies attest, turning to the community for assistance came at a severe emotional cost of shame and humiliation. Recipients immediately became second-class citizens. Huge stigma was attached to the word *sveitalimur*, denoting a person in receipt of poor relief. Writer after writer describes the struggle they or their relatives went through to settle their debts to the local authorities. Their desire to buy their freedom was often motivated simply by pride. But there were also practical considerations for people's often long and bitter struggles for personal independence, such as the desire to marry. One autobiographer, Hafsteinn Sigurbjarnarson (b. 1895), describes in detail the hardships his mother went through to be able to pay off her debts, as well as the satisfaction and relief once they had been paid: "Now I was no longer called a waif and a pauper, because my mother had repaid what she owed to the commune."²⁹

Paradoxically, the same independent farmers who collectively controlled the local government which often discouraged farm rental were tempted as individuals to divide up their land and rent it out. This was one of the few ways that an individual could capitalize on his assets and increase his wealth: it not only provided the owner with money for the land but in many instances the tenant was also forced to rent livestock. The economic historian Magnús S. Magnússon points out that "[t]he practice of cattle hire—sometimes with a rate of interest of 16 percent—became a widespread means to extract more income (other than land rent) by the landlord providing cattle for the tenant's farm."³⁰ This practice continued throughout the nineteenth century and was one of the reasons why farmers fought so vigorously against the spread of independent settlements along the coast where cottars could manage on much smaller pieces of land by supplementing their farming with fishing.

The Class Structure and the Economy

Despite the low productivity of each farm, the type of agriculture practiced in Iceland was highly labor intensive, largely because of the rudimentary technology available and the generally poor quality of the land.³¹ As a result, farming households remained comparatively large throughout the nineteenth century. At times when the population growth outstripped the demand for labor, the local authorities were generally ready to turn a blind eye when people with outstanding poor relief debts married and started farming marginal land. But for most years of the nineteenth century this outlet was unavailable and traditional farming society came under increasing pressure. Toward the end of the century, the pressure was relieved somewhat by the mounting exodus of people from the country to the coast. This, of course, created its own problems for the local authorities in their attempts to control the number of paupers and the activities of unattached wage earners and to regulate who could marry, and under what circumstances. The disruption caused by the population growth of the nineteenth century convinced the authorities still further of the need for tighter controls over family building. As Gísli Ágúst Gunnlaugsson points out, action was taken with the aim of both "maintaining the unit's highest production efficiency, and at the same time, keeping unemployment as low as possible."³² Legislation such as the poor laws and legal definitions of the social classes played a central part within this system of social control, working entirely in the interests of the taxpaying section of society. Farmers' representatives repeatedly lobbied parliament for stricter controls on marriage among the poor in both rural and coastal areas. The liberal government in Denmark, on the other hand, consistently refused to acknowledge the need for such laws, as they ran counter to their principles of granting their subjects increased freedoms. In the event, through the whole of the nineteenth century, little was done to narrow the great economic divide between those who owned their farms or were successful tenants and those who were at the mercy of the farming community.

Gísli Ágúst Gunnlaugsson identifies ten different groups within nineteenth-century agricultural society in Iceland:

> 1) Crown officials (*embættismenn*) (who were often farmers as well). This group can be further divided into several categories according to education, economic, social, and political status. 2) Landowning farmers (*sjálfseignarbændur*) who were not crown officials. This group can also be subdivided according to the value and size of land owned. 3) Merchants (*kaupmenn*) and artisans (*handverksmenn*). This was until the turn of the twentieth century a relatively small group, but grew in size during the last decades of the nineteenth century. 4) Tenant farmers (*leiguliðar*). This group can also be divided into two or three categories according to economic means, size of land, live-stock, terms of tenancy etc. 5 - 6) Sub-tenants (*hjáleigumenn*) and cottars (*búðsetumenn*). The position of these differed slightly. Their social and economic position was in most cases weak, but they enjoyed a household situation of their own. 7 - 8) Lodgers (*húsmenn*) and boarders (*lausamenn*). Although their legal status varied slightly, these groups enjoyed in theory, at least, a household status of their own, although (particularly in farming districts) they often resided within households where they worked. They could freely dispose their labor capabilities, live as day laborers in towns and villages or be seasonal workers in farming districts. 9) Servants (*vinnuhjú*). They did not enjoy a household status of their own and were forced to sign (although probably their contracts were often verbal) a contract with a head of household on an annual basis. 10) Paupers (*þurfamenn*). This group lacked several personal, political, and economic rights enjoyed by others. Paupers can be divided into sub-groups according to whether or not they lived (with the help of poor relief) in a household of their own or were cared for in the household of taxpaying farmers.[33]

Although agriculture remained by far the main occupation in nineteenth-century Iceland, many farmers who had access to the sea also relied quite heavily on fishing. Most fishing was done from open rowing boats that could be managed with a relatively small crew. Late in the century, the industry was revolutionized with the introduction of larger decked vessels powered by sail. The fishing season varied from one part of the country to another as cod migrated north from the south coast late in spring: in the north and northwest the season lasted from about April to September, with a break in summer for haymaking; in the southwest, the "winter season" as it was called ran from February to mid-May.

Inland farmers too, especially those in the south of the country, often supplemented their incomes with seasonal fishing. They left their homes in February and travelled to the fishing stations along the coast, staying on well into spring. In return for their labor, they took an agreed share of the catch, which was dried and taken back to the farm for domestic consumption. Often, the farmer was accompanied by his older sons and male servants, leaving his wife and younger children behind to tend the livestock. Fishing was treated as part of workers' normal terms of service at the farm, for which the annual pay was agreed in advance, with the farmer taking the workers' share of the catch. This arrangement had various advantages for inland farmers: it provided employment for the surplus workforce during the quietest part of the farming year, and it provided a ready market for some of the goods produced on the farm, such as butter and wool, which were bartered for dried fish.[34] Dried fish came to form an important part of the diet even on inland farms, used to tide families over when food supplies began to run low in spring.

Cottars or the landless poor also depended heavily on fishing. Through most of the nineteenth century, the local authorities attempted, with considerable success, to prevent landless cottars from moving out of the farming districts and settling on the coast. Permission to settle depended on control of enough land to support a cow. This land had to be rented from a landowner, and after 1863, landowners were obliged to obtain the permission of the local authority to rent land to cottars. An act of 1887 also required cottars to prove that they had assets of 400 krónur (a considerable sum at the time) and possession of land and household equipment, both measures designed to tie cottars to rural areas. As fishermen, cottars either worked on their own open boats or, more often, in the crews of coastal farmers. If fishing proved insufficient to provide for their needs, they took on work as day laborers in the surrounding areas or moved to farming districts for seasonal work. In general, the social and economic situation of cottars remained highly unstable and destitution was never far away: a poor fishing season could force them back onto poor relief, a fate that everyone was anxious to avoid.[35]

The rapid population growth in Europe in the middle years of the nineteenth century created a boom in markets. The increased demand for food, particularly for salted cod and shark liver oil, made fishing a much more profitable occupation than it had been up until then. Icelandic and Danish merchants had experimented with decked vessels earlier in the century but it was not until the latter part of the nineteenth century that such ships came into common use. These new, larger vessels could carry more fish and operate further out to sea and so exploit the richer fishing grounds surrounding the country on all sides. The change in actual fishing technology was minimal: work on the new decked vessels was still an individual occupation, with each member of the crew having their own hook and line and the catch being distributed among the crew according to traditional rules, basically the same as those used on the smaller oared boats. Despite this, the change from rowing boats to decked sailing ships encountered considerable resistance: certain conditions were necessary for the new methods to succeed, as Magnús S. Magnússon points out:

> Fisheries, on a larger scale than the customary rowing-boats could sustain, required a) good knowledge in both ocean navigation and fishing; b) fishermen to man the vessels for longer periods than previously experienced; c) high capital outlets, and d) a minimum of land-based facilities on private coastal land. Often these requirements could only be achieved through a partnership or co-operation of merchants, fishermen (captains) and financiers, which also implied that the risks were spread on many hands. The personal engagement of the Icelandic merchants was presumably a key-factor which spurred them to mobilize the available resources into modern fisheries.[36]

The decked vessels had little impact on Icelandic society before around 1880. They remained in use into the first decades of the twentieth century, when there was a further revolution with the introduction of motorboats and mechanized trawlers. A central part in this movement from oared boats to decked sailing ships was played by the Icelandic merchant-entrepreneurs. Several functions were often combined in a single person: as well as running their store and chandlery, they owned the new ships, processed their own fish, bought fish from smaller-scale fishermen, and formed the first stage in the export of fish to markets outside.

In 1854, all trade restrictions were lifted and henceforth citizens of all nations were permitted to trade in Iceland.[37] This had two important consequences: first, the growth in the domestic market encouraged more Icelandic merchants to set up in business, including farmers who started to band together in a cooperative movement in the latter half of the nineteenth century; and second, British merchants started coming to Iceland to buy livestock, especially sheep, for export to England. These British merchants paid in hard currency, something that had enormous significance for the development of the Icelandic economy as, up to this time, trade had been largely in the form of barter and the money supply in Iceland had been severely limited.[38] These changes provided the foundation for the expansion of the fishing industry in the late nineteenth century, led by some of the wealthier landowning farmers and the new class of merchant-entrepreneurs.[39] More importantly, the industrialization of fishing provided an outlet for the population pressure in rural society, especially in the last decade of the nineteenth century. From this point on, it became a realistic option for people who had previously been trapped in a life of domestic service to move away from the rural areas and settle on the coast, and this in turn provided the pool of labor necessary for the further expansion of the fisheries.

The Family

One of the main factors determining a person's social position was their status within the household.[40] The average family was a unit of production, reproduction, and consumption, and typically consisted of a husband and wife, their children, and quite often also foster children, relatives, and servants.[41] Gísli Ágúst Gunnlaugsson has compared household sizes in a number of farming and fishing districts during the period under study here. For 1845, he found that the mean household size (MHS) in five coastal parishes in the south of the country was 5.0, while in five farming parishes also in the south the figure was 7.9. This is much as one would expect, since the need for labor was considerably less in the fishing districts. During the next thirty years, and especially between 1860 and 1880, the population grew rapidly without new farms being established. At the same time, the authorities deliberately prevented people from settling on the coast through the strict enforcement of a series of laws aimed at maintaining the preeminence of the farming community. This, of course, led to an increase in MHS, especially in farming parishes. During the period 1880–1930, the MHS fell markedly in farming districts but only slightly in coastal parishes, the result of massive migration from the country to the coast. This change had other significant effects on household composition, most notably a sharp decline in the number of servants.[42]

Forming a household depended almost entirely on whether a couple could obtain land on which to farm. Land acquisition could take time; people could spend many years in service to others before they acquired the status and money to set up on their own.⁴³ As a result, the age of marriage in nineteenth-century Iceland was unusually high. As Gísli Ágúst Gunnlaugsson points out, "the mean age of bridegrooms was 30.8 years between 1890 and 1895 and the mean age of brides 28.2 during the same years. This was an extremely high average age at marriage by European standards."⁴⁴

The Icelandic household was strongly patriarchal, with the master of the household exercising absolute control over household affairs. He was the face of the home to the outside world and legally the only member of the household who could participate in public affairs. In practice, the farmer's wife often shared some—even many—of her husband's responsibilities, but only those that concerned domestic matters.⁴⁵

In 1746, an Edict on Household Discipline was issued, which made detailed provision for the relationship of the master with other members of the household, including bonded workers. Pétur Pétursson discusses the edict in his book *Church and Social Change*:

> The patriarchal order of the traditional farming society was legitimated by the ideological framework of the official religion, most obviously visible in Martin Luther's Minor Catechism. This book provided the basis for the religious socialization of the people, the preaching of the clergy and the pre-confirmation instruction of the children. Its social philosophy was based on the presupposition that there existed three ruling strata to which the common people were to submit themselves; the *Crown*, the *clergy* and the *master of the household*. The social order and any violation of this was sin and would be sanctioned by the proper authorities.⁴⁶

Children were raised by their parents at least up to the age of thirteen, and more often fifteen or sixteen. Learning how to survive the harsh realities of everyday life constituted a central element of children's education and they were expected to take an active part in farm work from an early age. This education continued after they took up positions of service, when, like all people who did not have their own household, they were required to commit themselves to bonded service within a household for a year at a time. Moving away from their parents and entering service did not change a child's legal or moral status. Between the ages of fifteen and thirty, most people had very limited rights and they were expected to follow the rules and orders laid down by the master of the household with unquestioning obedience.⁴⁷ People could, however, move from one household to another on the termination of their year of contract. The rigid hierarchical relationship between masters and servants was a product of the Lutheran Reformation and the centralization of authority that accompanied it. In the eighteenth century, the preeminent position of the master of the household was further reinforced through the principles of the Pietist movement. For most of the second half of the nineteenth century, workers in service made up 35–40 percent of the general population over the age of fifteen. One striking consequence of this social system was that, during the middle years of the nineteenth century, 40 percent of women aged between fifty and fifty-four had never married, most of them having spent their entire adult lives in domestic service.

Many Icelandic households included a number of foster children. Broadly, these can be divided into two very different types: "genuine foster children" and "private paupers." The first group enjoyed the same status within the household as the children of the head of the household; they were generally relatives taken into the home, either permanently or temporarily, as a result of some family crisis, for instance if their parents had died or were unable to look after them for some other reason. Private paupers occupied a very different world; they came from broken homes and, if the local authorities could not find any relative to care for them, they were often auctioned off to anyone willing to take them on. Since the local authorities were obliged to provide for the maintenance of such children, it was invariably the person who made the lowest bid in the auction that "won." Private paupers were expected to work hard and, in many instances, lacked emotional support of any kind.[48] Children described in the records as "foster children" often made up a significant part of the child population of a parish; for instance, in the records cited by Gísli Ágúst Gunnlaugsson from the years between 1801 and 1816, we find variation between 2 percent in one parish and 18.3 percent in another.[49] The records are hard to interpret and it is often difficult to determine exactly how many foster children there were at any given time: some were fostered for a short period with strangers, while others were registered along with a mother or a father in a household to which they did not belong. In reality, many of these children were effectively on their own.[50]

The number of children living without family support is not surprising when one considers the social predicament of people who were just setting out on their adult careers. This was the most fertile section of society and so tended to have many children.[51] They often started on a small farm, with the hope that, eventually, they might be able to work their way up the social ladder to something more prosperous. But their world was extremely fragile: death of livestock or a bad harvest could have a devastating effect on these people's ability to support themselves and lead to bankruptcy and the breakup of the family.[52]

In such cases, these families received little sympathy from the local authorities, as Gísli Ágúst explains:

> By splitting up families, the local authorities achieved several objectives: the reproduction function of the poverty-stricken family was cut short, a farm was made vacant for another family, support (and care) was provided for those members of the family who were not fit to work, and the working capacities of those members who were partially able to do so were utilized. Grown up and healthy members of the family were not categorized as paupers, but were required to seek employment as servants. This procedure also provided farmers with cheap labor, since many paupers were still able to perform some tasks within the households in which they were placed. Furthermore, the arrangement helped to maintain social discipline. The fate of the paupers was put entirely into the hands of the local governments. They organized the relief and tried to enforce the law, which among other things, made it illegal for paupers to travel around as vagrant beggars.[53]

Lastly, many Icelandic households included a number of more distant relatives. Gísli Ágúst Gunnlaugsson investigated two parishes, one on the coast, the other in a farming district, in the years 1845, 1860, and 1880. In the farming parish, the percentage of households containing relatives was 34.2 in 1845, 12.5 in 1860, and 25.0 in 1880. In the coastal parish, the numbers were considerably lower: 8.6 percent in 1845, 12.1 percent in 1860, and 18.5 percent in 1880.[54] These figures indicate that it was generally easier for people to provide for their relatives

Figure 3 Keldumýrar á Síðu.

on farms, where their often limited ability to work could be more effectively utilized. Additionally, it was easier in coastal areas for older people to establish or hold on to their own households or to continue to provide for themselves as fishermen or day laborers. Again, the figures are subject to distortion and hard to interpret. There are, for example, cases of more than one family sharing a single farm where it is difficult to ascertain the nature of the relationship between them. And many people who were classed as lodgers or boarders, that is, were free to dispose of their own labor, lived with the families with whom they worked, though, theoretically at least, they were deemed to have the status of constituting a separate household.

Contemporary debate may have had much to say about cultural and economic reform and the need for the people of Iceland to strive to improve their conditions. But the truth was that the opportunities open to ordinary people within the farming community were very limited in all ways. For some, a solution lay in the newly emerging urban centers along the coast, but for increasing numbers it was the prospect of a new start on a new continent, America, that captured the imagination. Rural society could no longer support the number of people living in it, and as time went on changes in employment patterns and culture became inevitable.

Part II

Historiography and Theoretical Framework

Figure 4 Reykir, Ölfusi.

1

The Biographical Tradition and the Icelandic School of Microhistory

The "Self" in the Icelandic Historical Context

In my research over the past decades, I have explored some of the firsthand writings in Iceland which I classify as egodocuments.[1] My initial focus in this chapter will be on the "travel book," which recounts some adventurous journey undertaken by the writer. It may be hard to distinguish between fact and fiction in these stories—the narrative is often far-fetched, to say the least. The first Icelandic book of this type dates from the seventeenth century: *Reisubók séra Ólafs Egilssonar* (*Travel Book of the Rev. Ólafur Egilsson*). The Reverend Ólafur (b. 1564) was captured in the Westman Islands off Iceland's south coast in a raid by Algerian pirates, known in Iceland as the "Turkish Raid." Many of the Icelandic captives were sold into slavery in North Africa.[2] Other examples of this genre include *Reisubók Jóns Ólafssonar Indíafara* (*Travel Book of Jón Ólafsson the India-Traveler* [b. 1593]) and *Reisusaga Ásgeirs Sigurðssonar snikkara* (*Travel Story of Carpenter Ásgeir Sigurðsson* [b. 1650]).[3] Professor Guðbrandur Jónsson, editor of the second edition of *Reisubók Jóns Indíafara* (1946), saw fit to point out in his foreword that "I see no reason to make an issue of Jón's tendency to exaggerate." On the contrary, he attributes to Jón many other virtues:

> The *Travel Book* demonstrates that Jón was outstandingly observant; and it is no less interesting to notice that he had an excellent memory—and the reader must not forget that Jón was nearing the age of seventy when he wrote the Travel Book, 35 years after the end of the journey. Despite this he remembers most of what he recounts so precisely that there is rarely any discrepancy.[4]

Guðbrandur Jónsson goes on to enumerate various sources which were available to Jón Ólafsson and demonstrates that he had a good overview of his journeys, although knowledge of exotic lands was generally patchy in those days.

Other writings in this genre include, for example, such famous works as those of the Rev. Jón Steingrímsson (b. 1728) and another by the Rev. Þorsteinn Pétursson (b. 1710) of Staðarbakki.⁵ Scholar Haraldur Sigurðsson wrote an introduction to an edition of the Rev. Þorsteinn Pétursson's autobiography, stating:

> The manuscript of the biography is huge, 764 sheets, in addition to some loose sheets—of which there were probably more originally. It is now in the keeping of the National Library manuscript collection, JS. 207, 4to. I do not know where Jón Sigurðsson acquired the book. No information is provided in the catalogue entry, and the manuscript itself offers no clue as to who its owners were from the death of the Rev. Þorsteinn until it came into the hands of Jón Sigurðsson. The Rev. Þorsteinn's manuscripts have arrived at the National Library from various different directions, which would indicate that they had been dispersed after his death.⁶

This story is an indication of how manuscripts are preserved and the randomness with which some end up in collections, while others are lost. Jón Sigurðsson, architect of the Icelanders' campaign for self-determination in the nineteenth century, was also a scholar and collector of manuscripts. He somehow acquired this manuscript, which thus came to be preserved in his archive in Copenhagen, where he lived and worked for much of his life. The story also indicates how extensive such self-expression in writing was in the seventeenth and eighteenth centuries, as the manuscript comprises 1,528 pages (Haraldur states that it is 764 "sheets"—i.e., twice as many pages of text).

Guðbrandur Jónsson also wrote the introduction to the autobiography of the Rev. Jón Steingrímsson, one of the best-known books of the genre in Iceland. The Rev. Jón Steingrímsson, known as the Fire Pastor, is renowned as an eyewitness and participant in the calamitous volcanic eruption of the Laki crater row in 1783. Guðbrandur Jónsson starts out by maintaining that curiosity—a so-called "vice"—is

> the basis of all human progress in all fields. All scientific knowledge—practical or otherwise—is thanks to the curiosity of mankind; without it there would be no knowledge. Man would be no more than a beast, and would probably sit naked, or scantily dressed in some garments of animal skin, with no fire, in a dark, damp cave, gnawing raw meat from the bones of wild animals, which he would have hunted bare-handed with no weapon—had divine providence not implanted curiosity in his breast, the spark of the divine, which drives mankind on to more and more discoveries. To decry curiosity is thus no less than blasphemy.⁷

This impassioned defense of curiosity served, of course, to justify an interest in knowing something about people's lives and how they felt. "One's neighbor is no less interesting," asserted Guðbrandur Jónsson, "than other natural phenomena, and knowledge of man and his nature is no less than a prerequisite for the possibility to maintain a healthy civil society, and to discern where people's habits and conditions require improvement. The concomitant inquisitiveness about the affairs of others thus also serves the cause of progress."[8] Guðbrandur Jónsson points out that the autobiography attained great popularity due to people's desire to learn things firsthand—and that the work in question was guided by the principle of truthfulness. All this argued, in Guðbrandur Jónsson's view, in favor of paying attention to this genre of literature.

The autobiography of the Rev. Jón Steingrímsson was a landmark work, in that it was far more outspoken and candid than most other writings of the time. As stated above, the book strikes a new tone in self-expression in Iceland, and the result is one of the most powerful works in latter-day literature.

In *Íslensk bókmenntasaga* (*History of Icelandic Literature*), the late Matthías Viðar Sæmundsson, associate professor in Icelandic literature at the University of Iceland, gave an account of the content of these books and their relationship to comparable writings from mainland Europe.[9] In a sense, travel books may be said to have constituted a springboard for individuals' self-expression, leading to the fully formed autobiography as seen in the nineteenth and twentieth centuries.

But we have not yet considered the literary forms which provided models for the biography. "The writing of biographies did not begin in earnest in Iceland until after 1700," writes Matthías Viðar Sæmundsson. He continues:

> although various genres of old Icelandic literature may be classified as biographies, the trail was blazed by the Rev. Jón Halldórsson of Hítardalur (1665-1736), writing *Biskupasögur* [Histories of Bishops], *Skólameistarasögur* [Histories of School Principals] at Skálholt 1552-1728 and *Prestasögur* [Histories of Pastors] in the diocese of Skálholt from the Reformation [in the 16th century] until 1730. Others continued to write such personal histories, but these were generally brief accounts or summaries. The most remarkable of these biographies is that of [scholar and manuscript collector] Árni Magnússon written by [his amanuensis] Jón Ólafsson of Grunnavík, in 1758-59, to which 'some few additions' were made until 1779.[10]

Indeed, a trail was thus blazed for an important literary genre enjoyed by Icelanders of different social classes in the eighteenth, nineteenth, and twentieth centuries. The biography became one of the most popular literary forms, providing a setting for the "þjóðlegur fróðleikur" (local tale tradition) in the nineteenth century—as I have explained in detail in my book *Fortíðardraumar* (*Dreams of Things Past*). Stories of interesting people, or of those who had experienced something unusual during their lives, enjoyed vast popularity among the bibliophile peasantry of Iceland, and that interest persists into the present day. Genealogy has always been a feature of the phenomenon.

Icelanders have been keenly interested in genealogy ever since the island was first settled in the Middle Ages. In the beginning, the role of genealogy was first and foremost a practical one: genealogy was used to ensure that certain families maintained possession of particular pieces of land. This was probably the main underlying reason for the writing of *Landnámabók* (*Book of Settlements*) and similar late medieval manuscripts. Over time, families became the fundamental units in Icelandic social structure and family dynasties reached their peak in the thirteenth century. The genealogical interest has lived on among Icelanders, even though the original purpose of genealogical knowledge has changed over time.[11]

The prehistory of egodocuments in Iceland, which lasts until the end of the eighteenth century, is consistent with the trends and developments in other countries. I am of the view that from that point, Icelandic literary culture diverges to some extent from that of Europe. This is especially true with respect to participation by the Icelandic peasantry: they may be said to have grasped the new thinking with both hands, and related it to their own sphere of experience and knowledge, from the beginning of the nineteenth century.

The nineteenth century was, for the reasons adduced above, a period of personal expression in a variety of ways. Paper, for instance, became readily available, and writing implements too were far more easily obtained.[12] Paper had, however, started to reach Iceland in the sixteenth century, after which the number of manuscripts written immediately increased. In the nineteenth century, most Icelanders could read, though fewer (particularly women) also learned to write. Increasing numbers of people became direct participants in written culture. The preservation of manuscripts is clear evidence of this.[13]

The progress of the scribal culture influenced people's possibilities for expressing themselves in writing in the nineteenth century. Two more factors must also be borne in mind when considering this history: first, the Icelandic peasantry had the advantage of familiarity with the world of saga literature— the sagas of Icelanders, legendary sagas, and chivalric sagas. Ordinary people could easily place themselves in the context of autobiographical expression, because their lives so closely resembled what they read in the sagas. While telling dramatic stories of feuds and bloodshed, the sagas also contained accounts of the lives of ordinary people, living much as they still did in the nineteenth century. For the average person, daily life in Iceland had not changed much over the centuries and so it was quite natural for them to identify with what they read. It is probable that many individuals in the nineteenth century found it easy to place themselves in a text—to place the self in the narrative of life. That did not require much imagination. But the existence of the model was important, and it influenced people's self-expression long into the twentieth century.[14]

Second, many educated Icelanders who had the opportunity to pursue university study in Copenhagen were influenced by international literary trends such as realism and romanticism. Both these movements certainly had an impact on the Icelandic intelligentsia's image of themselves. The worldview entailed by these movements influenced individuals' self-image and was first manifested in autobiographies of intellectuals and in due course in peasant writings. The distinction between the two groups—the peasantry and the intelligentsia—was, however, remarkably unclear, as both had sprung from the universal cultural background of the *kvöldvaka* or winter-eve gathering in Icelandic homes when the household sat together and worked at their tasks while someone read aloud.[15]

In the early 1900s, the publication of autobiographies boomed. It is fair to say that the twentieth century was the heyday of public self-expression as will be dealt with later in this book.

Scribal Culture

When the American historian Robert Darnton revisited his important essay from 1982, "What Is the History of Books?", in an article published in the journal *Modern Intellectual History*, he came to the conclusion that the study of the book had changed, among other things with the focus on the book people—those who in any shape or form had something to do with the book.[16] Darnton shows how the attention of some scholars looked past his own ideas about the development of the book once they focused on "the reworking of texts through new editions, translations, and the changing contexts both of reading and of literature in general."[17] By venturing off the beaten paths of book history, as Darnton puts it, one can expect to find new angles in this field of studies:

> Finally, I should acknowledge fields in book history that defy the urge to draw diagrams. Iceland had a printing press nearly a century before the Pilgrim

Fathers set foot on Plymouth Rock. But it turned out nothing but liturgies and other ecclesiastical works required by the bishops in Skálholt and Hólar. Secular printing did not begin until 1773, and even then it was confined to a small shop in Hrappsey. (I am drawing here on the work of Icelandic book historians such as Sigurður Gylfi Magnússon and Davíð Ólafsson). Iceland never had any bookshops between the sixteenth century and the mid-nineteenth. It also had no schools. Yet by the end of the eighteenth century the population was almost entirely literate. Families in farms scattered over an enormous area taught their own children to read—and the Icelanders read a great deal, especially during the long winter months. Aside from religious works, their reading matter consisted primarily of Nordic sagas, copied and recopied over many generations in manuscript books, thousands of them, which now form the principal collections in Iceland's archives. Iceland therefore provides an example of a society that contradicts everything in my diagram. For three and a half centuries, it had a highly literate population given to reading books, yet it had virtually no printing presses, no bookshops, no libraries, and no schools. An aberration? Perhaps, but the experience of the Icelanders may tell us something about the nature of literary culture throughout Scandinavia and even in other parts of the world, especially in remote rural areas where oral and scribal cultures reinforced each other beyond the range of the printed word.[18]

My own attempt—and that of my friend and colleague Davíð Ólafsson—has been to explain "the nature of the literary culture" in general, how new ideas were transported from one person to another, from community to community, and between regions—the role of "minor knowledge" in the development of the modern man. In order to achieve that objective, Davíð and I have looked to the rich manuscript culture in Iceland, as all archives are full of testimonies from private individuals about their life experiences. In our research, we have focused on what are termed "scribal communities." The term derives from the work of Australian bibliographer Harold Love in the early 1990s. In his ground-breaking study *Scribal Publication in Early-Modern Europe*, Love defines scribal communities as "groups . . . bonded by the exchange of manuscripts." Manuscript transmission, according to Love, had the important function of "bonding groups of like-minded individuals into a community, sect or political faction with the exchange of texts in manuscript serving to nourish a shared set of values and to enrich personal allegiances."[19] He argues that the routes by which handwritten texts travel from one person to another, based on personal agreement between the original supplier, the copyist, and the recipient, do not arise randomly but are more likely to coincide with

Figure 5 Miðgrund, Skagafirði.

preexisting communities such as a court, an extended family, a circle of friends, or a commune.[20] British literary scholar Jason Scott-Warren has since used the concepts "manuscript network" and "manuscript community" to describe similar phenomena: "Communities are brought into being through shared practices ... a manuscript community is a group of people who bond through the exchange of handwritten texts."[21]

Microhistory and Egodocuments

In large measure, an increasing appreciation among a group of Icelandic historians—microhistorians—can be traced to the wealth of popular sources—egodocuments—at their disposal, in particular autobiographies, diaries, and collections of correspondence from the eighteenth, nineteenth, and twentieth centuries. It was to this material that most of their attention was directed at the end of the twentieth century. From the start, interest in these sources centered on how they reflect the educational and cultural history of the country. Sometime in the middle years of the 1990s, I, for example, "discovered" a valuable group of sources for the life of ordinary working people of the nineteenth century, in the writings of the brothers Halldór and Níels Jónsson from the extreme northwest of Iceland. The brothers were prolific writers of diaries and letters and copiers of text from an early age until they passed away. They both left behind enormous amounts of written material which provided me with an opportunity to study their life courses in great detail. The research on this material led me to look in depth at the work of the Italian School of Microhistory and to the realization that the ideology and working methodology of the Italian microhistorians had particular relevance to the material I was working on. In 1997, the fruits of this research appeared in the book *Menntun, ást og sorg* (*Education, Love, and Grief*), the first historical study in Icelandic in which the methods of microhistory are applied systematically and to deliberate effect with the use of egodocuments.[22] In a collaborative study with my students, we continued to develop and apply microhistorical methods in the context of Icelandic cultural history.[23] An attempt was made to address the question of how historians can make the best use of egodocuments which, though difficult, and at the time in some ways unorthodox, have the magical power of opening up completely new vistas on societies that often challenge conventional wisdom among established historians.[24] This was followed by a spate of research into Icelandic manuscript collections conducted by a diverse group of scholars from various areas of the humanities.

One of the most important contributions to the development of microhistory in Iceland came from Davíð Ólafsson, who wrote his doctoral thesis at St. Andrews University, Scotland, about one of the most enthusiastic scribes of his time: Sighvatur Grímsson of Borgarfjörður.[25] Sighvatur's diaries hold a special place among the 300 preserved from the eighteenth and nineteenth centuries and the first decades of the twentieth century at the Manuscript Department of the National Library of Iceland, which Davíð has studied and published his findings recently.[26] Sighvatur kept his diary for sixty-seven years, first as a farmhand and later as a poor but independent tenant farmer. There, he recorded his literary activities over these almost seven decades, despite the daily entries being neither long nor detailed. Still, the diaries provide abundant information on the literary culture and manuscript circulation in his local community. Davíð Ólafsson's research on Sighvatur Grímsson's voluminous archive, together with my own work on Halldór and Níels Jónsson and Magnús Hj. Magnússon— another scribe from the same area of the country and the same time period— which I published in 1998, marked the start of our extensive research on the manuscript culture in Iceland from the modern period.[27] The writings of these men, as well as other "barefoot historians," as we refer to these scribes of modest means, are characterized by what we have called "minor knowledge."[28] By this, we mean material that has been largely ignored by the international academic world, which has tended to work primarily with sources that bear directly on the formal institutions of society.[29] Even when the focus has been on ordinary people and their lives, most of the attention has generally been directed to the formal framework that encompassed those lives.[30] It is difficult to accommodate Sighvatur and his fellows into work carried out with these kinds of research emphases—to find the right pigeonholes under which to file the products of their minds, the right names to put on the categories into which they might fit. Even in the context of "local knowledge," on their own home soil, they proved troublesome and inscrutable to the academic world, since the knowledge to be found there, when all is said and done, was classified and understood on the basis of the grand narrative—on the basis of emphases and analytical models that came from the international perspectives of traditional historical scholarship.

Manuscript Culture of the Modern Era

Set against the remarkable and internationally recognized manuscript and literary culture of medieval Iceland, the handwritten material of later times has tended to be regarded as second-class stuff—in a different league. Icelandic archives are full to bursting of material produced and circulated throughout the modern age, from the sixteenth century up to comparatively recent times. Until very recently, this material has attracted almost no academic interest.[31] Apart from the prestigious ambiance that is attached to the medieval heritage, there are other reasons for the neglect shown by professional historians to these manuscripts from more recent times. At the time when the formal collection of manuscripts and documents was starting in earnest, at the end of the nineteenth and the beginning of the twentieth century, the driving force behind the archival movement came from men whose origins lay in the very rural culture that had produced the barefoot historians—and, in many cases, were the same men themselves. They had a "gut feeling" for the importance of this material—it was an integral part of their lives and culture—and they were determined to ensure its preservation. But once the manuscripts had been removed from the hands of the common people of Iceland, that is, the people who had circulated them for information and entertainment, and into formal repositories, a sad and somewhat ignominious fate awaited them.

First, the material often lay in the archives, miscatalogued and inaccessible. Generally, the fault lay with the lack of staff and their limited expertise and training. Even in the place where manuscripts of this kind might have expected to receive the best care and treatment, the Manuscript Department of the National and University Library of Iceland, until recently conditions have left much to be desired. Second, as the twentieth century progressed a distinct rift occurred between, on the one hand, the popular culture that had had a formative influence on national life in Iceland in general, and, on the other, the world of scholarship. In the latter part of the twentieth century, Icelanders tended to be very anxious to throw off their traditional isolation and become part of the greater world outside, and this is also true as much for academic matters as elsewhere; Icelandic academics have in general fallen over themselves to embrace international currents in the sciences and humanities. So, there was simply no intellectual room for material like that which had emanated from the pens of popular scholars, and it tended to be regarded in the ways described above, as unfit for scholarly purposes.

Among the tasks undertaken by some Icelandic microhistorians over the last twenty-five years has been to identify and classify exactly what kinds of sources the manuscript collections contain. An example of this is the cataloguing and analysis done by Davíð Ólafsson, then an MA student in the history department of the University of Iceland, of the approximately 300 diaries preserved in the national manuscript collection. His research project was later turned into a book in which Davíð analyzes the development of diary writing in the country.[32] Another recent piece of research, carried out by Guðný Hallgrímsdóttir, has revealed that women have lost out significantly in the classification of sources—they have been systematically underrepresented in the figures, as will be discussed in Chapter 6.

A comparable project titled the Perdita Project: Early Modern Women's Manuscript Compilations has been carried out by a team of scholars based at Nottingham Trent University and Warwick University in England with the aim of creating a database of women's manuscripts from various parts of the world.[33] Guðný's identification of this "new" material and Davíð's work on the stores of Icelandic diaries, their nature and scope have revolutionized the ideas of Icelandic historians on the position of the individual in history and the approaches open to historians in researching such matters. Guðný Hallgrímsdóttir published a monograph in the book series *Sýnisbók íslenskrar alþýðumenningar* (Anthology of Icelandic Popular Culture) on one of the poor women whose testimonies she uncovered at the Manuscript Department from the middle of the eighteenth century.[34] In her work, she employs the methods of microhistory in a highly resourceful manner, bringing together in her analysis public documents, court records, demographical sources, and egodocuments, to draw up a very clear picture of the conditions of a working woman who had to fight for her existence in the male-dominated society of the nineteenth century.

The situation with diaries and women's manuscripts as historical sources is not unique; similar comments apply to other types of egodocuments. People in Iceland have in truth been aware of these egodocuments for decades. They have indeed sometimes been used for historiographical purposes—just as in international scholarship—but mainly in the context of work on named individuals, that is, in work done in the spirit of traditionalist-celebrant history (the history of "great men"). However, until very recently, their use among social historians and advocates of the new cultural history has been limited, as will be discussed later in this book. This changed with the arrival of microhistory, for example, into the Icelandic academic environment. A large part of the work of microhistorians in Iceland has been involved in coming to grips with egodocuments and comparable material—their validity as sources and how to use them. What precisely are we to make of sources produced by ordinary working men and women, who seem to have been driven by an urge to record their observations on life and existence or to copy out material that in some way gave their lives meaning, like the barefoot historians?[35]

A New Side of Microhistorical Development

Around the turn of the century, the debate concerning the significance of microhistorical methods entered a new phase among historians in Iceland, and in particular the question of how they could best be used to further historical study within the local setting—how they might open up new and unforeseen ways of addressing important issues in the lives of ordinary people. This led to a new phase in the development of these intellectual experiments. There was a determined attempt to move away from the traditional approach of microhistory and to look at it in a critical light. Behind this move was a dissatisfaction with the direction that microhistory had taken (or had failed to take) in the world of scholarship, particularly on my own part. As I saw it, the lack of interest shown by many scholars in the findings of the microhistorians was in large part the fault of the microhistorians themselves: they had been too timid to take the final step away from traditional history and to shift the main focus onto the individual and his/her part in history, and in doing so had failed to appreciate the potential gains to be won from an in-depth analysis of small units.[36] Their continuing perceived need to relate their subjects to bigger wholes (contextualization) resulted in microhistorical research being treated as an entertaining "optional extra" to "real history," rather than as an important and independent contribution to the advance of historical learning. I decided to take on the challenge of looking into the possibilities that might lie in the small units themselves and whether the knowledge that might come from them could, on its own, help us to better understand man's position in the world.[37]

Not to put too fine a point on it, these ideas on "the singularization of history" met with a chilly reception from many historians and found few to support them.[38] Just recently, two archaeologists—Dr. Charles Orser, Jr., and Dr. Kristján Mímisson—have shown interest in the singularization concept, and in fact, three PhD dissertations have taken the phenomenon a step further and used it in a very innovative way.[39]

The approach to the past developed by many Icelandic microhistorians has radically changed our understanding of the fates of ordinary people and their shaping of their environment. The research methods applied have provided opportunities for discussion about the past on the level of what might be termed "in-between spaces"—gray areas that open up between the institutions themselves and the people connected with them. Rather than simply assume that communications between the two are always "one way," from the institutions to the people, who hence become almost passive tools in their hands, devoid of will, we can identify a "discourse" within society that takes place within these "in-between spaces." Using this approach, we felt that we had managed to distinguish ways that made it possible for ordinary people to exert a genuine influence on the workings of the institutions through their ideas and actions.[40] This is what Davíð Ólafsson and I have tried to show in many of our studies—that the activities of the popular scribes of Icelandic peasant culture were an essential factor in the education and culture of the people of Iceland, working in parallel with the institutions that ostensibly directed these areas of society, with each influencing and being influenced by the other. Without the unique contribution of these people, which was based on unremitting toil and dedication to their self-appointed functions, we feel it inconceivable that Icelandic peasant culture would have been able to operate and flourish in the way that it did. The networks of contacts these independent peasant scholars built up extended far and wide and created much deeper and more varied connections within society than emerge from a purely institutional approach to the development of Icelandic society.

Our primary aim of a paper we published in 2012 in the Italian journal *Quaderni storici* was to present a picture of the activities of the "barefoot historians" of Iceland—the kinds of materials they worked on, how the networks that linked them operated, and how they and their work were received among their contemporaries.⁴¹ As yet, we have only managed to scratch the surface of this remarkable scribal culture; there is still a very long way to go. Before us lies the task of identifying this "minor knowledge" and analyzing what it has to offer, the kinds of knowledge it encompasses, and what effects it may have had on human life in the areas where it flourished. This we did in a book which was published by Routledge in 2017. Continuing research will allow us to look further and more precisely into the influences the manuscript reading material had on people's thoughts and actions. We anticipate that it will be possible to specify in much greater detail how this informal institution of scribal culture operated and how it interacted with popular culture in Iceland in general. This line of research promises to be particularly rewarding since, at this point in the history of Iceland, the formal institutions of education and culture were particularly weak. This weakness left room for another, informal structure to operate, a structure that was more closely shaped by and adapted to the people who came in contact with it. Working together and feeding off each other, the two—the official and the unofficial—managed to engender an unusual cultural ferment in a society that was almost entirely lacking in formal infrastructure but produced an astonishing amount of material that can be categorized as egodocuments.

Again, a New Beginning

A result of the changes discussed above is that in recent times scholars have utilized egodocuments from various angles and provided an opening for the multivocality of the sources to be fully appreciated. This historiographical development has meant, for example, that the methods of microhistory have been reinvigorated at the end of the twentieth century and in the early twenty-first century. Microhistory has been assigned far greater weight, because the attitudes discussed in the last section have fostered the use of methods that could elevate the worldview that egodocuments can create.⁴² In this environment, I developed the methodology the "singularization of history" discussed above. The general idea of the "singularization" method is based on the following: the model looks inward and studies all aspects in close detail, bringing out the nuances of the events and phenomena we choose to investigate.⁴³ The idea is that the focus will always be fixed on the matter in hand and on that alone: one egodocument or more—the focus is always on the subject matter under investigation. The ideology consists in researching with great precision each and every fragment connected with the matter in hand for which there are sources and in bringing up for consideration all possible means of interpretation that bear directly on the material. The main point here is both to study with the utmost thoroughness the material directly relating to the subject—to examine every detail exhaustively—and to strive to bring into the study the maximum of material that relates to the subject from its immediate environment. Such efforts often open doors to unexpected connections and "voices," which may offer competing explanations of specific aspects of the study.

Arguably, there are two ways to approach any matter: (1) work outward, looking for connections to other issues to create a larger synthesis[44]; and (2) work inward, exploring every nook and cranny—leaving no stone unturned—to fill out the "space" that the material at hand takes up. The latter way of doing research is not the most common one among historians, which explains why egodocuments are not high on their agenda. On the contrary, historians tend to be preoccupied with the larger context, sacrificing the gain that a detailed analysis might bring to their research. I argue for a more intensive analysis of the historical sources than historians have grown accustomed to—to deconstruct their context and inner being as minutely as possible. This is the reason why egodocuments have been extremely useful for this type of research in my own approach to the past.

Care is required here because the above almost reads like a call for total decontextualization. I try to separate the need to contextualize something I am working on, from the desire to expand that contextualization into realms of the abstract—where contextualization morphs into generalization. In fact, the argument here is about generalization—and even then, this raises all kinds of questions about what kinds of generalization, etc.

The problem with my approach is in many layers, so to speak: one might, for example, ask whether it is wrong to compare one piece of material with another one from the same study? One shard with another from a different historical site? From the same region. . .? Where do we draw the line, and why? Or, what level of generalization will we accept about the material we study: if we identify it in some particular way, is that not a huge generalization in itself?

The point here is that there are a tangle of issues which we too readily gloss over in our study of the past—contextualization, generalization, abstraction: I wanted to be more specific in defining and demarcating what counts as the *singular*. The problem is that the key concern—for historians at least—is the leap from talking about some specific phenomena and their concrete properties and relations to talking about society in terms of abstract processes and categories.

I do try to qualify these issues in many of my works—but that is hard to do when these ideas are discussed on this abstract level, as I am doing here. The discussions in this book draw out the importance of this approach when we move the focus to "in-between spaces" and come across the life and works of "barefoot historians"—the Icelandic lay-scholars. Thus, a new dimension opens up on past societies.[45]

Again, even if the scale is reduced in the way envisioned here, one must still expect some structural orientation within the frame of reference. But this structure must always be subject to laws other than those imposed by the traditional metanarratives and, because of their scope, must be more malleable—that is, the frames must be more limited and more easily controlled. What is proposed here is that the essential idea behind microhistory be taken literally: that scholars place their main emphasis on the small research unit, such as an autobiography or other types of egodocuments, and confine themselves largely to that. In this way, the opportunity arises to give the full range of voices within society a place in historical research. The singularization of history in this sense provides the researcher with a means of bringing out the contradictions that exist between the different "discourses" of individual groups, and that is a precondition for our being able to approach ideas and points of view that in the general run of events do not come to the fore. Egodocuments of all types offer a great opportunity to deal with complicated historical matters, because of their detailed description of limited and often well-defined circumstances.

Hence, this ideology brings into prominence the contradictions and inconsistencies in the mind of each and every individual, and heightens the paradoxes that exist within each living person and among people who live in close proximity. In order to allow the contradictions and paradoxes freedom of expression, the emphasis must always be kept squarely on the subject matter itself and on nothing else—on the existing historical sources such as egodocuments. The key word here is *singularization*; the singularization of history is first and foremost a search for a way in which history can research its subjects in their logical and cultural context, and thus dissociate itself from the "man-made" ideological package of the metanarratives.

The strength of the microhistorical approach is precisely that each subject addressed is discussed both with respect to known facts and to what is not known. The latter is, in other words, no less important to the historian's research than the former. But discussion of the unknown naturally requires research methods and approaches which are quite different from those used by historians whose narrative is broad-brush: those who work with the "grand narrative."

The approach often used in microhistory is called "the evidential paradigm."[46] The premise here is that research into small units calls for minute analysis of clues and signs in the sources—that in gathering evidence and proofs this principle is applied by detecting hidden clues in the text and deconstructing the position of the individuals involved. In such a case, proofs as such can hardly exist, as they may in a research project based on statistical analysis, for instance. But this approach can provide an indication of the way toward certain proofs and the path the case has taken. Thus, the microhistorian recognizes the *direction* of the case and seeks to follow up by analysis of clues and signs in the sources. The method is complex and demands great attention to detail; in applying this approach, it is necessary to bring out all the unique features found in the text—however trivial they may appear at first sight—and make them the subject of the study.

But how do we go about doing this kind of research? In a methodology that I have been developing in recent years called the "textual environment," I set out to address certain central issues regarding sources such as egodocuments and their use and meaning.[47] Subjects for investigation include how the individual is shaped by text; how scribal culture has, for example, had a formative influence on people in past times; and the nature of the interplay between texts (narratives) and life (reality).[48]

The central element of the analysis has been the manuscripts themselves, whatever type of egodocument the scholar can lay their hands on: their creation, their context within the events they describe, the opportunities they present for analysis, and how they tie in with events that take place when they are used. But we may have to ask: What kind of meaning can be attributed to manuscripts or texts of any sort that express people's personal opinions? And how can we justify their use in academic research? As a fundamental working principle, I have made an attempt to consider the interplay of *events, narrative (conscious and unconscious), analysis (conscious and unconscious)*, and *new events* that arise as life moves forward. This "living" research model I call "the textual environment" extends to all the aspects noted above. I say "living," since I take into consideration events that have an impact on the form of the narrative and the analytical process during the creation of each. This research model is certainly influenced by Ginzburg's "evidential paradigm," where the principle is to study the most minute details of each subject matter at hand.

A similar approach is found in the work of American historian Luise White in her book *Speaking with Vampires*, in which she tackles the history of peoples in Africa who in the vast majority of cases had no written sources from earlier times.[49] Here, "texts" of other kinds became a motivating force in people's lives: material that directed how they thought about and interpreted the past and their history. In these works, the distinction between public sources and oral sources, between sources that are part of the man-made landscape of societies and written sources in whatever form, breaks down; all that matters is how the sources are used in the context of time and space. The rationale for this approach lies in the perception that the sources are not solely pieces of information, but phenomena that are "alive." They are used to explain the background to specific conditions that are always contingent on the thinking and ideas of those who speak about them. They can be used if the "textual environment" is clear.

Let us take some examples of this new vision of the subject and the possibilities it offers: at its best, a diary is a powerful mirror of its age, as we have seen in this volume. It can reveal the constant interplay of everyday life, individuals, community, and institutions in a remarkably illuminating fashion. In this context, let us take examples which exemplify the dynamic power of such sources.

All these efforts to assess the value and place of egodocuments are worthwhile. But in the end they will prove ineffective if scholars are unwilling to accept the validity of egodocuments as testimony about past times on their own terms.[50] Autobiographies are subjective sources which can hardly be measured against a scale of objective truth, as many historians demand. Comparative approaches are, it is true, subject to various obvious limitations, as has been recounted here. Methods which offer an opportunity to assess whether specific autobiographies may be deemed a useful mirror of past times—or whether their subjective qualities rule them out as good scholarly sources—are grounded in an experiment which is in itself hostile to the autobiographical construct. Egodocuments are subjective sources, and their positive qualities consist mainly in the narratives formed by each writer in their writings. The methods of microhistory are connected to qualitative research, which is a very useful approach to studies where egodocuments can be used. That approach recognizes the strengths and weaknesses of this source and applies them appropriately.

I am of the view that in the final years of the twentieth century, microhistory led to egodocuments becoming sources that attracted the attention of a growing group of historians.[51] In a sense, both the methods of microhistory and egodocuments benefited from the academic position that had arisen: that the subjective experience was again valued as an important barometer for the exploration of life in the past. Both were revitalized, as I have recounted above, and established themselves as crucial sources and academic tools of analysis.

Hence, I see Michael Mascuch, Rudolf Dekker, and Arianne Baggerman as mistaken in postulating a connection between the development of microhistory and *"mentalités"*, the history of mentalities.[52] When microhistory took off at the end of the twentieth century, the history of mentalities had slowly but surely died out, as I argued in a paper in the *Journal of Social History* in 2006.[53] Before the demise of the history of mentalities, it was hardly possible to make a connection between these two schools, which were so very dissimilar and sprung from entirely different origins.

Baggerman, Dekker, and Mascuch's contribution, on the other hand, has been huge when it comes to the importance of egodocuments for historical scholarship. Namely, the trio have purposefully brought egodocuments to light with the publication of a number of books in the series Egodocuments and History, which they edit. In this series, the importance of egodocuments has been defined in various ways, as when Rudolf Dekker discussed the diaries of Constantijn Hygens, Jr., who belonged to the upper class in the Netherlands, and uses his writings to show how the diary as a historical source developed in the seventeenth century and became part of people's daily lives.[54]

If we look at the latest work in this series, it is a book that looks specifically at the autobiography in early modern French, and its author Nicolae Alexandru Virastau highlights the varied forms of self-writing by looking at four specific works that are classified as autobiography. In other words, an attempt is made to explain the development of this field in the early modern period, and the big

Figure 6 In Raufarhöfn.

news is that diversity reigned there immediately. The works are different and the focus is varied.[55]

It is quite possible to say that all the books in this series come to the conclusion that it is not possible to highlight any special characteristics of egodocuments because their content depends so much on social norms and the personality of those who hold the pen; customs and manners in each instance, as well as people's personal experiences, are usually the dominant factor.[56] It is therefore necessary to highlight as many aspects of egodocuments as possible, as they have tried to do in the Egodocuments and History book series.

2

Egodocuments in the Twentieth Century

Back in Time

Now it is important to go back in time and look at the development of autobiographical sources both in Iceland and globally over the last fifty years or so. The characteristics of the autobiography—that it is a work by one person, an account of the author's experience of their own life, and often a recollection of events that may have taken place decades before—make it a complex historical source. For much of the twentieth century, many historians were wary of the hazy boundary between fact and fiction in such writings, and this led to reduced interest in autobiographies as sources for most of the second part of the century. Historians have often seen themselves as unqualified to test the veracity of egodocuments—regardless of category—as other evidence is often lacking. For this reason, for most of the twentieth century relatively few historians made systematic use of egodocuments in their research.

The autobiography has had a major place in mainstream culture in Iceland for the last fifty years. The idea is to use the Icelandic case as a window on the world of egodocuments, and how the form has become the subject of a small but enthusiastic group of historians, and to explore the circumstances in which their interest intensified. In addition, a certain category of egodocuments from elsewhere in the world is also addressed below, and that is the starting point.

It needs to be kept in mind that in the past two decades or so some change has taken place in how egodocuments have been used, mainly because authors of egodocuments recognized that the boundaries between truth and fiction were generally unclear in their lives, and for that reason they started to work with those indistinct boundaries of the narrative in their writing. A considerable part of the scholarly world has followed their example.[1]

Historians working on the conditions of the working class in England and slaves in the United States made use of abundant autobiographical material throughout the twentieth century. For a long time, these fields of research were somewhat distinct from others with regard to their connection with egodocuments. The sources have given historians and scholars in other fields of the humanities who have pursued such research—especially in recent decades—the opportunity to highlight the viewpoints of both perpetrator and victim, in a highly effective manner.

This approach to research has transformed the way the subjects are addressed.[2] Through using egodocuments it has proved possible to develop convincing arguments that show the ideas and thoughts of individuals who had been seen as passive tools in the hands of others.

A priori the conditions of slaves in the United States gave scholars who studied the formal status of classes or social groups no indication that people who were enslaved had anything to say about their lives, nor the opportunity to control any aspect of their own lives. But research based on the autobiographical testimony of the slaves themselves demonstrated that, within the narrow confines that framed their lives, they succeeded in developing a culture which, in an extraordinary way, helped the oppressed find meaning in life. One of the outstanding examples of this method is Eugene D. Genovese's renowned *Roll, Jordan, Roll*.[3] Genovese demonstrates that within the constraints of slavery the oppressed succeeded in maintaining their cultural status and strengthening the infrastructure of their community. Their religious and spiritual dynamism flourished while they were subjugated in society.

The same is true of the working class in Britain. British historian E. P. Thompson wrote his classic *The Making of the English Working Class* from the viewpoint of the proletariat, making extensive use of autobiographical material and other narrative sources.[4] Until recently, these were the exceptions that proved the rule, as the use of autobiographies or other egodocuments that focus on the self tended to be quite random in most parts of the world.[5] The same accounts were, and often still are, cited over and over again, regardless of the specific subject under discussion. This is particularly true of research on political and ideological history, where autobiographies are often used to supplement a story with some colorful detail and not to deepen understanding. That application of egodocuments has also typified historical writing in Iceland, and this book is primarily concerned with that cultural environment.

In Iceland, at least four notable exceptions are found to scholars' lack of interest in egodocuments; all date from the last two decades of the twentieth century and from the present century. First, Guðmundur Hálfdanarson, professor of history at the University of Iceland, made use of more than 100 autobiographies, semi-autobiographies (memoirs), and conversational books in assessing the value of child labor in the nineteenth and early twentieth centuries for a paper which was published in the periodical *Saga* in 1986.[6] Guðmundur made a proviso regarding the use of such sources: he regarded it as unwise to use them for any other purpose than to assess the tangible aspects of individuals' lives, such as the work performed by certain groups in society, and their workload. He warned against uncritical use of the autobiography, pointing out that the use of such sources might "lead to a systematic distortion of the sources, which could be difficult to avoid, although the sample is a large one."[7] Guðmundur's use of these sources was very innovative in the Icelandic scholarly world of the 1980s, and it is a fine example of the ingenious use of egodocuments. I believe that by his reference to "systematic distortion," Guðmundur means that the autobiographical form has become so formulaic that the individual cannot avoid complying with the received structure. That is certainly a just observation, which remains valid today. But I feel that in recent years scholars have been more daring in their reasoning on the basis of egodocuments, especially after the entire scholarly world realized that all accounts of the past comply with certain rules of the narrative form—under whatever name—and this influences the outcome. What we call the sources is irrelevant.

Second, the late Loftur Guttormsson, a history professor at the University of Iceland, made use of travel books, autobiographies, and biographies in his study of childhood in the Age of Enlightenment. Loftur's study was naturally limited by the fact that very few autobiographies are extant from that period. Those which do exist mainly represent the social élite—who were, however, far from having mastered the creation of the self in writing.[8] For that reason, Loftur applied a rather controversial method, making use of autobiographies from a different period from the one he was studying (principally the mid-nineteenth century) in order to throw light on the *Zeitgeist* and state of affairs nearly a century earlier. The thinking behind an experiment of this kind is that little had changed in the intervening period, and hence that it is justifiable to use sources from one period about people's lives at another period. "In this context," writes Loftur, "it should not be incautious to look to writers who were children in the period 1850–1870; for well into the 19th century the spirit and the word of Domestic Discipline informed the parenting methods of the family."[9] Loftur's temptation is perhaps not as great as it seems at first glance, due to the ideological basis of his research. He worked with different types of grand narrative, and that approach gave him the green light to move fast between periods without paying much attention to the fine details of the historical development. Whatever the academic attitude to such methods, it is clear that as a whole Loftur's experiment is notable, as he puts forward many different forms of evidence in his study: subjective testimony, sources on the formal structure of his subject matter, and demographic variables from this time period. That approach opened up new possibilities for engaging with the period, despite its limitations.

Again, the most interesting aspect of Loftur's method is that it reveals his attitude to the past, or history: this is clearly evidenced in his transfer of evidence from one period to another. The grand narrative approach of the subject matter permitted such transference. Incidents within a unit, the small detail of human life, can scarcely be the subject of those who use the grand narrative to frame their research. In the grand narrative, a broad-brush approach is applied in recounting a story which progresses inexorably onward. In this case, the analysis is guided by both Pietism and the Enlightenment. The problem in this case is that self-expression of the kind that was common by the mid-nineteenth century was almost unknown in the late eighteenth century—that is, the time that is the focus of Loftur's study. For that reason, Loftur's methods overshadow his otherwise excellent discussion of the period.

Third, in my doctoral thesis, I myself used many different types of egodocuments in an analysis of the everyday life of people in the latter half of the nineteenth century and the early twentieth century.[10] I applied *life-course analysis* in my study of popular culture at that period. The method consists of dividing a human life into several life stages, and then applying egodocuments to an analysis of the nature of each stage in itself, and the relationships between them. The analysis is thus "horizontal" in the sense that a "slice" is taken of the life of each person who has left written evidence, and that is compared with the accounts of others. In that way, a detailed description is achieved of each life stage, and the main characteristics of each can be identified.

The advantage of such use of egodocuments is that a systematic analysis can be made of the ordinary aspects of people's daily lives, which are hard to address in other ways. Two birds are killed with one stone: a discussion of children in nineteenth-century society proves possible with this research method and in addition the daily lives of the peasantry form the foundation. The main drawback of the approach is that while narrative sources are used, they are processed through a demographic research model which is employed for analysis. Hence, the method makes very limited use of the egodocuments.

Life-course analysis opens up an opportunity to study and focus on some crucial turning points in people's lives. These turning points (moving from one stage to another) are important because they affect people's perceptions of life.

They influence not only the person who faces these changes but also those who are associated with that particular person. The experiences that each individual goes through differ from one person to another. But, at the same time, there is a structure, pattern, or cultural norm that people take notice of before they make decisions about their next step. This does not mean that every individual is conscious of the existence of these abstract phenomena; most of them do not think of themselves as a part of a certain structure or, for that matter, a cultural world. But these phenomena do exist, sometimes as learned notions, such as norms or values, and sometimes as external forces. Faced with a certain situation, people evaluate the alternatives given them and construct a way in which they want to deal with that particular situation. In this sense, each individual is not a passive participant who goes with the flow of the structure, or a passive receiver of ideas. They are at all times the one who makes the decision based on their own judgment, but always with normative and material constraints.

How can life-course analysis meet our objective when it has so many dimensions? How can we grasp the interrelationship among the timing, spacing, and nature of events through the individual's life course, and the historical factors that influence them, through life-course analysis? "The justification here is that the life course, as a socially organized process of growing up, is an abstraction that allows us to focus on a variety of simultaneously acting demographic, material, and cultural developments which are one coherent aspect of experience of contemporaries," writes US historian John Modell.[11] All social action will therefore be treated as constant negotiations, choices, and struggles of individuals who on a day-to-day basis are confronted with a formal structure that still leaves room for personal choices.

Marlis Buchmann explains this further in her book *The Script of Life in Modern Society*, putting forward three crucial assumptions for her analysis:

> (1) Neither discrete life stages nor specific transitions can be understood apart from the life course as a whole; (2) social changes in the larger society provide the appropriate frame of reference for assessing the significance of changes in the patterns associated with particular life stages and in the life course as a whole; and (3) understanding how society organizes individual life courses and how people direct and give meaning to their own biographies requires an approach that integrates a macro-sociological perspective with an actor-oriented one.[12]

It is necessary to emphasize the importance of linking together interaction among major historical events, structural and cultural transformations, and the individual's experience. This three-dimensional interplay greatly affects the life course of each individual. First, we have the formal institutions and their perception of the life course, based on rules, laws, and customs. Second, we have the individual who has to deal with this formal environment and their own motivation and desires. Third, we have what might be called "the rhythm of the moment": a historical event, which could be either big or small and affects to a great extent both these poles. It is safe to say that normally the individual is more influenced by a historical event than by the formal institutions. To put it another way: "the institutionalized life course" is a frame that surrounds people's lives and tends to direct it toward certain results. While the nature of the institutionalized life course is static, the nature of the individual life course is fluid, influenced from one minute to another by historical events. We may see this as something of a paradox, a restriction that opens up new dimensions.

It is important to realize that life-course analysis is a demographic tool by nature, that has been used as such by many historians and demographers.[13] In my doctoral dissertation it was used in a different way, because the focus was on culture or everyday life history, and the main source of evidence was people's personal testimony—egodocuments. It is different from the synchronic cross-sectional quantitative approach, in the sense that the biographical perspective gives us an opportunity to take an individual step by step through their transitions. We have an opportunity to investigate the effect of individual pressure for change in connection with their relations with social process and social change.

Fourth, over the past twenty years, scholars have increasingly turned to egodocuments for evidence about the past—and especially microhistorians, as mentioned before. They have applied such sources more boldly and imaginatively than had previously been the case, for example in Iceland. These microhistorians have gradually moved into using egodocuments as subjective or qualitative sources, and hence they have a much higher profile now than in the past.[14]

It should be mentioned that several other Icelandic historians have made use of firsthand sources in their work, although on a smaller scale. One of the best examples is Erla Huld Halldórsdóttir, professor of history, who wrote her doctoral thesis at the University of Iceland, based largely on egodocuments (collection of letters), with an indirect relationship to the methods of microhistory.[15] She has written extensively on the use of letters in historical scholarship.[16] Suffice to mention also is Anna Agnarsdóttir, professor emerita of history at the University of Iceland. A few years ago, she published a huge collection of the papers of Sir Josephs Banks, which I believe will set an example for high-quality editions of this kind.[17] Yet other historians made use of egodocuments earlier in the twentieth century in their research on political history, seeking out the testimony of individual politicians on specific events in political history.

As mentioned above, the problem with the analytical method I used in my doctoral thesis was that the research model lacked dynamism: the resulting picture was static, and changes from one period to another were hard to discern. In order to address this problem, at least in part, it is possible to apply a method that merges several life stages for each individual, and discuss them—analyzing the paths the individual has chosen during the course of their life. This method is certainly most applicable where the focus is on a complex social structure or a society in the process of transformation.

US historian Harvey J. Graff applies a similar approach in his *Conflicting Paths*, which he bases on a range of different egodocuments originating from over 500 people, such as diaries, correspondence, and autobiographies.[18] The method is essentially very similar to the life-course analysis model, guided by the principle of gaining an overview of people's long-term experience, and hence evaluating as a continuum the life of each individual from birth into adulthood. Graff divides paths in growing up among a number of categories and demonstrates how they change from one time to another (from the eighteenth century until the latter half of the twentieth century). Certain paths are dominant at certain periods, while others are added or take over in time. By this method, Graff reveals how society changed during the historical development of the United States.

Graff, who wrote the book in the early 1990s (it was published in 1995), was one of a group of historians who had embarked on experiments with using egodocuments in their research. This process was in step with developments in history and the other humanities which gradually undermined the idea that reality could be addressed in an objective manner, or that historical research could be pursued on the same premises as in the natural sciences (which many had, however, rejected decades earlier). Inspired by this, a promising group of scholars started to devote more interest to subjective sources, and how they could be applied in research.

Harvey J. Graff put forward, for instance, some fundamental concepts which became the *leitmotiv* of his study; these were designed to enable him (and others) to address the subjective qualities of egodocuments. He worked with such concepts as *conflicts, paths,* and *experience*, which form the foundation for the application of various other concepts, such as *integration*, which assumes a certain continuity in the life course of each individual; *inclusion*, which emphasizes that all possible voices be heard; *conflict*, which reflects the certainty that our entire process of growing up is full of paradoxes; *dependency*, which demonstrates that each individual is always dependent on others as they grow up, and that life is partly concerned with compromise between those who are so connected; and *historical constructedness* or *historicity*, which reflects the certainty that history contains our imaginary ideas about time and space. These concepts form the foundation for Graff's analysis of the process of growing up, with the emphasis on life involving constant compromises that take account of age, family, gender, class, ethnicity, nationality, and culture, to name but a few factors. All these elements give rise to *conflicts* between individuals or groups, which have an impact on the life course as a whole. The author stresses that the individual has, in spite of everything, an opportunity to choose—that they opt for *paths*, which Graff explores and applies to an analysis of the autobiographical material. It is vital to apply the individuals' *experience* in order to demonstrate the paths they took in life. Graff seeks to include most of the factors that influence the process of growing up as a whole and also to demonstrate the relationship between them. This very interesting approach offers historians great potential for viewing subjective sources in context and creating a new research framework for them.

I myself have applied a similar method in my research on gender roles in nineteenth- and twentieth-century Iceland.[19] I established three categories in order to analyze changes during the period—*traditional approach*, *redefined approach*, and *creative class approach*—making use of responses from over sixty informants to questionnaires sent out by the National Museum of Iceland. I based my research on the answers given by informants to a questionnaire I had prepared in 1995 in collaboration with the National Museum staff: *Daglegt líf í dreifbýli og þéttbýli á 20. öld* (Daily Life in Rural and Urban Communities in the 20th Century). The questionnaire was extensive, covering many aspects of people's daily lives, from cradle to grave.[20] Each reply was allocated to the abovementioned categories, reflecting characteristics of the informant's life course, and especially the internal coherence. Through these resources and the scholarly categories, I succeeded in demonstrating that Icelandic society remained very traditional almost throughout the period covered by the study, that is, well into the twentieth century. It transpired that this research method is exciting, and can, if correctly handled, provide scholars with opportunities to make use of the diverse flora of egodocuments in a new and creative way.

A New Focus on Egodocuments

At the end of the twentieth century, historians' attitudes began to change, initially with great caution. They were clearly reluctant to follow the example of literary scholars and embark on textual analysis of autobiographies and discuss such matters as the structure of the works. Scholars such as US historian Mary Jo Maynes, who had long been focused on research on historical demography, turned to using autobiographies by working-class people from Germany and France in her research.[21] Through autobiographical sources, she has analyzed classic demographic factors such as the relationship between parenthood and work, sex and efforts to restrain it, and many more. Sometime before that, Danish historian Bjarne Stoklund had studied 270 diaries and account books from the period before 1920, all written by farmers and laborers, with the intention of reconstructing their social world and everyday life at the time.[22]

Research of this nature clearly had an impact, although the vast majority of social historians were entirely opposed to the use of such resources. A famous debate arose, for instance, on childhood research, between those who focused on the use of qualitative and quantitative methods, respectively, involving such scholars as Edward Shorter and Linda A. Pollock. The latter cited egodocuments in order to refute Shorter's conclusion that parents had not displayed appropriate affection for their children in the early modern age.[23]

Autobiographical material received attention from scholars in other disciplines early in the twentieth century. For example, the use of personal documents in academic research (in the humanities and social sciences) can be traced to the heyday of the Chicago School in social sciences in the first part of the century. The so-called "life story approach" was widespread in the 1920s and the 1930s, but then it mostly died out (though critical monologues and essays have been published over the years).[24]

In the 1980s, the "life-history approach" received considerable attention from scholars in different disciplines, such as anthropology, psychology, and sociology; this approach was very much based on the example set by the Chicago School earlier in the century. Briefly, the life-history approach is an attempt to acquire reliable information about the past through repeated oral interviews with people who belong to the same social class, occupational group, etc. These interviews often then form the foundation for a comparison of the relationship between individual and collective action and sociohistorical changes. Theoretical discussions about the importance of the life-history approach take up considerable space in this literature, where scholars debate the strengths and weaknesses of this methodology. These theoretical and conceptual discussions are relevant and useful when dealing with the importance of the autobiography, because of the similar nature of these sources. In general, it is safe to say that some social scientists in the last forty years or so have turned to the life-history approach out of frustration with the use of quantitative data in human studies, and when they try to measure processes in time.[25]

The autobiography has also been viewed from another angle. An enormous body of literature has been published under the aegis of literary theory. Unfortunately—for historians and in fact also for literary theorists—most of these studies show little interest in historical context and whether or not the autobiography is a successful reflection of everyday life.[26] The form, not the content, of the autobiography is their subject matter.

In the late twentieth century, such literary research became far more relevant for historians—as discussed later in this book—when the latter increasingly realized that the resources they were dealing with were subject to much the same principles as any other literary text. For that reason, in the latter half of the 1980s and the 1990s, most historians sought to apply egodocuments by means of quantitative methods; they tried to promote the scientific use of such sources through systematic analysis. I myself thought the same way, as explained above, when I was working on my doctoral thesis. At that time, scholars did not look to individual autobiographies and what they might have to offer, but saw these sources as part of a large whole, a unit in a bigger set.[27]

Once again, others have placed more emphasis on utilizing the subjective qualities of the autobiography to the utmost. They have sought to bring out the creation of the *self* in this literature, as was done above in examining and defining individual manifestations of the self.[28] Through their research, literary scholars have fostered increased interest in the autobiography as a phenomenon, and many have emphasized its use in analyzing previously unknown subjects relating to humanity.[29] All this has had a considerable impact on people's ideas about history and the past.

Despite the abovementioned academic trend, historians long made little use of the resources contained in autobiographies. This may be because of the fact that history remained highly traditional almost throughout the twentieth century— including even social history. Historians based their work primarily on formal or official sources, regardless of whether they were working in political history, cultural history, or some other historical field: the structure of society was their subject, although in variable ways.[30] The influence of German historian Leopold von Ranke and the research tradition he established around the mid-nineteenth century may be widely seen in the writings of historians and their discussion of their discipline. One of his trademarks was to demonstrate the limitations of so-called *narrative sources*, and the importance of using official documents in history writing. As a result, institutional history has tended to receive detailed attention, at the expense of the individual viewpoint. Institutional history, naturally enough, pays little attention to individuals' attitudes and their understanding of life and its vicissitudes—with the exception, needless to say, of the handful of *males* in a position of power. However, despite historians moving away from *positivism* to some degree, and turning to theories and models, the influence of empiricism remains potent even today, and it certainly affects the research of the vast majority of historians worldwide. Within that research tradition there was little space for egodocuments, which have even been met with skepticism from historians. The latter half of the twentieth century saw the advent of the new social history as the standard-bearer of avant-garde history, which for a long time made no allowance for individuals' personal testimony, as discussed below.[31]

In the early decades of the twentieth century, the "objective approach" was the rule, emphasizing that a certain distance from the subject must be observed. This approach to history underwent some change due to the influence of historians who were outside the mainstream of traditional academic institutions. The best known of these are Norbert Elias, and later Philippe Ariès: the latter wrote his magnificent *L'enfant et la vie familiale sous l'ancien régime* (*Centuries of Childhood*)

Figure 7 In Hvammstangi.

in the early 1960s, using egodocuments among other resources. Another is Roy Pascal, whose *Design and Truth in Autobiography* led to considerable change in ideas of how egodocuments might be applied in scholarly analysis. He stressed the point that the autobiography must be approached as an autonomous world—a work which should be judged on its own terms. It was not subject to any requirement of factual responsibility, as in the case of most sources; all it had to do was to present a comprehensible picture of its subject that met reasonable standards.

The Individual Central Stage

It may be said with some accuracy that in the late twentieth century, scholars gradually started to look favorably on subjective experiences. The writing of autobiographies has a long and remarkable history, evolving from devotional autobiographies of the seventeenth and eighteenth centuries, in which gentlefolk came forward to describe their inner spiritual life, into accounts by working-class people in the twentieth century, recounting how they grew and lived their lives, citing a multitude of contributory factors.[32] It is important to give more attention to the evolution of autobiographical expression in recent times. In this part of the book, I explore developments in the writing of autobiographies, primarily toward the end of the twentieth century; there are various indications that changes of attitude to memory had an influence on people's self-expression. The plan is to focus mostly on one interesting scholar who has used autobiographical writing in a very productive way in her studies.

American scholar Mary Jo Maynes, who has been cited above, worked extensively with the autobiographies of people of low social class in France and Germany in the last decade of the twentieth century. In her *Taking the Hard Road* (1995), she points out that the books written in those regions were generally the result of outside encouragement from political groups.[33] Socialist leaders, for instance, urged people to write about the exploitation and injustice they observed in their everyday lives. In that way, personal narratives became political tools. What is more, Maynes claims to be able to chart the different types of autobiography in those countries according to political movements of the time. From the mid-nineteenth century to the mid-twentieth century, after the Second World War, autobiographies tended to be informed by a certain political climate in daily life. That was a period of rapid change, when the means of production were industrialized, inevitably entailing massive negative impacts. Class conflict broke out—and one aspect of campaigning for social change was to encourage individuals to tell their own stories as they experienced them. After the mid-twentieth century, according to Maynes, such systematic promotion of working-class history declined, to be replaced by the superficial impression peddled by the media. And it was not until the advent of *history from below* that such subjects attracted attention for historical study—and scholars with an interest in working-class culture started to seek out material about such social groups.[34] These historians were admittedly few in the 1970s and 1980s, but their numbers were rising.

Maynes, a representative of the quantitative approach in social science history, had worked with autobiographies in her research before her book was published.[35] She writes:

> These subjective and personal sources have a great deal to add to history, for they allow us to view and assess historical transformations from the perspective of people who lived through them. The subjectivity of autobiographical accounts provides a place from which to interrogate and refine the categories through which the past is understood. The autobiography's personal emphasis, moreover, points to the significance of private life in history—a significance that historians are only beginning to appreciate.[36]

Maynes also deals with this subject in her paper "Autobiography and Class Formation," published in *Social Science History* in 1992. In the paper, she mainly addresses two issues raised by critics of autobiographies: To what group do the autobiographers belong? And are autobiographies reliable as scholarly sources? On the first question, Maynes is of the view that the autobiography must be approached on other principles than the quantitative approach. It is not possible to assume a specific structural link between the individual and society, which informs the study. Instead, it is important to give the autobiographer the opportunity to express their own perceptions of institutions and relationships, which may be of use.

Also the researcher must seek to show, through a comparison of many autobiographies, how social relationships can exist on entirely different premises from those presumed by formal institutions. This ideology proposed by Maynes is, of course, grounded in the principles of quantitative research methods, as explored above. Maynes, like many other demographers, has difficulty in throwing off the methods which belong to the technical approach of quantitative ideology. This is obvious in all her arguments, despite her sincere desire to explore new avenues.

With respect to the credibility of the autobiography, Maynes remarks that, of course, in many cases the author's testimony cannot be verified, but that it is the author's insight which is crucial: "In other words," writes Maynes, "to use autobiography and other personal narrative evidence well, we cannot take it at face value but must be prepared to read it in a context, to interpret."[37]

I have absolutely no desire to belittle Mary Jo Maynes' scholarly experiments, and, as witnessed in the above quotation, she made a huge leap away from the demographic approach—a daring and unexpected one. But despite that, Maynes was by no means sailing under false colors. Her writings continue to smack strongly of quantitative thinking; I return to this matter below. That was also the way of many historians who were taking their first steps in using such sources, at the end of the twentieth century.

Maynes' systematic analysis of about ninety autobiographies focuses on the formation of class identity in France and Germany. She stresses that each and every individual is influenced by countless other individuals who belong in various groups to be found at different levels of society. In addition, she is of the view that various traditional social institutions with which people have links, direct or indirect, contribute to their social development. In Maynes' view, the autobiography throws light on that process, and that is how scholars should apply it. She argues:

> But the construction of identity that occurs and is recorded in these autobiographies, while it is the product of individual imagination, is also very clearly marked by the social, economic, and political, and cultural institutions that shaped the authors' lives. These institutions also influenced how and which subjectivities found expression in autobiography. These autobiographies thus demonstrate the fluidity of the boundary between the individual and the social.[38]

Maynes stressed that, by a systematic analysis of autobiographies, it is possible to identify the paths and processes followed by individuals as they formed their common perception of life.[39] Here, we see ideas informed by the social sciences, which were a strong influence on those who worked with autobiographies from the mid-1980s to the mid-1990s, cropping up in Maynes' thinking.[40] Those are the norms that are applied to exploring the veracity or strength of the categories formed by demography in the analysis of phenomena and processes in society.

In the introduction to his *The French Worker*, Mark Traugott is keen to demonstrate, first, that autobiographies are unreliable in the analysis of large-scale developments in society, and second, that they are invaluable in bringing out other aspects of those same processes and people's experience of them. He is of the view that the latter cannot be attained by using other sources.[41]

Like other quantitative scholars, Traugott and Maynes emphasize in their writings that these working-class autobiographies are not typical of the European proletariat. Maynes draws many comparisons, for instance, between these autobiographers and ordinary workers—in order to place them in the correct context, as she says. Maynes discusses the problem perceived by many historians in the use of autobiographies, that is, the difficulty entailed in verifying the truthfulness of accounts. She goes on to undertake a comparative process similar to the one I describe later in this book under *subjective truth*, *historical truth*, *social truth*, and *comparative truth*; all with the aim of reinforcing the status of autobiographies as scholarly sources, and trying to counteract the objections of those who were opposed to the use of such evidence from the past.

Maynes warns against scholars undertaking an excessively strict comparison with outside sources. The virtues of autobiographies, she maintains, are primarily a matter of their subjective viewpoint, that is, "more in the clues they offer about how people made sense of and reconstructed the course of their life," rather than in views on specific events or circumstances.[42] She stresses that autobiographies cannot be used in their "raw" state. They need to be remade, deciphering their symbolism and imagery (semiotics), in order for the researcher to make the best use of what the text has to offer. The remaking cannot be carried out on objective principles; on the contrary, such a process must be grounded in a relationship with the context from which the autobiography has arisen.

In this context, Maynes cites her paper in *Social Science History*, in which she discusses the view of Italian historian Luisa Passerini that the autobiographical memory is always true; it is only the scientist who needs to show in what sense they are right.[43] I wholeheartedly agree with this view; and I believe that this constitutes an important understanding of the potential of egodocuments in social research. The "problem" of veracity is, in the end, not a problem at all, but an opportunity for creative approaches to diverse subjects.

Mary Jo Maynes had, in other words, at this point departed from the path of strict demography. Instead, she sought to evaluate the text on its own terms, holistically. Maynes was certainly cautious in drawing conclusions and wanted to proceed one step at a time, but she realized that autobiographies cannot be used creatively unless they are acknowledged as a valid subjective measure of human behavior. Maynes recognized that this literary form is subject to certain laws, and takes on a form and shape that she attempted to prove were analyzable.

Within the limits of language, a domain of discourse is created in autobiographies which is unique, and important for scholars to study.

These views expressed by Maynes bear clear witness to new ideas in history regarding the potential of a qualitative approach. The reason why I have chosen to trace the development of Maynes' ideas in such detail is that she was one of the first scholars from the demographic camp to take that step over into subjective sources. As stated above, Mary Jo Maynes' scholarship is firmly rooted in the strong American demographic tradition, linked to the Social Science Historical Association, a group which prioritized the development and application of qualitative methods.[44] Maynes was thus true to her roots when she focused in her study on the comparison of the positions of specific groups, such as women in Germany and France, and underlined the importance of having a broad cohort for comparison. Maynes thus saw the comparison of certain groups who wrote their autobiographies in their respective countries as helping to explain certain social attitudes in which the stories are grounded, "but these stories cannot be taken to mirror somehow the working-class populations of France and Central Europe," maintains Maynes. "After all, only a restricted group of people came to write these autobiographies. Moreover, generalizations based upon these stories, however large their number, can always be contradicted in individual cases and even ultimately overturned as an increasing number of texts come to light."[45] Maynes' remark sums up in a nutshell the scholarly tradition from which she came.

In this context, I want to take an example from my own experience, which will throw some light on the attitudes discussed here. For most of the twentieth century, scholars who were interested in working at the University of Iceland submitted applications supported by the relevant documentation: books, papers, a curriculum vitae, etc. Having received these, the university appointed a selection committee of three people, who examined all the applications, and often wrote extensive opinions about every applicant: they would assess the quality of the applicant's individual works, and then place the applications in order of qualification for the appointment, in the judgment of the committee. I cite here two committee opinions which I received after applying to the university's Department of History.

The committee opinion which I received from the selection committee in March 1994 made reference to my use of autobiographies (invariably referred to, however, as "biographies"), making various criticisms of my use of egodocuments (often referred to in the report as personal sources or firsthand sources). The findings I had reached in my doctoral thesis on the basis of those sources were also criticized. The committee's opinion contained much that was favorable with respect to my thesis—and all the discussion was more or less conventional. But the inferences drawn from the thesis by the author of the committee opinion caught my attention; and they must be deemed enlightening about scholars' attitudes to sources of this nature in the 1990s.

According to the committee opinion:

> This ... demonstrates the problems to be dealt with when working on the basis of biographies [the author's reference here is to *auto*biographies, as elsewhere in this quotation] as key sources on mindset and philosophy. There is a lot of scope for interpretation of the documents by the scholar. The author clearly explains the limitations of these sources in Chapter I, but in his work with the sources, on the other hand, he does not always adhere to the necessary reservations. *Authors of biographies are not typical representatives of the population; and while biographies may contain examples of specific phenomena (way of life or mindset), it is not possible to extrapolate on the basis of such examples for all the people of the country, regardless of their circumstances and social status. The story of one man is not the story of the entire nation. Nor is the story of 200 authors of biographies the story of the nation, unless they are typical representatives of the people—in fact reflecting the entire nation—having remembered their past perfectly, and told it all truthfully.*[46]

As witness in the footnote below, I here cite a committee opinion from 1997. That paragraph was repeated verbatim from the committee opinion from 1994, when I had applied for an assistant professorship at the University of Iceland's Department of History.[47] Having recycled that paragraph cited above, the 1997 selection committee added: "The present selection committee is in agreement with the above words." Hence, six members (historians) of two selection committees, in the early and later 1990s, put their names to the ideas stated.

It is the latter half of the cited paragraph, which I have italicized here, and the views it expresses, that is particularly striking. It puts forward a strictly positivist view, which in 1994, when I received the committee opinion, I had believed to be on the way out, not only in Iceland but around the world. These words express a view that assumed that the past could be magically conjured up by use of sources: the past as it was. What is more, the opinion blithely ignores the decades-long debate in international academia on the position of the narrative in text, how best to approach the past, and whether that is even possible. Demographers were among the last to enter that debate—but even they were by that time starting to pay attention to egodocuments, as witness the case of Mary Jo Maynes.

How is one to understand a sentence like: "Nor is the story of 200 authors of biographies the story of the nation, unless they are typical representatives of the people—in fact reflecting the entire nation—having remembered their past perfectly, and told it all truthfully"? The attitude expressed here is pervaded by the views of the positivists—an unquestioning belief in quantitative methods, and a willful blindness to anything that may be termed a qualitative approach. Yet, for some time, scholars had been working on the assumption that all sources were based in fallible human memory, and that language was a limited medium for people's experience in the past and present.

The viewpoint expressed above severely restricted the potential application of autobiographies. Maynes went on to pursue a similar course to mine in my doctoral thesis in 1993, that is, to follow the life course, emphasizing the transitions that took place when people moved from one life stage to the next.[48]

The innovative aspect of Maynes' approach lies in her efforts in reading into the language symbols and meanings that throw light on the shared mindset and ideological ground of the working class in these countries: the self-perception of individuals of the same social class. The author is essentially addressing the idea of the collective memory of the working class in the two countries, and the fundamentals on which it was based, and seeking to identify the crucial factors that shaped the worldview of people of that social class. Throughout her discussion, Maynes is engaged in a debate with the demographic research findings of previous decades, which historians had been keen to gather. Maynes' approach thus offers a range of opportunities, although it misses out on perhaps the best that such sources offer, that is, the opportunity to examine the content of a single autobiography and gauge what may be learned from it without any reference to generalized processes or developments that govern people's lives, which are the product of society's formal institutions.

Mark Traugott, mentioned above, who edited the anthology *The French Worker* in 1993, takes a scholarly stance similar to Maynes'. He is of the view that the autobiographical form circumscribes the author. He cites a number of factors that are required by the form in a working-class autobiography, especially in France: (1) the family history is recounted, with the emphasis on internal coherence; (2) stories are told which are intended to reveal various interesting aspects of the autobiographer's life; (3) a tale of triumphs is told: how the autobiographer overcame challenges and achieved success; (4) an apologia regarding certain aspects of the autobiographer's life, in which they have been unfairly judged; (5) the autobiographer looks back, and shares their experience, knowledge, and wisdom; (6) one who can look back on changing times, and often urges their class to radical action; (7) the autobiographer sees a need to identify themself as a worker, or a participant in the working-class struggle for better conditions.[49]

Traugott sees the last of these factors as highlighting the tendency of many autobiographers to maintain that they speak for the masses—that they represent a class of people who have had similar experiences. Traugott points out that the autobiographical form demands a very specific regimentation of events, with the aim of organizing the life story—presented as consistent with the experience of the group and its collective memory. But Traugott adds that this is also true of other types of source. "Official statistics, for example," writes Traugott, "apply universal categories that shape and channel information, giving it the appearance of consistency and comparability."[50] Here, the author has entered the realm of the historical memory, that is, when institutions and other public bodies determine what is to be remembered—what is deemed beneficial and important for the nation to know.

Traugott does not subscribe to the opinion that narrative sources can be set free from the coordinated effort to understand and elucidate history. Like Maynes, he takes the view that it is important to compare individual narratives with other viewpoints. The idea here is that reality can be recreated. But recreation of an autobiography, he says, is problematical, largely because it is written down long after the events described. Traugott goes on to enumerate all the "problems" which are inevitably conjured up by quantitative thinking—simply to remind the reader that such sources are risky, and must always be handled with caution.

The ideology of Traugott, Maynes, and others whose background was in the quantitative research model—some of whom were trying to break free of it—was grounded in the conviction that the world comprised a set of systems which could be studied using "scientific" methods of analytical demography. The problem they saw with such analysis for those who were interested in using egodocuments was that it was hard to see how a *"strategy of selection"* could transform autobiographies, "initially fascinating for the insights they offer into the subjective world of a particular individual, into a tool for understanding large-scale changes which affected the lives of the great mass of society's population over time," as Traugott put it.[51] In the end, he was of the view that autobiographies are perfectly serviceable for the purpose, despite their obvious drawbacks.

In other words, historians have, even into the twenty-first century, had major reservations about the use of such sources; but ever-increasing numbers have felt compelled to recognize their strengths and possibilities when exploring such subjects as the mental world of women, or of other social groups who have been sidelined in conventional history. But all the innovative work has been informed by a desire to have a firm footing—leading to a cautious approach. This is the spirit of most historians' scholarly experiments relating to egodocuments. Swedish social historian Britt Liljewall probably speaks for many historians when she expresses this view of autobiographies and comparable sources:

> Writing a life story implies the development of a logical pattern of past events based on a reality, which is perceived in the light of interpretation formed over a long period of time and gradually influenced by the experience of life. Autobiography might, therefore, be seen as the frozen reconstruction of the never-ending cultural interpretation of reality realized by people over the span of a whole life.[52]

Liljewall's assumption here is that an autobiography is a reflection of something bigger—some "whole" to which the autobiographer belongs. The same applies to other historians, as discussed above.

A medium for the aesthetic resolution of the self, that increasing numbers of writers have turned their back on in attempts to objectify their lives, has entailed a major change in many historians' approach to their subjects. They have thus increasingly acknowledged that it is not possible to create an objective account of the life course that has any significance.

The same is true of readers of such stories: they know that in order to enjoy and understand the self they must apply their senses—whether through looking at images, text, photographs, or some other narrative form. The perceptual potential of the work has thus taken precedence. This development arises from an increasing understanding that the boundary between reality and virtual reality is unclear—and both author and reader handle the text on those terms. In this, literary scholars have led the way, as so often before. They embark without hesitation on a detailed analysis of individual autobiographies, *inter alia* with the aim of explaining what kind of phenomenon the autobiography is, and apply a range of perspectives to that analysis. Such new ideas have had a huge impact on the evolution of the humanities in the late twentieth century and the early twenty-first century.

To conclude this discussion of the historical approach of Mary Jo Maynes, it is interesting to point out that she published a book in 2008, *Telling Stories*, with coauthors Jennifer L. Pierce and Barbara Laslett.[53] The objective of the book is to work from an interdisciplinary perspective, as her coauthors are both sociologists. The focus is on individual human agency, which gives an indication of the direction this book took. The authors are here approaching more closely what may be termed the "cultural turn," where each work is recognized on its own terms, though assuredly with a definite connection with "the social." This development is certainly interesting, and demonstrates how a fine scholar such as Mary Jo Maynes has taken account of changing emphases within the discipline, and through her initiative and emphases has had an impact on how our approach to the past has developed. The authors sum up their priorities as follows:

> Finally, personal narrative analysis pushes the investigator to move beyond the distinction between what sociologist call the macro and micro levels of analysis (or, put differently, between the social and the individual realms of experience) and instead to focus on the connections linking them. Once the individual life is explored in its subjective detail and temporal depth, the line between individual and social tends to dissolve.[54]

Their approach is grounded in an attempt to understand the importance of the individual and their narratives of the formation of the self in this interaction. This work marks, effectively, an entirely new view on the use of personal narratives in historical research, which would develop in various different ways in the twenty-first century.

Discussions on historiographical issues in this book mostly focus on the late twentieth century and somewhat into the twenty-first century. As we have already seen, this is when the use of autobiographical material started

Figure 8 Grímsstaðir, Eyrabakka.

slowly but was gradually considered for historical analysis. The purpose of this emphasis is to show how these historical sources garnered the attention of many historians, particularly after grand narratives of any kind were called into question.

The historical development in the twenty-first century and up to the present is, of course, both complicated and thought-provoking. By complicated, I mean that the impact of egodocuments like varied autobiographical material, affected many fields of historical inquiry. To name just a few: the history of emotions, memory studies, and everyday life history, as well as microhistory. For the sake of the argument in this book, I am however focusing almost entirely on the methods of microhistory in the twenty-first century to demonstrate how the use of egodocuments has enriched historical analysis across the globe.

In Chapters 3 and 4, I examine how autobiographical material can be applied effectively. In the following chapters I bring micro and macro approaches together, in an attempt to show how we can best use egodocuments in historical research.

3

The Autobiographical Expression

So far in this book, we have learned a little about the structure of society and how the biographical tradition developed in Iceland in the seventeenth, eighteenth, nineteenth, and twentieth centuries, and into the twenty-first century, in the hands of the general public, as well as how the scholarly world made use of its existence. We have also learned how egodocuments have been used, both in Iceland and elsewhere around the world; the kinds of opportunities this source material has created and how the methods of microhistory have revolutionized the conceptual framework of works of that nature. In this chapter, the idea is to consider how the autobiography comes into being and how it is created. It is important to understand how we can use autobiographies, or egodocuments in general, for historical scholarship and to shed new light on the society with which they deal.

Whose Evidence?

The backstory of autobiographical expression, as it has been recounted in the previous chapters, and the manifestations of the self in the seventeenth, eighteenth, nineteenth, and twentieth centuries raise exigent questions regarding how egodocuments can be used as evidence from the past, or to better understand people's attitudes toward themselves. As we have noticed, in recent times, scholars have started to look favorably on egodocuments and to see various possibilities in their use.[1] This material has been seen as ideal in order to shed light on past times and to better understand the processes that are followed in an analysis of events, phenomena, and individuals. It is important to consider well the arguments of those who saw egodocuments and other narrative sources through *quantitative* spectacles, especially in the context of the rise of social history within the discipline of history in the late twentieth century.[2]

Egodocuments had been in an academic "straitjacket" in the last decades of the twentieth century and even into the twenty-first century, as recounted above: recognized neither as "reliable" evidence of life as it "really" happened, nor as evidence of the quotidian and the recurrent. In the 1980s, social historians sought general information using the methods of social science, as Icelandic historian Guðmundur Hálfdanarson maintained when he pointed out that social historians were dealing "with the recurrent and the involuntary, rather than the unusual."[3] Guðmundur refers here to social historians all over the world being compelled to seek out resources that could be used to demonstrate the recurrent, which was likely to be a manifestation of the systems and processes involved in human life. As stated earlier, Guðmundur Hálfdanarson did not shrink from making extensive use of egodocuments in his study of child labor; however, he did so precisely by focusing on factors that recur over and over again in sources of this kind, with comparison in mind. Earlier, a similar view was expressed by the renowned French historian Roger Chartier at the beginning of the 1990s. "It is clear, moreover," said Chartier, "that since the *histoire des mentalités* (considered as a part of socio-cultural history) takes as its object the collective, the automatic and the repetitive, it can and must employ quantitative methods."[4] In this context, the status of the autobiography has been quite unusual: autobiographies have enjoyed great popularity among the general public, while at the same time social historians have seen them as problematical.

Despite many scholars' negative view of egodocuments, a certain group in the scholarly world started to make very effective and successful use of such resources. Scholars in this group have, however, felt the need to address the matter of the methodological strengths and weaknesses of the sources.[5] Use of material from autobiographies has, for instance, been grounded in the same quantitative methodology as has been applied by social historians who have been strongly influenced by the social sciences.[6] Their use consisted primarily in studying a range of egodocuments (such as autobiographies) and arranging them so that large-scale subjects that occurred could be identified—as I did in my doctoral thesis and Harvey J. Graff in his *Conflicting Paths*, as discussed earlier in the book. That quantitative approach has entailed at least three focuses which scholars have discussed, relating to the reliability of the sources (Figure 9).

First, many scholars asked themselves whether it is even possible to dredge up from people's minds memories of events and people relating to their lives. Is it feasible to illustrate in writing a comprehensive picture of an experience from past times? Are such memories perhaps nothing but the writer's state of mind at the time of writing, or can they provide insight into the author's mind, decades

Figure 9 Vallakot, Grímsey.

after the events took place? Many scholars have also asked whether memories of past times may perhaps best be used as descriptions of impersonal events: in that case, the memories are seen as less likely to lead the reader into the maze of the writer's mental and emotional life. That is often deemed simply impossible. Others reject such arguments, taking the view that memories of past times are most valuable precisely because they disclose the thoughts and ideas of people from the past. These are all worthwhile issues, to which there is no clear answer.

Second, questions were often asked about the significance of the fact that egodocuments are, first and foremost, *subjective* sources. The inference of the questions is that egodocuments are not to be relied on, as it can be difficult to verify specific events and actions recounted there. But, in recent years, another question has been asked in return: is there really so much difference between the subjectivity of egodocuments and of other sources? In addition, in recent years, increasing numbers of scholars have maintained that it is precisely that subjectivity which makes egodocuments valuable resources. In order to win over the skeptics, certain methods have been adopted in order to enhance their belief in the potential of such sources. These methods will be explored further below, demonstrating how attempts have been made to ensure that the source will be taken seriously by those who have hitched their wagon to quantitative thinking.

Third, many scholars gave thought to the motives behind autobiographical writing. There is nothing strange in asking about the impulse that has led people to engage in airing their opinions, attitudes, and personal experiences in a public arena. Such an analysis is deemed likely to determine where individual stories belong on a scale of veracity—to locate the boundary between the credible and the incredible. What stories are to be trusted? And how can we identify those that are not to be trusted according to "scientific" academic principles?

The first two issues are concerned with whether, and how, autobiographies could be used as scholarly resources. The third focuses on the value of each autobiography *per se*, regardless of the bigger picture. In brief, the first two may be classified as essentially methodological, while the third is practical.[7] All three entail attempts, at the time, to evaluate the sources on the scale of quantitative thinking, accepting the arguments on which that approach is based.[8] The premise is accepted that it is possible to determine whether, and how, a specific autobiography is consistent with the bigger picture. Scholars constantly asked how they could be sure that an autobiographer is part of a larger group, and in some sense a spokesperson for that group. In the 1990s, they were keen to ascertain what group the writer belongs to and stands for, and how they may be said to reflect the group's views. The testimony of the individual alone is not enough, according to this ideology.[9] That is because it is individual—not recurrent and involuntary—contrary to the preferences of social historians, as discussed above. For that reason, many scholars saw it as important to explore the motivation for the autobiography, in order that all the source base of egodocuments may be sorted into categories, thus facilitating an analysis of their source value. In other words, the quantitative approach requires from scholars a clear analysis of whether there is any truth in the account in question. This gives rise to a complex discourse on *veracity* as the basis of quantitative science or the "scientific" arguments of the discipline.[10]

The abovementioned arguments and the concomitant frame of discourse are the main focus of this chapter. An attempt will be made to examine the arguments that have been adduced in favor of, and against, egodocuments as testimony about people's lives—and especially the factors emphasized by scholars until the 1990s. In this context, I explain how I developed a discussion on a quantitative approach to narrative sources such as autobiographies when I was working on my doctoral thesis in the United States in 1985–1993. The quantitative arguments were radically revised in America in the late 1990s, and I return to that step-change later in the book. In that context, I state the main arguments regarding the place of egodocuments as *qualitative* sources which have been put forward in international academic debate as it has evolved in the last few years. Entirely different principles apply in the use of sources, and scholars' way of thinking in their research is in sharp contrast to the previously accepted norms in the discipline. The reader will also have the opportunity to compare in clear terms the quantitative and qualitative approaches. The focus will be on the evolution of scholarly thinking in the twentieth century, which is directly relevant to the position of an analysis of the autobiography at the beginning of the twenty-first century.

Reliability of the Subject

In his well-known book *Aspects of Biography*, written in the late 1920s, André Maurois pointed out that there are "several causes which tend to make autobiographical narrative inaccurate or false."[11] One reason for the weakness of the autobiography as a source is, in Maurois' view, a generalized problem with memory, and especially the individual's systematic "censorship" of their own memory. That alone has sufficed for scholars to shun such sources, entirely or in part. Maurois' ideas spring from a trend in historic scholarship from the nineteenth century and into the twentieth century, which may be briefly summed up as follows: in the eighteenth century and before, argument was made that the biographical form was worth something if the subject had a close connection to the author. But as Michael Mascuch, Rudolf Dekker, and Arianne Baggerman point out in their important article on the development of egodocuments, "nineteenth century scientists stressed the importance of critical distance between subject and writer. Hewing to this new empirical and objective orientation, professional historians slighted both biography and the emerging secular autobiography for their subjective perspective."[12] The authors went on to point out that for the rest of the nineteenth century, egodocuments were left in limbo, as a marginal phenomenon in historiography. "On account of historiography's embrace of positivist objectivity, egodocuments of any sort were deemed unreliable sources of history."[13] This was precisely the basis of André Maurois' views on the importance and value of the autobiography as a historical source material.

Maurois maintained, for instance, that it was all but impossible for an individual to remember anything from childhood: that what people think they remember is invariably based on the memories of others—people who were part of their life and were witnesses to their childhood, such as parents, siblings, other relatives, friends, and neighbors. Maurois goes on:

> Yes, all that remains to us of our childhood consists of just such tiny things—confused feelings mixed up with associations of which the origin is lost in

obscurity. This is not enough to explain the complex individuality which we all acquire by the age of six or seven. Of the vast accession of vocabulary, ideas, and emotions; of our introduction to the world outside, of the successive pictures of society which are formed in the mental vision of a child—of all this we retain practically nothing; and so an autobiography of childhood is nearly always commonplace and untrue, even when the author himself is sincere.[14]

The author took the view that the individual continues to forget through the whole course of their life, although the impact of forgetting is greatest during childhood. This is because "his recollections are linked on to certain fixed realities which surround and absorb him."[15] Here, Maurois upholds the view that every person goes through such enormous change in their early years—changes apropos of emotions, intellect, and general experience relating to the child's surroundings that extend to factors such as language, ideas, and visual reality—that it is impossible to trace the process of development. Due to these emotional and intellectual upheavals, he maintains, childhood memories are completely unreliable.

Maurois is not alone in this view, which has affected ideas about the autobiography right through to the end of the twentieth century. Let us consider some important voices in history—people who had the courage to make use of egodocuments in their research in the 1980s, such as Icelandic historian Guðmundur Hálfdanarson, who pointed out in his paper on child labor cited above that autobiographies are appealing but untrustworthy sources: "This is true not least with respect to the autobiographer's childhood. This is testimony written many years or decades after the events described took place. The writer puts down what he remembers, as he remembers it. But memory is an unreliable tool for historians. It stores up special events rather than daily routine."[16] The other Icelandic historian previously mentioned, Loftur Guttormsson, had reservations regarding the use of autobiographies and also pointed out the problems involved in recalling past events.[17] Loftur expresses the view that in the case of childhood memories, "the account is colored by reinterpretation in later life, which takes place more-or-less involuntarily as one grows older."[18] Loftur adds that it is also debatable how much can be extrapolated from descriptions in an autobiography, "and what it says or does not say."[19] In other words, it seems to me that scholars who addressed this issue in the early and late twentieth century were of the view that it was risky to take such sources too literally, because their very existence and their reliability are predicated on the author's memory.

There is nothing surprising about this attitude among social historians, in view of the requirement within the discipline at the time when Guðmundur and

Loftur did their research, that issues must be addressed in quantitative terms, and that the "scientific" reliability of the sources used must be demonstrated.[20] It is beyond dispute that Guðmundur and Loftur displayed considerable audacity in their time with their use of egodocuments, in a most effective manner.[21] The research work of both demonstrated what rich sources these can be. The reservations they stated with regard to the use of autobiographies are quite understandable in view of the trends and ideas that were dominant in the 1980s.

Literary scholar John A. Garraty threw some doubt on childhood memories in his *The Nature of Biography*, published in the 1950s. Garraty's main issue concerned how the truthfulness of such memories could be verified. But, in spite of these drawbacks, he saw at least one strength in childhood memories:

> However, memories of childhood are often very frank. As psychologist Edwin G. Boring once wrote: 'You can be proud of your childhood or sorry for yourself as a child; in either case you are free to say what you think without evolvement because childhood is separated off from manhood. But when you get into your twenties, then the responsibility for the mature continuous individual comes in and you are constrained'.[22]

In other words, it is possible to maintain that children's memories are a function of constant change, so that is impossible to expect any individual to discern the series of thoughts and ideas that are involved. But the image that forms in the mind of a person passing through the upheavals that are part of childhood is likely to be honest and truthful, according to Garraty, and thus stands out from people's latter-day memories. The problem is hence not deliberate deceit, as maintained by the abovementioned skeptics; instead the subconscious is at work, and can adversely affect memory. People tell themselves they will remember this or that, but the conclusion is often lost in the chicanery of memory.

The inference of these arguments is that the inevitable fate of all autobiographers is censorship. It is of three kinds: first, *considered censorship*— that is, the universal experience of those who set out to recall past events. Selecting some memories and rejecting others is a process of considered censorship. This is one of the principal characteristics of the autobiography: the writer must consider which facts and events have been important in their life, and how they have been applied in life. Considered censorship is a manifestation of the limitations of the autobiography, and at the same time of its strengths: the selection always lies with the author themself, who is responsible for what is included. The limitations consist of the author's decision not to tell the whole story, to winnow the grain from the chaff. Hence, the writer may not focus on the matters that are most interesting to scholars or others who wish to make use of this testimony. The content is selected by the author on their own terms.

Second, there is what may be termed *unconscious censorship*; many scholars have found this a stumbling block and have seen it as a fault in the source. Some people view it as a universal human tendency to deny our less pleasant memories, so that they disappear from our minds. Nearly every single person does this systematically, from cradle to grave (or almost). Such memory-filtering prevents the author from being able to throw light on "reality" as it appeared to people at the time of the event.

Third is a factor which we may call *linguistic limitations*—the restrictions imposed by language on all expression that aims to recount "what happened, as it happened." Even if we had the capacity to recall with precision everything that has happened to us, it is impossible to express that in words in such a way as to illuminate the "reality" as it was. In that sense, the language "censors" what we do and imposes on the narrative natural restrictions which cannot be overcome.[23] So, the question is: What is the reality recounted in the text? Does it have anything in common with the person's experience, or is experience tangible only in language itself?

All these factors have led scholars to engage in extensive speculation. Unconscious censorship, for instance, has received much attention from those who study autobiography and those who focus on memory. In recent decades, various lawsuits have arisen regarding alleged past sexual offenses against young people. In these cases, with the assistance of psychologists (sometimes using hypnosis), victims have recovered memories of events alleged to have taken place when they were children—and in many cases the allegations have proven to be well grounded. The reliability of recovered memories has been fiercely disputed in many of these cases, and doubts have been cast on how it is possible to forget such experiences. The debate on these questions has been interesting, focusing especially on the methods applied in recovering memories. At one time, many such cases were energetically prosecuted, for instance in the United States, often with extensive media coverage. And the plaintiffs were often vindicated in court. In more recent years, however, there has been a backlash, and law courts have become increasingly skeptical of evidence recovered in this way. This is primarily because experience has shown how easily memories recovered from the subconscious through psychological methods can be influenced and altered. Psychologists, and their role in memory recovery, have been subjected to rigorous scrutiny.[24]

In the same way, the Holocaust of the 1930s and 1940s has also been a focus of attention in recent times, and especially the role of memory, and memories, in the formation of personal and national identity.[25] Around the turn of the twenty-first century, both scholars and members of the general public almost seemed to be in a competition to settle issues relating to the Holocaust—reawakening memories that had been suppressed for decades. One of the principal questions that arose was how it was possible to remember anything at all, for people who had lived through the excruciating suffering inflicted on Jews, Gypsies, homosexuals, and others during the Nazi genocide.[26]

The truth is that unconscious censorship, however it happens, is a matter that remains controversial today. But it is clear that the way unconscious censorship works may be classified as a normal defensive response in people who have experienced grave psychological trauma. When individuals have been through such horrific experiences as genocide, sexual abuse, "ethnic cleansing," or other crimes against humanity, in many cases their only option is to carry on with their lives, suppressing their memories and the emotions they awaken. To learn to live with one's bad experiences is often the only possible way to cope in societies that do not offer opportunities for the expression of emotions. Such a decision not to speak—whether conscious or unconscious—becomes a part of that person's identity and affects the rest of their life.

The point has been made that when people reject unpleasant memories, that need not necessarily involve any very dramatic event. In an individual's thinking about themself and their sense of identity, there is a tendency to skim over events that are inconsistent with the personal identity one has forged. According to André Maurois, if an event gives rise to overwhelming feelings of shame, memories of that event will be erased. It is rare, for instance, for autobiographers to frankly discuss their sexual lives, as—at least for most of the twentieth century—it was not deemed appropriate to make one's sexual experiences public. Yet, it is safe to assume that emotional life in its many forms may have played an essential role in the mental landscape of the autobiographer (and in many cases certainly did). For André Maurois, memories—or the process of memory—are nothing but a logical justification of the person's life, and invariably a considered review, looking back:[27]

> When the crisis is past, he looks back, rationalises, and says to himself: 'I am a socialist, I am a positivist, I am a conservative.... The development of my ideas was as follows. Such and such a process of reasoning convinced me.' Later, in his old age, he finds himself (if he examines the past) in the presence of this series of incoherent and contradictory crises, and, since he cannot tolerate the idea of not

being able to understand himself, he makes a system out of his life and organises it in order to make this system coherent.[28]

Maurois' description of memory following a certain course makes interesting reading. His conclusion is simply that it is impossible to get close to the past, by any means. If we accept his arguments with respect to the autobiography, we must at least ask whether the same may apply to all other sources, of all kinds, regardless of how much time has passed from the event before it is recorded. Does not every text entail some kind of justification of actions, by individuals or those in power—and does not such justification tend to follow a certain course within the limitations of language?[29] In that case, what is the difference between egodocuments and other historical resources? This is a question that must be considered.

Sources

I am fairly sure that today the majority of critics of egodocuments would not agree with Maurois' arguments, as that would involve establishing some kind of scale for determining when the memory is most likely to fail and when it is reliable.[30] Is it in the same minute that the event takes place, or two hours later? Two months? And so on. No such scale exists, of course, and scholars must simply accept that each individual source or fragment exists on its own terms. Hence, it must be judged by itself, bearing in mind a range of factors which may influence the outcome. Time is, naturally, an important issue in all discussion of sources in the study of history. But ideas such as those put forward by Maurois have a tendency, on the other hand, to cast doubt on anything that involves memory and its relationship with self-awareness.[31]

Problems relating to memory have given rise to the view that the autobiography itself faces another, graver, problem which was mentioned above: the *limitations of language*. The challenge of putting each thought into words is not conducive to scholars having confidence in the reliability of memory. Not only does language restrict the narrative, but also phenomena such as the autobiography must conform with certain norms as a literary form, as will be discussed later in the context of Iceland's cultural heritage. Such formulae have been said to direct the narrative along a certain path, compelling it to comply with certain "rules" of form, which have emerged over the centuries.[32] The claim has thus been made that the form itself almost takes over control of the narrative, shackling it into a framework of convention.³³ This is a function both of the character of the autobiography as a literary genre, and also aesthetic factors. It is probable, for instance, that many autobiographers fall into the temptation of "spicing up" their accounts, adding events and heroic feats to make for a more interesting read than unaltered reality. Elements of style thus affect the outcome, and writers can be expected to apply oratorical skills when presenting their work. Characters may be created or sacrificed in order to illustrate an improved and sharper picture.

Models have great importance in autobiographical writing, as in other literary genres. The characterization seen in published autobiographies may influence authors in their accounts of people and issues in their own books. Hence, in the autobiographical tradition certain *archetypes* emerge, which become models for other books of a similar nature. Benjamin Franklin's autobiography, for instance, not only became a model for other autobiographers, but it also had a pedagogical influence on its readers, who used it as a template to live by. For that reason, some people see endless drawbacks to using such sensitive sources because in their view they are simply not to be trusted.

André Maurois' conclusion about the past need come as no surprise: "It is impossible, then, to retrieve the past; it is impossible not to change it unconsciously, and, further, it is impossible not to change it consciously. Such are the obstacles which make one fear that an authentic autobiography can never be written."³⁴ Maurois here states a principle with which many late-twentieth-century scholars who are called postmodernists can agree; however, they differ from him in extending the argument to all historical sources!³⁵

As mentioned above, other scholars have reached the same conclusion as Maurois. Some recognized that an autobiography can be useful where it refers to specific events "that need no interpretation in order to reveal their importance," as Georg Misch says in his *History of Autobiography in Antiquity*.³⁶ He frankly states his view that "in the reproduction of inward and especially of religious experiences, autobiography is a field of auto-delusion."³⁷ Nor is Misch in any doubt—like many later social historians—that the autobiography is "the self-knowledge of the individual at the time when, looking back on the past, he attempts to survey and assess his life as a whole."³⁸ But some difference is evident between Misch and Maurois' views, in that Misch's work is predicated on conventional positivist views that egodocuments are neither usable nor reliable because it is impossible to verify them. Maurois, on the other hand, takes the view that the past cannot be recreated regardless of what sources are available. While Misch is certainly faithful to his positivist views, he approached the subject from the viewpoint of his father-in-law, German philosopher

Figure 10 Hólakot, Borgarfirði.

Wilhelm Dithery, who maintained that the scholarly community should study autobiographies in order to gain insight into the culture of individuality in the Western world. That approach would be influential later in the twentieth century, when egodocuments began to attract more scholarly interest.

All the criticism discussed above provides an opportunity to address the character of the autobiography, and other related resources, from an interesting viewpoint. It is precisely such debate that has ultimately reconciled many skeptics to the idea of using autobiographies in the resolution of issues within the discipline. Scholars have gradually realized that such sources offer a viewpoint that cannot otherwise be achieved in scholarly research. It is important, nonetheless, to bear in mind this criticism which emerged in the mid-twentieth century, as it had a strong influence on many historians until the end of the century.

Memory and the Concept of Time

The reliability of memory has been called into question by historians and others working in the humanities, and has led to scholars hesitating to make use of sources based on the memory of one individual. But opinions differ. A certain group of scholars have approached egodocuments with a more favorable attitude. Let us recall the three main issues that arise with respect to using egodocuments in scholarly research:

(1) Can any person retrieve from memory reliable memories of past times?
(2) Does not the passage of time ensure that little is left of the memory, except perhaps fragments, which can hardly form the basis of study?
(3) Are "memories" not simply testimony about the time and place where the writing took place? In other words, is it possible to remember events from decades ago?

In later modern times (1750 to the present), conditions arose in which people were able to see themselves as vital elements of society—individuals who had references in time and space. This way of thinking, which was regarded as new in history (at least with regard to the peasantry) according to the ideas of the adherents of modernization theory, meant that people increasingly engaged in examining themselves and the life they led as autonomous beings.[39] This was partly attributable to a fundamental change in the status of time as a phenomenon: in the early modern period (1500–1750), individuals in traditional agrarian societies were seen as having perceived time as cyclical. In the modern period, in contrast, people started to see time as having a direction, progressing ever-onward. The outcome of that process was that ever-increasing attention was paid to progress or development. *Change* thus became a key concept in people's mindset from the latter half of the eighteenth century to the present. Everything was contingent on changed circumstances. The individual began to see themselves as a person setting off on a journey—a journey that is meaningless without constant reference to the past, present, and future. On the journey, a person met with challenges which called for changes in thought and deed. Life, and the preparation for it, consisted largely of being able to deal with new circumstances and get one's bearings in a new environment. The aim was to deal with these changes in such a way as to promote personal growth and progress.

It goes without saying that such ideas about time have been much criticized: the sharp division envisaged between the agrarian societies of the early modern period and the modern societies that followed, with urbanization, industrialization, the emergence of the nation state, etc., was deemed to have been less clear-cut than the adherents of modernization theory had maintained. A group of historians noticed, for example, that before the days of real industrialization, a phenomenon they termed "proto-industry" had existed: this was a stage of economic development that was the premise for the industrialization of societies that took place from the late eighteenth century until the early twentieth century.[40] It has been maintained, in other words, that there was much more professional specialization in such "agrarian" societies than had previously been believed, and that paved the way for the Industrial Revolution. This pattern of specialization in rural society was diverse in nature; in some cases, it entailed that raw materials were gathered together in one place and used in a production process by a family who had excess time and labor available for some portion of the year. This offered the opportunity for specialization in some specific work. Ongoing development meant that the owners of the raw materials increasingly sought out a stable workforce, which could focus exclusively on that branch of production.

Another step toward industrialization was taken when production was transferred to urban centers, where the workforce was less subject to seasonal factors. However, that did not alter the fact that the period in question (after 1750) called for major changes of mindset for most of the population.

The Life Course in Real Time

In this context, I want to tell a little story which relates to arguments I put forward for the use of autobiographical works in historical research. In the early 1990s, I was in the United States working on my doctoral thesis. Among other things, I considered the significance of autobiographies for historical research. That was unavoidable, as the scholarly environment to which I belonged at that time had little faith in narrative sources such as egodocuments. Historical demography was the name of the game for the majority of social historians I mixed with, and that fact spurred me to give serious thought to the importance of such sources. And, what is more, the demographic focus of social historians in the United States provided me with the quantitative research model that I used in my thesis.[41] But how was it possible to expect life-course analysis to succeed in bringing to light the relationship between individuals, time, space, the nature of specific events, and the historical development that affected the life course?

The individual life course of ordinary people, especially in nineteenth-century rural and twentieth-century urban societies, was the focus of my thesis. And the protocol for my study derived precisely from the application of the *life-course analysis* model, based on the principle that the life of each individual may be divided into several stages—life stages, each of which has its own attributes and significance in the individual's development. Such life stages are imposed by the formal institutions of society and are designed to control people's development and role in society in relation to time. They are thus shaped by the needs of society, which also has a decisive influence on its function. The life stages make up a sort of framework around human life from cradle to grave, dividing a life into chronological units taking account of development, action, and ability. Within the limits of each life stage, the individual has a good opportunity to deal with their own circumstances, and in a sense the life stages are a support network for each person as they engage with society's expectations and the general routine of everyday life.

In nineteenth-century Iceland, the life stages were as follows: the period from birth until the child's first tasks is generally seen as one life stage.[42] In Icelandic agrarian society at that time, children were put to work from the age of about five to seven. A child's first task was a landmark in life, as they had to stand on their own feet and rely on their own initiative and resourcefulness. For many, this was hard to achieve and might affect their entire lives. "I was young when I began to be expected to 'do something useful,' for in those days it was taken for granted that children would start working as soon as possible," wrote Bernharð Stefánsson (b. 1889) in his autobiography.[43] Another autobiographer recalls falling asleep as a boy when he was watching over ewes one evening, and thus lost control of the herd of sheep: "It was far beyond my capabilities at such a young age, but the responsibility was placed without hesitation on country children in those days."[44]

The next life stage, from the age of about seven to fourteen, ended with confirmation into the church as an adult, which was a life-changing time for most. This period was varied and complex. In my thesis, I divided this stage into two, taking account of the customs of most homes in connection with the combination of work and education for children, which has already been discussed here. Dividing the stage into two was helpful in identifying striking aspects of children's lives between these two principal factors in rural society and also brought to light the autonomy enjoyed by most children with respect to both work and education.

Most autobiographers write in detail about their work and what it entailed at that stage of life. The accounts indicate that work played a very important role in the life of any individual. Finnur Jónsson (b. 1842) developed rickets early in life, which permanently affected him physically, as he discussed in his autobiography titled *Þjóðhættir og ævisögur* (*Customs and Biographies from the*

Nineteenth Century). He reports on various tasks assigned to him at that period of his life:

> It was also my job to round up horses and drive them. Every evening I had to drive them a long way west by the Hólaá river to a gully on the boundary of the Laugardalshólar and Miðdalur estates. Often I didn't get home until everybody was asleep. I was often tired and cold, during the chills of spring, because I had to go the whole way through marshland without waterproof footwear, even in frosty conditions. Because I often got back late in the evening, I couldn't get enough sleep, as my mother didn't want me to get into the habit of lying abed in the mornings. Like many people of old-school thinking, she tended to allow youngsters rather little sleep. Though I often felt that my mother was unnecessarily censorious and strict, I never answered back at that time.[45]

The life stage from confirmation to marriage was both long and important, as people had an opportunity to live their lives independently, though at the same time they enjoyed few formal rights. People in service had the legal status of children. They strove to establish a basis for living an independent life, until they married, at an average age of about thirty for both men and women. By that time, they had reached a point where they could set up home as a family. But prior to that time, their position was severely circumscribed, and they had little freedom of action due to the old system of bonded labor, whereby landless people were compelled to work for farmers under yearly contracts and had no freedom to seek employment on their own terms.[46]

The situation of the individual on the basis of life-course analysis—a subjective evaluation from the experience of hundreds of authors of egodocuments—can best be visualized in the following schematic diagram.

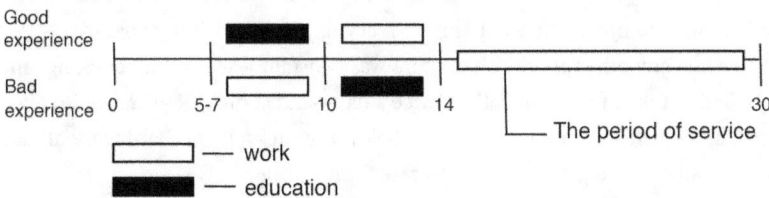

The final life stage is from marriage to death. That stage was naturally characterized by the individual's efforts to achieve and retain autonomy, and many authors of egodocuments see it as a time of action. Stories recounted from that time of life tend to have a bittersweet tone, reflecting the fact that the person succeeded in what they had set out to do—to seize control of their life and achieve security—although many sacrifices were necessary along the way. There are, of course, also cases where the opposite is true—recounted by those who had not succeeded in making their way, or whose progress had been halted by illness, or by the multitude of injustices ingrained in society. Such stories too can be compelling, leading the reader to consider the relationship between the individual and the community.

All these life stages can be subdivided into smaller units than are specified here. All the stages are mutable and their relative significance varies from one period to another—not least in different societies.[47] I focused primarily on the earlier stages of life, but it is clear that the later life stages are far more complex than scholars have generally recognized, and it may be regarded as certain that their importance will increase in the future.[48]

There is no doubt that people's lives in the latter part of the nineteenth century and the early twentieth century were complex and burdensome. Work took over almost all of a person's life, and for parents the demands were great. Tryggvi Emilsson's account of his parents' workday in the early 1900s provides insight into family life. At this point, the couple have eight children and they are living in dire poverty in a small cottage on the outskirts of Akureyri, an urban center in north Iceland:

> It was the autumn of 1906. My father was working in a fish plant at Oddeyri. He got up at an early hour each morning to stoke the fire under the boilers, and he often got home late at night. In bad weather he was often soaked to the skin, for there were no waterproofs, but people had to put up with those conditions, and they were glad to be in work.
>
> My mother took good care of the home. She fetched water from the well or from the brook that flowed out of the marsh by the field boundary; she saw to the cattleshed and took care of the sheep, and kept the farmhouse so clean that it was remarked upon; she went almost every day to buy fish to cook, carrying it home like any other goods. Then there was constant washing and cooking, and she had to take food to my father twice a day—and sometimes she would take a shift at the fish-drying site on the spit below the rocks. It was hard work all day, yet she always had plenty of time to care for her children.[49]

Those who mainly pursue life-course analysis focus on the *transition* which takes place when the individual passes from one life stage to the next. Such transitions often entail major upheaval. Dealing with new circumstances then reveals the personality traits of the individual and the demands that society makes on them. In such a situation, every person must examine their own character and make a decision about what to do. That stocktaking process lays the foundation for the person's future, a "road-map" that will be followed in life.[50]

A life course of this kind, in the nineteenth-century world that was changing, though slowly, explicitly required people to take stock at regular junctures of their lives. It is necessary for all conscious people to look back over their past and take stock, in order to achieve a better understanding of their life. "Where do I stand, at this point in my life?" people may ask, and "How should I live my life in future?" And it is certainly possible to maintain that such questions are likely to assail people going through a period of change, passing from one life stage to the next.

After reading, at the time, well over 300 works that may be classified as egodocuments, the vast majority dealing with the latter half of the nineteenth century and the first half of the twentieth century, I became convinced, as I carried out my doctoral research, that as one life stage ends and another begins, with new obligations and problems, every individual realizes that they must consider their place in life. In that way, people acquire the necessary strength to deal with the daily tasks and challenges that lie ahead. In such stocktaking, a person sums up the most important elements of their life, and then goes on to face new challenges, armed with what has been learned from experience. I felt that this was revealed in one way or another in almost all of the Icelandic autobiographies I used in my research.

As the life course comprises a number of stages, as enumerated above, the individual will take stock as one life stage follows another, cumulatively adding to the summary of their life. The stocktaking may take place at an unconscious level: the person may not sit down to think over the past and their options, or meditate deeply. The process usually takes place as the life change is approaching, and that preliminary period is "formalized" in the sense that it takes place in the context of the formal elements of the life course, which are determined systematically by the social structure.

But such stocktaking can also happen unexpectedly, without any prelude or warning. This is what French scholar Roland Barthes called *biographème*: an event in a life, no matter how small, which throws light—or is made to throw light—on the personality and life of a person, *in toto*. The idea is that some event has had such a decisive influence on a person's psyche that it informs their life history ever afterward. But such transformations have nothing to do with the organized stocktaking involved in the formalized life course. The formal institutions compel the individual to consider their position, and that process of thinking may be a result of inner conflict or other mental consequences of change. Hence, this is a focused process, and it should be reiterated that the stocktaking that takes place is a vital premise for the well-being of the individual, and the way they choose to go in the next life stage. Stocktaking that arises from the unexpected, such as a death or accident that has a great impact on the person's psyche, may have precisely the same consequences, that is, to require a reevaluation of the person's life.

In this context, a number of examples may be mentioned: in Icelandic agrarian society in the nineteenth century, confirmation, following on from infant baptism, was a typical example of a formal "institution," as mentioned above. Prior to confirmation, youngsters received instruction from the parish priest, generally over a period of weeks. Confirmation instruction essentially compelled them to consider their place in the world, especially since so many of them would be leaving their childhood home after being recognized as adults through the confirmation ceremony. This was thus a decisive turning point in their young lives. The ceremony itself was designed to underline to the confirmand and the congregation the magnitude of the change. This was ensured by a combination of their own actions with those of the ecclesiastical authorities and the congregation—including parents. Before God and their neighbors, the children were tested on their knowledge of Scripture. That event is often recounted in vivid detail in egodocuments, which is attributable partly to the fact that the youngsters were encouraged to think deeply about its significance. Tryggvi Jónsson (b. 1864) describes the roller-coaster of emotion he experienced on his confirmation day:

> Finally the big day came around. The lead-up to it had been quite prolonged—with many grave admonitions. It seemed to me that the ceremony ahead was very serious and important.
>
> —Before the mass, the pastor spoke to each of us in private, and gave us various advice. He pointed out to us the great responsibility for our lives that we were now taking on ourselves, making a promise about it before God and men.
>
> —I felt I understood how important this was for me, and I was seized with fear and trepidation. I did not manage to properly control my feelings, and I burst into tears. I cried for quite a long time, convulsed with sobs. The pastor was kind to me, and he managed to console me.[51]

Tryggvi's fear was concerned with the unknown—with what would happen next when he had entered on a new life stage. Such a feeling can often be read between the lines in egodocuments, and it may be regarded as certain that Tryggvi's tearful outbreak was attributable to the emotional turmoil commonly experienced by confirmands. But that anxiety about the future and what it might bring was precisely what motivated the individual to make peace with themself. Most autobiographers seem to reach the conclusion that they must take stock of their lives in order to be capable of taking the next step. And that quest was often beneficial, so that people looked forward to undertaking the challenges ahead. Ágúst Jósefsson (b. 1874) describes that feeling in his autobiography: "My confirmation was in my mind a very solemn and significant ceremony, which changed me, as it seemed to me, into a grown man, and required of me that from now on I should myself be responsible for my deeds and all my actions during my life."[52]

The impact of the changes that would follow the confirmation day was not confined to stirring up feelings of anxiety, fear, or pleasurable anticipation; in other cases, the psychological effect was far more dramatic, almost like an out-of-body experience. "All at once I was overcome by joy and peace, which I felt flowing into my consciousness," wrote Friðgeir H. Berg (b. 1883) in his autobiography, recalling the time just before the confirmation ceremony when the pastor was testing the children's knowledge of the Catechism. Moments before, Friðgeir had seen a ray of sunlight burst into the church, bathing the deserted space with a mystical glow. "That joy and peace had nothing in common with doctrine or religion; it was far deeper and more rapturous. I felt it brought with it everything a mortal man could desire of spiritual riches. That moment has lived on evergreen in my consciousness."[53] Friðgeir's potent experience of his confirmation day is of a nature that leads one to consider how events and circumstances can have an impact on people, and how that life experience can be put into words.

When I was developing my arguments in favor of the use of egodocuments in the early 1990s, I was approaching the completion of my studies in the United States. I was quite preoccupied by the question of what would happen to me once the thesis was completed, and the *viva voce* examination was over. And those thoughts grew more insistent as the day of the *viva* approached. And all at once, I was overcome with feelings of anxiety and a sort of anguish because that period of my life was coming to an end—a period that had lasted nine years. Now it was time for me to take the next step, out of the community that had nurtured me as a doctoral student—and where I had been happy, under the sheltering wing of excellent men and women—into another and less secure existence, where I was expected to play my part as a fully fledged historian. Night after night at one time, I was plagued by nightmares which I immediately attributed to this watershed in my life. But it took me some time to realize that I was going through the same process as many of the autobiographers I was studying. I also recognized how my subconscious resolved the anxiety attacks by looking back in time and retracing the process that my doctoral studies had entailed, to draw a picture of the experience

I had gained. I thus grappled with a period that extended from the beginning of my doctoral studies (and even earlier in my life course) until their conclusion and reconciled my inner forces which were in conflict over my feelings about the future. My internal turmoil was so overwhelming that I felt a need for a fundamental rethink of my own sense of myself and the reality around me. In a sense, the changes that my personality underwent may be likened to a *metamorphosis*. I was, at any rate, never the same again: my life was turned upside down. And—more than that—the arguments that I had been dealing with in the context of the autobiographies were suddenly brought to life in my own emotional life.

In the end, I was able to put myself in the place of the Rev. Gunnar Benediktsson, who we will deal with later in this book, who had said after he was confirmed that it had been "as if I were being born into a new world, in those spring days of the Year of Our Lord 1907"—because that summed up exactly how I felt at the end of 1993.[54]

Such emotional experiences, and other less sweeping ones, gradually give rise to a fully formed idea of the life story of each person. My hypothesis is that the synopsis that is made at landmarks in life "create the person" in that period and that it remains with the individual throughout their life. And the individual calls upon those synopses or some version of them, in due course when looking back over their life. Certain people go on to put their life-synopsis down on paper for

Figure 11 A farm in Fljótshlíð.

a range of reasons, to which I will return below. The most important element is that the synopsis is shaped in the person's mind, simultaneously with a period of change or shortly afterward; and, due to its existential significance for the person, it must be deemed likely to be stored in their memory. Thus, the result of the stocktaking—the narrative that is created in the mind—may be seen as a force which shapes the individual and their existence. It is useful to everyone at such milestones in life and gives shape to the person's identity at that stage of the life course. Synopses of life stages are thus part of the subject, to be summoned up when the need arises, when a person's life or some aspect of it is under scrutiny—*inter alia* when writing an autobiography in the autumn of life.

4

The Formation of the *Self*

Individuals Are Born!

One of the findings of my research is that a human being is, in the end, not one but many. Every individual goes through such colossal changes in the course of life that one can hardly compare the same person at two different life stages through their whole life course. We are, however, always striving to hold the fragments together, to reconcile the *many* who dwell within us. These efforts often give rise to emotions that have a unifying influence on disparate forces in people's lives. That tension is precisely the reason why the individual and their history make for such a fascinating subject of research for those who study the past.

One of the most enchanting descriptions by an autobiographer of the emotional impact of milestones in life was written by the poet Matthías Jochumsson (b. 1835) in his autobiographical masterpiece *Sögukaflar af sjálfum mér* (*Short Tales of Myself*):

> The most difficult part, perhaps, was to write the story of one's childhood years. The adult has nothing to rely on but his own memory, or those of others. But for most people, that part of memory has disintegrated. And it is mainly the larger transitions which retain in the memory some life or color, something of the
>
> sensation of sorrow and joy, some sense of cause and effect. For it is certain that man's pulse never beats as fast as in childhood—the phenomena of life are never relished more rapidly as then, and joy and sorrow are never so close to each other again. A child's smile has been likened to a flash of sunlight, and his tears to the morning dew.
>
> But is that so? Does any force, any impact, vanish without trace? Would not all the impacts of the child's inner life emerge in some way in the web that forms the inner and outer character of the adult? That is my view, though I cannot demonstrate or prove it.[1]

It would be hard to describe more effectively how a person comes to be, how they shape their own personality from the materials supplied by memory. The formative process is continuous and is at its most prolific during the childhood years. These continual fluctuations in the child's mind, whenever something new and unexpected arises, are often more effectively stored in memory than other events that occur later in life. Many autobiographies allude to this, and the accounts are often dramatic. Childhood is the life stage when the individual goes through the changes that have the most lasting impact—whatever the person experiences later in life. But there are variations in whether, and how much, such memories shape the personality and how their manifestations are reflected in daily life in adulthood.

As stated above, many social historians have dismissed autobiographies as dependable sources on the grounds that they are primarily evidence of the mental state of the author at the time of writing. In my doctoral thesis, I maintained, on the contrary, that the content of the life story derives from the synopses which people must often make at the time of transition from one life stage to the next. The individual who has been formed at one stage disappears and another takes over at the next life stage, in a constant process of revising the norms and attitudes that are applied at different stages of life. Of course, this does not lead to an unchanging, immutable identity which endures lifelong, pure. and untainted for the historian's scrutiny. On the contrary, experience and its scope undergo change through memory; however, the essence of the memory persists to become part of the ongoing process that informs the life course of the individual.

I am well aware that there are variations in how far those who collect a store of memories have succeeded in developing their sense of their surroundings and themselves. That perception is a function not only of personal factors but also of environmental and cultural circumstances. Sensitivity to odor, taste, visual interpretation, and other "aesthetic" factors relative to emotional life demands conditions which hardly existed in the latter half of the nineteenth century and the early twentieth century.[2] In a sense, all of a scholar's study and training consist of developing a "feel" for the subject matter—learning to spot what is important and nurtures the imagination. The key to this is to apply the senses in the most productive way, in order to develop one's understanding of life. The same is true of individuals, wherever they are: some do better than others at gaining an overview of specific periods of their lives—although all may be said to try to do so. Individuals' emotional development is simply variable. Those who succeed in strengthening their sense of life by relating events and phenomena to the life of the mind and their life course are often good at expressing themselves about their identity and how it has taken shape. In such cases, it becomes a natural act to put this down in words. "I still remember," writes Matthías Jochumsson in his autobiography:

> when I first spelled out the Book of Job and the prophetic books of the Bible, and also when I first read Homer's verse with his 'lowering night,' 'boundless ocean' and 'bounteous earth'. I understood it all well, for I had seen it all myself—and more, far more! Who has comprehensively described the child's soul with its morning dreams, midday merriment, evening mind and night dreams? Or its grandeur and sensitivity, its cataclysms and transfigurations, and its mystic empathy for all things living or dead, small or large—No! not dead—for in the eyes of the child everything is imbued with eternal life: the great, shifting, mysterious sea; the stilly lakes; the barren wildernesses; the monumental mountains! And all the animal kingdom! An internal mental response is first sparked by three factors: the sunrise, the starry skies, and night or darkness [...] At an early age I was astonished by the transformation from summer to winter—being already accustomed to the daily variations of light—but for a long time the autumn evenings had a heavy and melancholy mental impact upon me.[3]

The objection may be raised that this dramatic description is inadmissible as evidence, as it expresses the experience of the master of poetry Matthías Jochumsson. The poet achieved, admittedly, great skill in the perception of his own emotions, but it is no less interesting to observe how people who are not poets often express themselves with great sensitivity and insight.

Níels Jónsson, a young farmer at Grænhóll near Gjögur in the West Fjords, for example, pens this account of the weather in his diary on November 13, 1893:

> Northwesterly light wind, and more-or-less calm in the middle of the day, but lowering skies everywhere, and black as tar to the east, with snow flurries. By early evening fog was settling over Kálfatindar, and thick frosty snow as everything began to freeze. Now there is a chill northerly wind and thick snowfall, and quite blind—and only now is the wind starting to rise.[4]

Even a weather report can be infused with the grace of a person who goes about with their eyes open and has learned to know the changing hues of nature and understand what they mean. Peasant diarist Níels Jónsson is an example of people who impart to their descriptions of the weather an ambiance of mysticism and sensitivity; and he is far from alone in this among the diarists of his time.

Everybody, of course, has a tendency to forget; and it is arguable that every person must forget, in order to grasp their identity. But for that very reason, people are likely to remember the stocktaking that has taken place at turning points in their lives. These are, after all, the conclusions of a mental process of filtration—the picture that remains when fragments of memory deemed irrelevant to the person's daily life have been discarded. But what is left, on the other hand, is a vision of the past that is vital to the views and cosmology of the individual. The "feel" of a person's life, so to speak, is more likely to live on in memory, because the concomitant stocktaking is, in a sense, the weapon with which one arms oneself, in order to face new challenges. That self-confrontation does not alter the fact that the memory is by no means infallible—and each individual forgets a large proportion of the series of events that inform their life. Forgetfulness or "selective memory" of this nature is one of the fundamental premises of human life; without it we would be inundated with our own and others' memories. It should be stressed that comparable selective memory applies in other fields of human life—and is evidenced in all sources used by historians and other scholars of the humanities.

Such considerations about memory and people's memories have been given extensive thought by many: Friðgeir H. Berg (b. 1883), for instance, discusses the nature of this brain activity at length in his autobiography, *Að heiman og heim* (*Away and Home Again*). He was a peasant man from a poor family who, like many Icelanders in his position, ultimately emigrated to America with his father. He points out *inter alia* in his autobiography: "The age of people's earliest memories is said to be very variable. I have asked many people how old they were when they had their first memories, and the answers have varied. Some have memories from when they were two years old, others not until three, and the rest from the age of four or five."[5]

Certain scholars want to take this argument a step further, to ask: Is there anything special about sitting down to write one's autobiography, when most people process their lives as expounded above? In his classic work on the autobiography, British historian David Vincent maintains that there is little difference between the two processes—sitting down to write one's life story and, on the other hand, engaging in a regular process of recollection: "The mere fact, therefore, that the action of recollection was translated into a written form and then, in the majority of cases, published, does not in itself isolate the contents of an autobiography from the experience of those who have remained silent."[6] Vincent's argument has value, but there is no reason to take this comparison too literally. His point is simply that the process of recollection is more or less a given in human existence, in the cultural environment which is the premise of modern life.

For obvious reasons, certain conditions must be met in order to write one's own story—for instance, a fundamental requirement is the ability to read and write. There is a difference between making one's life story public and confining one's self-examination to private thoughts. Despite that obvious difference between the two behaviors, the common features are interesting, as Vincent points out in his study.

Another Icelandic peasant, Hannes J. Magnússon (b. 1899), proposes a similar idea in his book *Hetjur hversdagslífsins* (*Heroes of Everyday Life*): "I do not compose poetry, and I have nothing in common with great poets; but we must all have our perspectives, each for himself, whether we write our poems and stories on paper, or simply in the sands of time."[7] Hannes demonstrates here that memories find an outlet; that they demand attention, for "we all desire more or less passionately to know what is on the other side."[8] These ideas put forward by Hannes Magnússon and David Vincent are definitely conducive to boosting the confidence of those who are interested in using autobiographies as scholarly sources.

The cultural environment in Iceland reinforces the position of egodocuments, as mentioned above. The interaction between people and their surroundings is precisely the subject of all historical discourse. Journalist Jóhanna Kristjónsdóttir (b. 1940), the widow of renowned Icelandic author Jökull Jakobsson, wrote a book about their marriage, long after his death. Discussing the sources she used, she remarks on memory: "But above all I sought information in my memory, and discovered to my astonishment that there was a lot stored there, which emerged fresh, and was remarkably consistent with facts for which I had pretty reliable evidence."[9] In recollecting memories that are placed in the context of life, or the life course, people can often recall vital aspects of their lives—some distorted and others that confirm the evidence of other sources.[10]

At any rate, it must be reiterated that the relationship with time is vital here. Time demands stocktaking in each person's life, and time puts the source in an amorphous context of time and place in the minds of most readers. Every single stocktaking is personal, accompanying a person from one life stage to the next, combining into a whole which we call life. That whole comprehends much more than just memories—including the bonds with what we do not remember. The limitations of what is recalled, forgetfulness, and the certainty that something has happened to one in life that had significance for people other than oneself, always entail some reference to time. The consequence of these facts is that the narrative has an appeal for the reader. In recent times, the personal perspective on time has led to many scholars being reconciled to the autobiography—

Figure 12 Bræðraborg, Seyðisfirði.

mainly because the traditional chronological framework has broken down, with the consequence that modern life appears to be nothing but a random series of events. Personal testimony thus gains greater value, on the premise that it reflects entirely subjective links with reality. Hence, egodocuments have proved important for contemporary people, in order to trace their way through a welter of factors whose existence is based on a complex interplay of power and influence. No one else can express precisely the same perspective as the storyteller. Scholars cited below are also starting to understand that all other sources share similar attributes—having been written by people who had a certain viewpoint and perspective on life and existence.

The Subjectivity of the Self

The discipline of history evolved in the nineteenth century and well into the twentieth century in such a way as to marginalize personal testimony, as recounted earlier in the book. The personal perspective was seen as insufficiently scholarly, not meeting the standards for the scientific study of history. Scholars asserted that it was impossible to verify the testimony of egodocuments, and it was also deemed difficult to judge how far the writer was "representative" of their cohort. Not until the 1990s did historians—and in fact many social scientists—start to seek out sources that would be likely to offer scholars an opportunity to look beyond the statistics, to ask questions that could not be answered by historical demography. Thus, attention turned back to egodocuments.

It goes without saying that *subjectivity* is the crucial attribute of egodocuments. An autobiography is, for instance, an evaluation of events from the writer's viewpoint, generally based on their own experience. This is precisely what makes the autobiography an invaluable source material, and it is on those terms that I have dealt with egodocuments in my own research. Not only do they establish a temporal connection between past and present—evidence of how the individual has grown and developed—but they are also written on the basis of the development of the society to which the writer belongs. The writer selects events that were important to them from the early years of their consciousness, and through to old age. This selection gives the reader a unique insight into a world that would otherwise largely be lost. But the main point here is that the narrative has significance primarily for the writer and their own vision of their life—both the process (recollection) and the conclusions (the story in its final form). This source material opens up a totally new line of thought into past times and gives us an important opportunity to understand part of the society we have had little to say about for a long time.

The self-images projected in egodocuments have attracted scholarly attention for some time. This is confirmed by arguments put forward more than forty years ago by British historian John Burnett: he maintained that, while autobiographies do not completely meet the historian's demand for truthfulness, "in all such writings the hopes and fears, joys, sorrows, ambitions and frustrations of ordinary people are revealed to a greater or lesser extent."[11] In most cases, asserted Burnett, interested scholars, and others with an eye for human behavior, should find something for them in every single autobiography. What is interesting about Burnett's assertion is that he made it at a time when the vast majority of historians favored the statistical analysis of historical subjects—at least those on the social-history side, researching people of lower social classes. Ten years after Burnett's remark, times had changed. By then, many more historians had changed their views, and ever-growing numbers focused on qualitative research methods, where the concept of truth had been redefined in a different context.

Many autobiographers are preoccupied with the idea of truth and strive in many ways to convince the reader that they are telling the truth. Some even go so far as to attest that they can call on other individuals to corroborate their stories. This is evident in many Icelandic autobiographies.[12] The reason for this is, naturally, that every person discusses their own time in their own way. In the 1980s and 1990s, the question was often asked: What does the subjective quality of autobiographies mean for their application as historical sources? Can a scholar verify whether an author is giving a true account when the subject is the mental development of that person and the people around them? Can we apply the yardstick of history to a text when the content is as personal as self-expression—especially in view of the fact that there may be no other witness than the writer themself? These were all seen as important questions that had significance for the majority of scholars (especially historians). What is quite certain is that the questions were assigned an unusual weight when discussed in connection with the concept of time in an autobiography: Can people remember things from the distant past?

Historians who did not want to give up on the autobiography as an important source about the individual sought ways to grasp the subjective qualities of the narrative. They attempted to convince their colleagues that such sources were reliable, and that it was possible to seek out scholarly means of assessing the position of egodocuments under consideration in a particular study. In other words, attempts were made to use a yardstick on the phenomenon. But the drawback of such yardsticks is that they themselves are based on subjective principles. It is safe to say, however, that historians and general readers tend to apply them in their reading and research—regardless of when the research work has taken place.

So, the four different approaches explored here are, in fact, quite well known, and are among the recognized methods used by historians, although they rarely apply them to the autobiography. All these ideas arose from systematic efforts by literary scholars to study the impact of the autobiography as a literary genre, as discussed further below. The studies related to an exploration of the idea of each individual's "self-creation" or even "refashioning" of the self, which took on an entirely new form in the latter half of the twentieth century and ultimately had a powerful influence on how historians handled their sources.[13]

(1) *Subjective truth*: Literary scholar Martin Kohlin addresses the first approach in a paper written in 1981. He applies the concept of *subjective truth* to assessing the importance of the autobiography. He takes the view that it is up to the reader to assess the significance of each autobiography. Following a systematic but informal assessment based solely on common sense, he maintains, a decision can be made on how seriously the work should be taken.[14] This is a well-known viewpoint, based on old-established ideas about the structure of a narrative and the techniques used. Another literary scholar, John Garraty, addresses the position of the narrative in a study carried out in the mid-twentieth century, in which he considers the actual act of making a text. He draws the reader's attention to some fundamentals:

Does the story hang together? Is the use of detail precise and assured or vague and doubtful? Is the author plainly attempting to justify himself, or is he at least trying to be fair and candid? Does he tend to magnify his own exploits and deprecate his foes, or is he plagued by false modesty that gives too much credit to others and seems in effect to say: 'See how generous, how magnanimous am I!' [...] The perceptive reader can learn a great deal from the way an autobiographer treats this 'hard and nice' problem.[15]

A detailed reading of an autobiography can give the reader a good idea of the position and significance of the work. This method is applied automatically by readers as they read. We consider whether this or that recounted event falls within the parameters of the credible. Our evaluation is generally not deeply thought out but tends to take the form of fleeting thoughts that lead us almost unconsciously to an impulsive conclusion. The reader then tends to turn to the next part of the story, and evaluates that in the same way, and so on. When the entire story has been read, people rarely devote any thought to the significance of the individual items they have considered along the way. But a general impression remains, of whether the book is credible, or not.

Similar impressions are revealed even more clearly in an assessment of the impact of modern phenomena such as advertising in today's society. Advertisements appear without warning, and a subconscious snap decision is made on whether the object or product advertised is of any value. The same is true for many other phenomena, both large and small. Decisions are made on their credibility and their significance for life, and those data are stored up with other memories, in the appropriate place. The vast majority of information acquired in this way will be forgotten in time.

In working with autobiographies, scholars may make a conscious decision to place this automatic process of attention in the context of a formal procedure—and raise the automatic response to a higher level, seeking to apply it within a systematic process. In this way, scholars are likely to have a more robust basis for their conclusions. This happens even where the scholar has nothing to work with other than their own experience and the text in question. The crucial point is that a similar process is taking place in the individual's mind almost every moment of their waking hours—consciously or unconsciously. It simply forms part of the thought processes of each individual, although it is more active in some than others and influenced by circumstances and personalities.

The way to so-called "subjective truth" is only the first step in the process of assessment applied by readers of autobiographies. While this approach can be useful in the analysis of the value of individual writings, it is clear that many scholars distrust the findings of such studies. More is needed.

(2) *Historical truth*: Martin Kohlin explores the second part of the evaluation process, which may be termed *historical truth*. He sees this as another useful tool for evaluating the value of individual books. In this second stage of the process, the assumption is that the autobiography is only one of many sources that throw light on the autobiographer. This approach is familiar to all scholars: it entails searching out other sources on the most diverse aspects of the personal life of the individual in question. A wide range of sources may have something to offer: the subject's medical records, evidence from other family members, correspondence of the autobiographer or diarist, documents relating to public bodies such as court papers and church registers, and demographic data of various kinds. Today, public bodies are crammed with data about the population of a country. All such data can be useful. Genealogy may open doors to unexpected relationships that are constantly being formed. The story of the subject's family can be told together with the personal experience of the autobiographer. In that way, the subjective truth of the autobiography can be reinforced. The method aims to place the writer in their surroundings and to seek confirmation of their specific deeds and actions. How much such a process yields is variable from period to period and person to person. The method can hardly be applied to the evaluation of an individual book, but it is often used in large projects, such as the creation of a biography. This approach is a characteristic feature of many microhistorical studies: specific aspects of the social phenomena in question (people, events, small communities) are studied, as are all their relationships with their surroundings, in as much detail as possible. Historical truth is the method predominantly applied in such microhistorical research.

(3) *Social truth*: In evaluating an autobiography, the work is often compared with prior knowledge about the period, which may be termed *social truth*. The general reader often has quite extensive knowledge of that past—perhaps more than they realize. That knowledge is useful in this general analysis and is likely to be illuminating with regard to individual autobiographies. A historian, with their specialized knowledge, is, of course, even better equipped. And every scholar who makes organized use of autobiographies knows where to look in order to place a specific story in a macrosocial context. This brings us to the essence of the historian's work, as it is understood by many historians. The quest to gain an overview, to link individual events to a larger whole, is a fundamental principle in the work of the vast majority of historians—although I have criticized various

aspects of that activity.[16] All such comparison is regarded as helpful, and it is part of the recognized methodology of the scholar.

Attempting to place an autobiography in a macrosocial context can be risky if taken too literally. It must always be borne in mind that the autobiography is a one-off source and primarily expresses one individual's view of a reality which they have experienced on their own terms. That view can be entirely different from what is expressed in other sources. It is helpful to keep in mind that most other contemporary sources have been written by a more or less homogeneous cohort. Here, we deal with people whose experience may differ from the average person's norm. Those who wrote official documents were people who enjoyed a certain social status; they tended to be educated and they generally had obligations to public institutions. The documents are informed by the interests of those individuals, the institutions they represented, and their social class.

The autobiography is quite different in nature from official documents. There are certainly major differences, for instance, in how certain issues and subjects are addressed in autobiographies and in official documents. The opportunity that arises for a comparison of such dissimilar categories of sources is precisely what makes the autobiography such a valuable source. For that reason, individual autobiographies must not be excluded solely because they may differ from other sources, either with respect to specific events or as a whole. In other words, comparison between social truth and individual autobiographies is fine, as far as it goes. But it must always be subject to the proviso that the autobiography as a scholarly source has quite a different place from official public documents.

(4) *Comparative truth*: The fourth approach which may be useful in evaluating the value of autobiographies is concerned with the source itself, and the respective position of a specific book vis-à-vis another of the same kind. Here, one might perhaps point to *comparative truth*, which essentially entails a comparison of aspects of a number of books, for instance from the same region, or products of the same social class, by authors born at the same time, or of the same gender, to name but a few possibilities. It is in that way that Harvey J. Graff and I have made use of the category of sources, referencing a large number of books for comparisons regarding aspects of the authors' lives or other matters related to them.[17] In a large study using many hundreds of autobiographies the opportunity arises to compare individual autobiographies, just as I shall do in this book. In such cases, it is also possible to compare the experience of people from the same social groups, writing on similar subjects. That kind of comparison can be most productive. It enables us to identify stories based on

norms other than truth—for instance, where the author tends to exaggerate and entertain the reader, sacrificing credibility.

I have pointed out before that a new type of autobiography has appeared. This is known as *auto-fiction*, whose position as egodocuments is unusual. In the twentieth century, such stories were not recognized by most historians as valid historical sources. But today, at least some of them would surely welcome such writings.

The comparative mode provided some security to those scholars who wanted to be able to identify writers who are in some way impaired—those who have some personality defect which is deemed to make their account a usable historical source. An example is the autobiography of Icelander Jóhannes Birkiland (b. 1886), *Harmsaga ævi minnar. Hvers vegna varð ég auðnuleysingi* (*The Tragedy of My Life. Why I Became a Failure*), discussed further later in the book.[18] This autobiography is not a good source on work and growing up in the rural society of the nineteenth and twentieth centuries, but it is an excellent source on the mental state of a man who went through psychological problems. And that is how every autobiography must be approached—seeking out its strengths, while also recognizing its weaknesses.

Comparative truth was thus yet another attempt to reinforce the use of autobiographies as scholarly sources. The advantage of such a comparison was that it offered the possibility of attaining a good understanding of historical processes by juxtaposing a large number of books, bringing out by comparison what may be termed a *cultural evaluation* of some specified regions or periods, and people's attitudes to their daily life. This approach went some way toward meeting the desideratum of many scholars, that it should be possible to demonstrate how far egodocuments can be used to generate generalized conclusions. The more authors and the clearer the testimony of the many, the greater the likelihood that twentieth-century scholars would be prepared to take such sources seriously.

Why Write an Autobiography?

The preceding chapters have addressed both the subjective attributes of the autobiography and how humans apparently have an innate need for a reckoning of their lives. It has been proposed that both these factors entail certain problems which may distort the final version of written memoirs—that the narrative in autobiographies is a reflection of the author's notions about life as they believe it has progressed. Despite the obvious limitations of egodocuments, many scholars find it worthwhile to overcome them systematically and to make use of these remarkable sources in scholarly research. I have also pointed out that scholars have maintained that there is nothing remarkable in writing down one's memories—as that task closely resembles a process of thinking resorted to by most people at certain stages of life. However, account must be taken of the momentous nature of the decision to start writing one's story, which is entirely different from a person's generalized, unspoken thoughts about their life. In my efforts to persuade people to have more confidence in these sources, I have suggested various methods of evaluating each work individually. This is all grounded in what may be termed common sense—a detailed scrutiny of the content and composition of each work. Such a process, which is within the capabilities of the majority of readers, provides a good indication of the reliability of the work.

One factor remains to be addressed: the incentive behind the writing of each book. The reader can often tell where the motivation lies by asking: What led the author to decide to take on the subject of their own life and put the conclusions down on paper? It is safe to say that all authors have something in mind as they write. A systematic exploration of the reasons for the writing of egodocuments yields important information that may be crucial to the application of such works as scholarly sources. I am of the view that scholars who subscribe to the quantitative school of thought within the humanities and social sciences must inevitably prioritize such scrutiny, in order to justify their use of the sources.

Were autobiographers to be systematically asked the reasons for their writings, most would probably reply that they have experienced a good deal and have much to recount, and want to share it with others. This must be deemed a healthy and reasonable attitude, to which there is no reason to object.[19] Undeniably, however, people have many and diverse reasons for writing their life stories. The magnitude of the task alone tends to indicate that people must have something to say. For that reason, it is important to consider the incentive behind the writing in evaluating the reliability of autobiographies, while also taking into account that the incentive is to be found in the text—in life itself. An analysis of this factor may be crucial to the assessment of the reliability of the work, and how it may be used.

I have established several *categories*, each of which has its own attributes and is intended to bring out important reasons behind the production of egodocuments.[20] These categories could be subdivided; and it is clear, for instance, that many autobiographies belong in more than one category. This is far from being a definitive classification system that can be imposed on egodocuments of all kinds. I carried out this experiment more with the intention of creating a tool for use in reading the books and analyzing the value of each book. It is unnecessary here to examine each category individually in order to demonstrate the diversity of ideas relating to the forms of egodocuments, mainly autobiographies and semi-autobiographies; it is sufficient to mention the principal attributes. Behind each category lies variable numbers of *metastories*—narratives about a narrative—and no attempt is made here to mention all the works that might be placed in each category. The categories are as follows:

Political Autobiography: The author of a political autobiography is invariably either a person involved in politics, having taken part in the political sphere in one way or another, or one who has witnessed political events which they feel are worth recounting. In many cases, authors of this category of egodocument are seeking through their writings to influence political developments in their time or to have an impact on public perceptions of the past.

Book of Justification: An author of this type of book sets out to explain how they succeeded in becoming a good citizen, often under challenging conditions—or to recount the reasons why they failed to do so. This is a well-known category in the Icelandic egodocument tradition—especially the former type. The justification tends to relate to the author's economic status and attitudes to poverty among their contemporaries. Authors maintain that they recall "the two times," that is, the good and bad times. They recount how they managed to find their way out of poverty and misery to establish themselves in society. This is the story of the Icelandic farmer who grew up, almost with exception (as recounted by the narrators), in poverty, then worked as a laborer from his teens until his thirties, and ultimately managed by great efforts to acquire farmland and marry a wife.

Book of Propaganda: The author of this type of book tends to be quite frank, rarely trying to conceal their intentions in writing the book. This type of metastory is usually confined to a specific subject, such as religion or teetotalism. The author is depicted in the condition which led to their downfall, before they "saw the light." The account is detailed, concealing nothing. It is seen as important to place all one's cards on the table, and not to gloss over the way of life that sent the author off the rails. The next stage of this type of autobiography is to recount how the author succeeded in getting their life back on track. How they managed to overcome harmful urges and feelings that had led them into trouble. Often, this is an internal battle that places a great strain on the author's mental well-being and those around them. The final part of the book of propaganda describes the "sunlit upland" days, weeks, months, and years after the author has got a grip and is living a healthy life once more, having learned from experience. Most of these works follow this formula, which is sometimes identified with the kind of Twelve-Step Program pioneered by Alcoholics Anonymous.

Book of Confession: This category has much in common with the preceding one, but refers more to writings that address life as a whole—they are one comprehensive confession. The best-known examples of this genre are the autobiography of Jean-Jacques Rousseau, who set an example followed by many, and the *Confessions* of St. Augustine.[21] The motivation for such writings tends to be highly personal, the author focusing on a reckoning with themself for their own sake. The motivation is thus to confess and the objective is the formation of the self. Such writings may be said to be very interesting, as they are invariably candid and sincere.

Book of Reckoning: As a rule, the author of a book of reckoning is generally carrying out a computation of their life with respect to some specific events, which may not have haunted them all their life, but have had an impact on their life—whether positive or negative. The author is often settling scores with certain individuals or families and sending them a message through their writings.

Book of the Life Course: In this type of book, the author conscientiously recounts their life course from cradle to old age. Such autobiographies are, as a rule, well-constructed and clear. They show the interplay of different factors in the author's life, the relationship between them, and disruptions between one period and another. Autobiographies of this type are numerous and are outstanding as historical sources. They contain a mix of personal descriptions and the author's evaluation of their own worth, alongside well-written accounts of the material world that was part of everyday life. They are thus characterized by an interesting combination of the author's surroundings, other people, and their personal life, which deepens the reader's understanding of the period in question.

Book of Tales: Authors of books of tales generally have no specific objective other than to tell a good story. This type of metastory is very familiar in Iceland, generally written by self-educated people who have been brought up in the traditions of the sagas of Icelanders and legendary sagas. They simply want to tell a story, even if they do not feel they have anything important to say. The narrative has significance only of itself, and often belongs to the tradition of *þjóðlegur fróðleikur*, the local tale tradition.

Book of Nostalgia: Authors of these kinds of works have a strong tendency to view the past through rose-tinted spectacles. They constantly compare the present with the past, often favoring the latter. Such egodocuments tend to have a strong moralistic undertone, maintaining that people in past times were morally superior to the author's contemporaries. Adversity and poverty served to enhance their moral strength—especially at times when every step was dogged with problems.

Book of Heritage Conservation: This category of egodocument has a single declared objective: to rescue valued aspects of cultural heritage from oblivion. This category has much in common with metastories that are imbued with nostalgia; however, in this case, the author is of the view that times have changed so drastically that it is necessary to provide an account of the lost world, with the aim of preserving ideas and thinking which are on the brink of oblivion.

Book of Self-Glorification: The author has a strong desire to glorify themself and enumerate their own virtues. The narrative is uncritical and tends to be characterized by empty words of praise in recounting the author's achievements. This type of metastory is unappealing, as the book shows the author's character in a bad light. These stories are also easily identified: the author is blind to their own qualities and never judges anyone else fairly. This type of egodocument is uncommon, but elements of it are found in many autobiographies that fall within other categories. This may perhaps be seen as characteristic of many egodocuments written or otherwise produced by middle-class people in the postwar years—the fear of telling the story plainly is blindingly obvious to the reader, often overshadowing an otherwise interesting life. Autobiographies are characterized by the author's desire to see themself in the context of their surroundings; however, books of self-glorification are a travesty of that quest: the subject of the book is presented all alone, without any bonds with the surroundings or other people.

Book with a Global Perspective: These are writings which take place partly or entirely outside Iceland, or have a broader relevance than in Iceland. A remarkable number of Icelandic autobiographies belong in this category. They may relate to global historic events such as participation in war, specific events that affected others as well as the author, or they may be concerned with the author pursuing a career abroad, whether temporarily or permanently. Autobiographies of Icelanders who emigrated to the New World in the nineteenth century belong in this category.

Book of Life Experience: A large number of books fall within this category. They are focused either on one specific event that had a crucial impact on the narrator's life or on a series of events that affected their entire life. Such books are often interesting and exciting, recounting conflicts that affected not only the author in question, but many others. A good example of this category are books set during the Second World War or that relate to the events of the war. These books are numerous and recount a wide range of personal experiences. They also relate to other categories of autobiography, as most people's lives include some kind of conflict that they see as the equivalent of a war! In this context, books may be mentioned that recount an exciting life course and the individual's remarkable exploits—in faraway places, for instance.

Travel Books: Many of the earliest Icelandic autobiographies were primarily travel books. Written in the seventeenth and eighteenth centuries, they tell true stories of Icelanders' travels at that time. These stories are unusual in that they recount one adventure after another, without any clear indication of the purpose of the journey, other than to travel from place to place as a sojourner. Travel books have much in common with books of life experiences and books with a global perspective, and share many of their attributes. This category also includes some of the best-known books in the flora of egodocuments, which influenced the development of this kind of story. Some Icelanders' travel books recount perilous adventures in the uninhabited central highlands, or other tales of confrontation with the elements. These are often heroic tales that relate to the author's profession or a leisure pursuit, such as horse-riding. The common factor that binds these stories is that they are entertaining and often exciting, with a generous helping of machismo. This category also includes many stories of seafaring and fisheries: the life of the fisher. A common feature of these stories is that the authors are heroes who have faced the prospect of death and have generally been victorious.

Unpublished Autobiographies: This is not a category as such, but a collection of material whose common factor is that it has not been published. The motivation for the writings is, naturally, diverse. It is clear, for instance, that authors of this type of autobiography considered publication but had concerns about the implications. For that reason, a certain number of authors simply decided not to publish. The intention of this group is primarily to put together an autobiography so that their descendants will have some documentation of the writer's life and experiences. Such works are often written at the urging of family and friends, in order to ensure that the grandchildren will have some opportunity to learn about this ancestor. It is not unlikely that women have been more reluctant to seek publication than men, but it is impossible to say. And we do have women's autobiographies, published after their death, which are outstanding examples of this literary genre.

In other cases, the author is elderly and intends to leave a manuscript that relatives can publish after their death. The motivation for the writing is often to ensure the family's financial security, and in such cases the author may embroider and exaggerate, hoping that this will enhance sales.

It must be pointed out that the intention of this classification is primarily to give the reader an overall sense of this kind of system of categorization. Behind each category lies a far more precise analysis; I illustrate this by exploring one of the categories in more depth, in order to give the reader a clearer perception of the classification system. I have selected the category *Book of Justification*, as this spans, in a sense, a characteristic element that is shared by many other categories.

Book of Justification: An author of this type of book sets out to explain how they succeeded in becoming a good citizen, often in very demanding circumstances—or to show how they failed to do so. The author explains how they rose up from poverty and misery and made their place in society. The first part of such an autobiography is thus a story of struggle and adversity, where the prize is no less than the author's mental and emotional well-being. The second half of the autobiography then generally reports successes in the fields of agriculture and social progress. Books of justification tend to blend with the history of the nation—shaped by the nineteenth-century campaign for self-determination—as it progressed until the end of the Second World War. The underlying tone of the stories is generally that Iceland's ultimate victory in gaining independence from Danish rule and other foreign powers was the achievement of the narrator and their generation—in face of the adversities they had to overcome. This type of autobiography thus recounts the story of great social achievements.[22]

This type of autobiography may also tell the story of outstanding talents and how they developed in the face of adversity. A famous example is the story of Hannes Þorsteinsson (b. 1860), who grew up in poverty with a domineering father in rural areas in the southern part of Iceland. Despite his clear talent for learning, he saw little opportunity to develop his gifts, except by studying on his own at home in the *baðstofa*. Before long, he had gained such expertise in genealogy that he could readily trace the descent of people he met, without particular effort.

On one occasion, he was on his way to a seasonal fishing station on the south coast when he met with students of the Latin School outside the school building, and got into conversation with them. His knowledge and talents drew the students' attention: "because I had learned their names from reports in [national paper] *Þjóðólfur*, I knew something about most of them, and in some cases I could tell them something of their descent. They were surprised, but nothing significant happened on that occasion."[23] Hannes was about twenty at the time, and he would in due course have the opportunity to study at the Latin School himself, with outstanding success. He became a nationally renowned parliamentarian, editor of *Þjóðólfur*, and then director of the National Archive. His autobiography is, in a sense, one long book of justification, in which he explains his own good qualities.

Books of justification can be very useful sources, as more often than not the author has lived an eventful life, and had many opportunities to examine their own character. The author's reckoning with themselves and others is the framework of the book. A book of justification often has a political undertone, mainly manifested in the author's links with Iceland's campaign for self-determination. Authors have thus often seen themselves as part of a larger whole. All these factors strengthen the position of books of justification in the flora of Icelandic autobiography. Occasionally, however, embellishment is seen, with the aim of magnifying the stature of the author. In a sense, all books of justification fall prey to such stylistic mannerism—which is an inherent risk of the narrative form. As a rule, the message of self-justification is obvious in such stories.[24]

Sometimes, a person is inspired to write an autobiography by rather uninteresting events in their life, which would not normally be deemed worthy of a book.[25] In other cases, the author is spurred by some special events or by their own character to tell their story and rectify matters. The Rev. Gunnar Benediktsson, for instance, realized at the age of eighty-one that he had been a promising writer. An old play by him was staged in Iceland at that time: "This seems to be the last chance," he writes in the foreword to his autobiography, "for me to clarify a little to myself what is the place of writing in my life's work, and the part it has played in spinning the thread of life."[26] Gunnar's rationale for writing the book evinces something of hubris—which is often an element of the book of justification.

We have yet to consider the autobiographers who seek to rectify their missteps in life—why they "became a failure" as Jóhannes Birkiland put it in his well-known autobiography, cited above. In his foreword or *Address*, he writes about his life:

> In recent years various people have expressed their astonishment to me regarding the fact that I have fallen prey to fantasy and misfortune. I shall seek to answer that question in this book.
>
> I have now, at last, succeeded in breaking out of all my lifelong fantasies, and chill reality faces me as it is.

> In that context I shall assert, with absolute self-criticism, that if someone who reads these lines had offered me the directorship of a large commercial or industrial enterprise, that would have been a turning-point in my life. I have, in my own judgment, reason to believe that I had the talent for such work. But Icelanders mistrust of my talents felt by Icelanders meant that my splendid desire to be a director was not to be fulfilled. It was a terrible oversight on the part of the Icelanders not to offer me the opportunity to direct a large commercial or industrial enterprise. They have missed the opportunity to know with what excellence I could have performed tasks of great responsibility. Instead of being a director, I am the greatest outcast of the Icelandic nation.[27]

The focus of Jóhannes' argument is that he was spoilt in his youth by the indulgence of his parents, especially his father. From that point, he had no hope of recovery. Thus, he attributes his misfortunes to his early years, and takes on the guise of an anti-hero. He finds nothing but debacles wherever he goes. He travels widely, always meeting defeat: shunned by society, he finds himself marginalized. Jóhannes recounts his mental struggles with unusual frankness. His unconventional conduct "left me socially dead!" he writes in his autobiography. "And thereby I was literally dead to human society! I was in a desert!"[28] Jóhannes follows these dramatic exclamations with two photographs of himself to illustrate how he was treated. One shows Jóhannes in his finest clothes—white tie and tails—with the caption: *J. Birkiland (at the beginning of this period)*. The other photograph shows a ragged man, clearly in a wretched state, who has all the sorrows of the world on his shoulders, and the caption reads: *J. Birkiland (a year and a half later)*. Here, Jóhannes makes an unusual attempt to document his mental and physical condition, showing the reader how rejection by society has truly affected him. The use of photographs is highly effective and unconventional; photographs are generally used to show the setting of the storytelling, and not to illustrate and elucidate the import of the text.

Jóhannes' autobiography is highly unconventional, and it is difficult to place it in the autobiographical flora, principally because the narrative is so clearly marked by the author's mental condition. Yet, that very quality makes this one of the most impressive books of justification ever published in Iceland.[29] Jóhannes sums up his place in the world as follows: "My entire life has truly been a terrible *suicide* from beginning to end!"[30]

The classification system explained here is not intended to be a final frame of reference for egodocuments—on the contrary, it is intended to be a constantly evolving analytical tool that can be adapted to the requirements of the subject. It is, in fact, simply one way of approaching egodocuments, of whatever form, as has been done in the preceding chapters of this book. It would be entirely possible to build the classification up in a different way, for instance with four main categories, which are then divided into subcategories.

One category, for instance, might be *Famous Icelanders*, and under that heading the subcategories of *politicians, artists, entrepreneurs*, and *eccentrics*. Another category might be *Changing Times*, which would include books about the experience of migrating from a rural to an urban environment and changing times in society. A third category might be *Stories of the Ego*, embracing books of justification, confession, self-glorification, propaganda, reckoning, etc. This classification system is mentioned here simply to show the different potential ways to work with such sources, and at the same time to carry out a certain quality assessment of a category of egodocument based on certain premises. This is what scholars (and readers in general) usually do: they classify their sources into categories, and try to assess the importance of each group. It is also possible to eschew all classification, focusing on one work at a time—which is something that has been emphasized in this book.

The following factors are worth reiterating: First, when individual autobiographies are measured against the above categories, the reader is likely to discern qualities of works in several categories within each story. Second, it is important to bear in mind that, even where an autobiography has some of the negative elements attributed to the categories, that does not make it unusable as a source. Hence, this discussion of categories is not intended to exclude books with certain attributes, but to encourage readers to consider the motivation that

Figure 13 Blómsturvellir, Eyrabakka.

lay behind the writing of each autobiography. Such an analysis can provide the reader with a good deal of information about the content of the book and the author's place in it—information that is often helpful in the possible use of the book. Assessment methods such as this provide clues to the potential uses of the book. Third, it should be reiterated that books that are deemed by many to be historically flawed may provide us with a view of the author's emotional life and mental state—subjects that rarely feature in other kinds of egodocument. Together, these books open our eyes to the world of ordinary people, which would otherwise be closed to us—enabling us to address the subject of events that relate to people's everyday lives. In these pages, I have sought to bring out the subjects and factors in the lives of ordinary people which have influenced the development of Icelandic society in the eighteenth, nineteenth, and twentieth centuries.

In Chapters 5–7, I examine how autobiographical material can be applied effectively. In the following chapters, I bring micro and macro approaches together, in an attempt to show how we can best use egodocuments in historical research.

Part III

The Autobiography and Life

Figure 14 In Glerárþorp, Akureyri.

5

Icelandic Egodocuments

The Autobiography

One might argue that the character of egodocuments is essentially the same all over the world. But special conditions prevailing in Iceland (and elsewhere) mean that egodocuments such as autobiographies are quite unusual resources. There is good reason to believe that the tradition of egodocuments is stronger in Iceland than in most other parts of the world.[1] That may be attributable to the strong cultural position of most of the Icelandic population in the nineteenth century—as literacy rates were exceptionally high among the general public—as well as the perennial popularity of saga literature, which continues today.[2] The sagas are, directly and indirectly, an intrinsic part of Icelandic popular culture. Helgi Einarsson (b. 1870) explains this connection with the Icelandic saga in his autobiography:

> I don't suppose I was more than about 7 or 8 years old when I started to read aloud at the evening gatherings, and I enjoyed it very much. I loved reading books and papers. I ready everything I could get hold of and could borrow from nearby farms. I treated books with care, so people were willing to lend me all their books. I don't remember anyone ever refusing to lend me a book. In that way I read more or less all the Sagas of Icelanders, all the folktales and the Thousand and One Nights, and much more. I was also quite well-read in the Bible, and read most of it, though I didn't like it, at least not the doctrines of the Old Testament.[3]

The strong narrative tradition has been widely manifested in Icelandic national life in recent centuries, as will be discussed in later chapters in this book. The art of telling a story, or giving shape to a readable text, has played a major role in Icelandic culture from early times, and the evolution of the tradition is informed by saga literature.[4] Hence, many authors of egodocuments tended to address difficult philosophical questions that related to their memories and their life:

how memories were formed and how they were stored in the brain. Friðgeir H. Berg, cited in Chapter 4, writes:

> Memoirs are the diary of the mind. A systematic man, with a tendency to keep records of weather and health in his home district, and of other events, large and small, that occur, will write an informative diary, where he and others can later find a continuous series of the events that took place during a whole human life.
>
> People's minds, and their conservation of memories, varies greatly. Some people remember everything they have heard, seen and participated in, from childhood to old age—even insignificant facts, such as what they ate on a certain day.
>
> Nobody knows for sure how memories are formed. They are believed to be fixed and stored in the folds of the brain. I am ignorant of such matters, but from my own experience it has occurred to me that the part of the brain that receives what is to be remembered, may not be unlike a camera with film. The clarity of the image depends upon certain conditions and influences. For a mental photograph, there is just as much need for favorable conditions, so that the image may be developed when one wishes to recall the memories it keeps.
>
> Mental photography can only be accurate if the person's consciousness is correctly attuned. The person must have receptive capacity for that which their vision sees, and other senses have perceived.
>
> In many cases the receptive capacity is dulled, or even entirely absent. Important events may pass us by, without our acquiring any memory of them. Insignificant events, on the other hand, may seize the mind, leaving an indelible mark.
>
> The minds of some are so focused on certain specific matters that the stream of daily life flows past them without their hearing its burbling. That state of affairs has its drawbacks, but the life of the individual is in no way impaired; and many people who are made in that way would not wish to exchange their way of thinking for the fleeting impressions of the passing day.[5]

Behind this lie extensive ideas about how memories are formed and how they get onto the writer's page. Such reflections take place because the author is prepared to undertake fairly abstract thinking about the nature of such writings. The writing is important to him, and he wants the reader to understand that behind his writing lies a way of thinking that is not unfounded. Poet Matthías Jochumsson writes about his recall of the past:

> But for the reason that I have been, so I believe, more of a freethinker than is common, I feel myself compelled by an inner duty to undertake this experiment, though it may never reveal more than some outlines of my internal story—all

unclear and half-pickled, or fragmented, and most without vivid tones of color. That is the near-universal tendency of autobiographies. Our consciousness is divided, and much that reaches it, one way or another, goes missing, for the memory varies in terms of veracity, reliability and richness; only a small part of what we perceive is stored in memory. . . . I have reached an age when I should shun all pretension and all secrecy, but do my best to display reality.

But thereby it is not my intention, nor my duty, to tell all that some people might deem relevant to my internal or external history. No sane man would attempt such a thing. My purpose is principally this: to strive, by my memory and might, to explain to my descendants and friends my origins and spiritual growth from the blank slate of infancy, my character, and my internal and (partly) external circumstances, as well as my relationship and dealings with the outside world.[6]

This is indisputably a very mature approach to the deed of writing one's autobiography. But Matthías had more to say:

I know that the most difficult thing is to find and preserve the continuous thread that accompanies the life of the mind and the personality, and keep it together. When some contradiction or frank exchange of opinions emerges in what a person says, composes or writes, the problem is to give a clear account and explain the background to such viewpoints.[7]

And Matthías had not finished, when he addressed the place of autobiography:

But while lack of memory gives rise to a lot of hesitation and many misconceptions and misstatements by those who wish to give an accurate account of their own and others' experiences, the other aspect—to write objectively about oneself—is yet more difficult. And no doubt for that reason do so few good, reliable autobiographies exist—stories which are not blemished by egotism or self-delusion. And I do not recall reading any such autobiography that did was not marked by the author's eccentricity or oddity, even when they have been the wisest and most truthful of men.[8]

Matthías points out that the reason for this is that it is, in fact, impossible to know oneself utterly. The principal point here is the maturity of this contemplation of the value and significance of writings of this kind.

The ability to tell a story well was valued: a vagabond who had this skill would generally be welcomed into any home—even if they tended to meet with the disapproval of the authorities. Many autobiographies recount regular visits by vagabonds; and while some may have found such drifters eccentric, and perhaps even disconcerting, they certainly added color to the routine of country life.[9]

The *kvöldvaka* or winter-eve gathering was a regular element of Icelandic home life until the first two decades of the twentieth century. In the dark winter evenings, after all outdoor tasks had been completed, the household would gather in the *baðstofa* (communal living/sleeping loft) to continue their work, mostly woolworking such as spinning and knitting. As they sat at their work, a member of the household would read aloud from some saga, or *rímur* might be chanted. All this was a powerful stimulus to the imagination, as well as enhancing productivity. The evening gathering generally concluded with a reading from a religious text and singing hymns. In his autobiography, Jósef Björnsson vividly describes the intensity of the work carried out during the winter-eve gatherings; his parents set stringent standards of diligence for the household:

> In the household, work took priority over everything else. We got to work as soon as we awoke, and in the evening we worked until bedtime. The winter-eve gatherings were more formalized, and different from what they are today. When the lamps were lit, everybody was by their bed with their work, except the cattleman, who did not come in until after 7. It was a matter of course that one person was exempted from work to read to the household. In those days, there was no private reading, there was no time for that. This arrangement was most efficient in terms of productivity, and the knowledge and cultural influence of the books was better utilized, as those who were not readers listened like the rest.[10]

In his book, Jósef explains the ideology of work and people's ideas about it:

> Nowadays work is sometimes spoken of as a necessary evil, that destroys both health and enjoyment of life. I never heard anything like that when I was growing up. Work was sometimes deemed to be the main necessity, but never a necessary evil—rather a source of satisfaction, when one worked hard and with motivation. To fall asleep tired, after a good and productive day's work, is something that few people who have experienced it would wish to lose from their lives.[11]

Jósef also points out that the people of the household worked from early in the morning until ten at night: "To take one's seat in the *baðstofa* for the winter-ever gathering with no work in hand was almost unknown, except in the case of those who were reluctant to work. Sometimes I heard my mother remark: 'What a shame to see grown men idle.' Then they would start doing something, rather than be shamed."[12]

The winter-eve gatherings were influential in many ways, and it was in this setting that children started their education.[13] Here they learned to read and write, as before schools existed in Iceland parents were responsible for teaching these skills. Magnús Helgason (b. 1857) from the farm of Birtingarholt in southern Iceland recounts in his autobiography how he was taught to read at the age of four. Initially, his father taught him his letters, after which his mother took over: "She sat at the spinning-wheel and spun, while we sat by her on the bed or on a chest at her feet, holding the book. While we were not yet independent, she chose books for us that she was familiar with, so she could correct us and help us without having to take time to look at the book."[14] Magnús was one of fourteen siblings; after the eldest had been instructed as described above, they took over from the parents to teach the younger. Tuition did not take place at any specific time of day, "but opportunities were seized for teaching and study when time was available between other tasks."[15] And, slowly but steadily, they learned to appreciate the value of a good story and the skill of reading aloud.[16] It is arguable that these factors led to people of all classes feeling the need to sit down and write their own stories. And that became a practical option in the latter half of the nineteenth century, when writing materials were available quite cheaply, and the publishing sector was expanding fast.[17]

This background to Icelandic egodocuments means that latter-day readers have an unusually good opportunity to address the history of the Icelandic peasantry on their own terms. Let us take the example of a traumatic event in the life of several families in the mid-nineteenth century and the potential offered by such a narrative for an analysis of the relevant community. The narrative, of infant deaths within a community, is written by autobiographer Matthías Jochumsson, whom we have met before in these pages. Death recurs later in the book:

> The couple at Staður had a large family of children, all fine and promising. But in the spring of 1851 they lost six of them to diphtheria, which was then an epidemic. It was said that neither of them, and especially not the mother, ever fully recovered after that terrible blow. My wife, who also caught the illness at the age of 11, said that shortly before she became ill she dreamed that she saw a ball of fire rolling about the *baðstofa*, halting at the beds of all the children who died, before disappearing when it reached her bed. Around that time four children of my uncle Guðmundur died within a few days, I was staying with him at the time.[18]

This account is riveting, raising many questions about people's emotional lives in the past. How could one go on with one's life after such a calamity? Many autobiographies give some indication of an answer to such questions and other difficult ones that may arise. That is precisely the virtue of this literary form: the autobiography often indicates historical questions which historians cannot otherwise adequately address. Jósef Björnsson, quoted above, recounts the death of his nineteen-year-old sister after a difficult illness, in the *baðstofa* of their home; they were two of ten siblings:

> It was as if death, silent yet sibilant, met me at every step. I went upstairs and over to the bed. Everybody, except we children, was assembled there. All were silent, and I saw that some were weeping. A final farewell was being given to the one who had now bidden farewell to life in this world wracked with sorrow. My mother was sitting on the bed. She was still holding the hand of the departed, having held it all morning. That was her farewell. She was not crying, but the weight of grief in her face was so huge that I was spellbound; I hurled myself into the bed opposite and burst into tears. Then Anna came to me, bent down to me, and said: 'Don't cry so much, lad. Your Mama can't take it.' I did not immediately obey, and she had to repeat the request. Then I got up, wiping my tears, though I had nothing for the purpose but the sleeve of my jacket, stopped crying, then went downstairs and out. Time is quick to dry the tears in a child's eye.[19]

The household's response to the young lad certainly indicates that this community was faced with grief in a powerful way; one could not allow oneself strong expressions of sorrow, as we shall discuss below. The priority was simply on daily life; one could not allow much time to experience grief when there was always work to be done.

All over the world, social historians faced the problem that their searches for working-class people's direct testimony about their own lives yielded such meagre results, as we have discussed earlier in the book.[20] Hence, the majority of historians resorted to focusing on the institutions that marked out the framework of the daily lives of the peasantry—or the formal structure of society. But there have been departures from that research mode, in very interesting scholarly experiments around the world, known as the *cultural turn*. The objective of these is similar to that of research that makes use of egodocuments, that is, they focus on *agency*, offering an individual in the past the opportunity to contribute to the study. As I discuss below, I have taken a slightly different path to the same goal, mainly by applying the methods of microhistory in historical research. But these have much in common with the *cultural turn* in history.

Icelandic egodocuments certainly offer the opportunity to gain insight into the world of other people who belong to different social and economic groups, and challenge the institutional bias that has characterized social history for many years.[21] Such resources will come into their own when scholars start to analyze them on their own terms, disregarding the requirement of scientific methodology. That is where the methodological opportunities lie.

Why Autobiography?

"The biographical turn," the history of popular culture—everyday life history, the new cultural history, and microhistory—as these scholarly approaches are practiced today, is largely based on personal testimony.[22] And the same is true of many other branches of history: they are reliant on egodocuments as was mentioned at the end of Chapter 2. This applies especially in cultural and social-historical research, in a broad sense of those concepts: scholars in these fields often seek out personal testimony, whether directly or indirectly. As discussed above, people's subjective testimony from the past is manifested mainly in the form of autobiographies, diaries, private correspondence, memoirs (semi-autobiographies), conversational books and interviews, auto-fictions, scholarly questionnaires, illustrations, and films, along with art works or what might be called "perceptual sources." Naturally enough, such sources are far more likely to originate with social groups who have had an education and are financially secure—individuals who in their professional lives have become used to expressing themselves in written or artistic form. In past times, such activities often led the same individuals to write about their daily lives in diaries or in personal letters. In other words, their working environment was conducive to the individual thinking and writing about life and existence—which naturally reflected their own lives.

That same group would often, in later years, look back over their lives, writing about the most noteworthy events. This reflected a desire to sum up one's life and work, as well as a need to explore one's own development and position in society. In the latter half of the twentieth century, this form of self-expression underwent some change—both the nature of it and its timing. The media, along with ever more rapid modern communication, provided new platforms and opportunities to share one's experience—consciously or unconsciously. Technological advances such as photography, film, and later computers (digital outlets) enabled all kinds of people to tell their stories, in a range of formal and informal ways. Individuals around the world, for instance, set up devices in their homes that enabled strangers to observe their lives around the clock, via the worldwide web. Families made video recordings of family gatherings and could watch them on their own small screen. The distinction between an original and a copy was eroded, and that led to a revolutionary change in the attitudes of many scholars in the humanities toward sources and their use. In that context, egodocuments acquired an entirely new significance, which has had an impact on how we address the subjects of the discipline in the present day. That interaction of words, imagery, thinking, and scholarship will be among the matters addressed in the following chapters. The main point here is to understand that people's everyday experience of every kind of self-expression in the present day has opened scholars' eyes to the potential of such mediation—hence, egodocuments attract ever more attention in scholarship.

The late Bergsteinn Jónsson, professor of history at the University of Iceland, wrote about Icelandic biographies and autobiographies in a short paper in the history periodical *Saga* in 1987. Among other things, he had made a rough survey of (auto)biographical writing of Icelandic parliamentarians:

> *Alþingismannatal* (Register of Parliamentarians) *1845–1975* is at present the latest volume. I estimate, after a cursory examination, that of the 611 people who had sat in parliament during that period, 18 completed, or almost completed, their autobiographies; six have died leaving them incomplete; another six have been the subjects of detailed biographies; and finally, seven have contributed to conversational books which focus principally on their lives and work.[23]

Such writings have undergone some change in the years since, and it is generally true to say that scholars have become interested in undertaking the biographical form more resolutely than before, with the objective of making it a respectable medium.[24] Bergsteinn's survey gives some idea of the scale of such writings among the upper classes in Iceland.

In olden times, the peasantry of the Western world were not in the habit of writing down their thoughts and desires, or of expressing themselves about current events. For them, their everyday toil had precedence. That, at least, is the argument that used to be adduced by many historians specializing in book history. The crucial element of the argument was that the advent of printing had eliminated scribal culture, thus making books the preserve of the educated classes.[25] Lack of writing materials was also presumed to have precluded many from expressing themselves in writing, until the later nineteenth century. Nor could the average peasant in the Western world be assumed to have the skills to express themself in writing, as in most agrarian societies literacy was a privilege of the wealthier classes. All this led to the assumption that the philosophy, values, and emotional life of the vast majority in society in past centuries were largely a closed book to a present-day person.[26]

While it is true that most of the peasantry had no opportunity—and perhaps no particular desire—to express themselves in writing about their lives, it is quite obvious that a considerable number of people of the peasant class left written sources, in Iceland and elsewhere in the world.[27] Recent studies have revealed that scribal culture flourished until the end of the nineteenth century, and even longer in some parts of Europe.[28] It is reasonable to assume that this group of peasant scribes was relatively large in Iceland, especially in the later eighteenth and nineteenth centuries—due to the high level of literacy. Hence, it is surprising to observe that of these categories of resources, only a handful have attracted the attention of historians who have set out to work systematically with them. Historians have tended, for example, to consult an autobiography in search of confirmation of some event, or to demonstrate that certain individuals were participants in some field of national life, such as politics. Hence, it is fair to say that egodocuments have been much underused historical resources, in both Iceland and internationally, as has been mentioned above.[29]

The autobiography is in many ways an apt context for a discussion of the existential basis of the humanities in general and especially history as a scholarly discipline. History, like autobiography, is based on individuals' memory and their personal experience of their environment and actions. Each narrative or self-expression, of whatever kind, is thus full of personal experience—even in those cases where the author makes a conscious effort to avoid declaring an attitude to their environment. In the end, it is a truism.

In his foreword to *Brautryðjendur* (*Pioneers*), published in 1950, the late Vilhjálmur Þ. Gíslason, a former director of the state radio station and a cultural giant in Iceland, wrote: "History has in fact always been molded to some extent by the history-writer's thinking, judgment or prejudice; and to that degree all history is a kind of autobiography. In a sense, an autobiography also tends to become a general history of a kind—it becomes a book of memories about people and issues."[30] To most minds, however, it makes no sense to assume equivalence between historical research and autobiography. Historians are taught to verify exhaustively, and never to trust the memory of one person (as the autobiography usually does), but to seek out the testimony of many witnesses of different kinds. To my mind, this is not a matter of a difference of kind (as both are grounded in the personal evidence of certain individuals), but rather as a difference of degree—but one that may be crucial.

It is interesting to pursue this difference further: Italian microhistorian Carlo Ginzburg, who is renowned as the international embodiment of *microhistory*, wrote a noteworthy paper published in the periodical *Critical Inquiry* about the beginnings of microhistorical research.[31] He explains how he came to think of this research ideology in the 1970s, recounting the ideological history of a scholarly discipline. He originally set out to do this by working with his own memories. Ginzburg regarded this as natural, as he was one of those who had developed the methods of microhistory in the 1960s. Hence, his account of this historical approach is also the author's autobiography. This unusual task placed Ginzburg in an unexpected quandary, which came to light when he set out to explain one of the defining features of microhistory, *reducing the scale of observation*. He had difficulty clarifying the genesis of the idea:

> The motives that impelled me at that time to make this choice are not totally clear to me. I am different about those that come to mind today because I would not like to project into the past intentions that have been maturing in the course of these many years. Gradually I came to realize that many events and connections of which I was totally unaware contributed to influencing the decisions that I thought I had made independently: a banal fact in itself but always surprising, because it contradicts our narcissistic fantasies.[32]

Ginzburg goes on to consider whether the political climate in Italy in the 1970s may have influenced his views and concludes that it is impossible to say. He adds: "but I suspect that the motives for my choices should be searched for elsewhere."[33] The approach chosen by Ginzburg was to apply the research methods of microhistory in order to determine how the discipline itself has evolved. His own memory, that of a man who shaped that historical practice, was not sufficient in itself, in his judgment. Thus, he searched for the meaning of the word *microhistory*—where the word, or some variant of it, is used in historians' texts, and the varying conditions in which it was used. In this way, he gradually built up a coherent picture of the evolution of microhistory and the meanings that influenced its development.

This leaves us with the question: Do Ginzburg's arguments mean that the autobiography must be rejected as source material on the grounds that memory is fallible? It is quite clear that Ginzburg's attempts to base his analysis on memory lead to consideration of the function of memory in general, and what purpose it serves in our efforts to understand the past. The storage of memories is, obviously, imperfect, and that can influence in many ways how they are remembered. Accident, injury, illness, and mental strain of various kinds can transform our memories in an instant, or even erase them. Even in ideal conditions, when an individual has lived at peace with themself and others, there is no guarantee of the undiminished power of memory. Ginzburg's ideas call above all for the memory and memories to be considered as analyzable concepts, seeking to throw light on their function and importance, while also addressing their limitations. In my view, Ginzburg's arguments focus on the limitations of the autobiography as a source while also pointing the way to some of autobiography's strengths. Clearly, Ginzburg's own memories played an important role in his study of the beginnings of microhistory, even though he did not trust them implicitly. While he opted not to define the memory and memories in his analysis, he finds a way to use them in conjunction with other sources.

In the end, it seems to me that Ginzburg applies here a method that is, in fact, used by most autobiographers: to rely first on their own memory and then to consult other available sources when it transpires that forgetfulness has misled them. Hence, autobiographers may be said to apply, unconsciously, the methods of microhistory in their work. They seek out fragments of memory from their lives, which, as witness the example of my own experience recounted earlier in the book, can often be recalled in the right circumstances (e.g. finding a cache of letters). They then embark on "reading" their own lives armed with the weapons of textual analysis. The skill with which autobiographers apply this method varies—yet individuals make an arrangement of fragments of memory using *texts*, found either in their objectified reality (walking about the streets

Figure 15 In Skagafjörður.

and squares around them), or in written form, put away in desk drawers or other storage places. Photographs or film of certain events can be helpful in recalling them. Innumerable details in individuals' daily lives can summon up memories which would otherwise be hazy. It is, for instance, well known that old chess players retain clear memories of chess games they have played, and even the circumstances in which they took place.[34] Hence, these aspects of their lives stand as landmarks on which they can "hang" memories of other events as they recall them. These variants of *text* combine with the individual's personal memory, giving rise to a work of writing which defines the author's *self* as they see it.

What Kind of Source?

In my view, there are many possible ways to use egodocuments in scholarly research. It does not matter whether one work is used, or many; whether the qualitative methods of microhistory are applied, or the quantitative methods generally used in social history—especially by those who work with historical demography on a macro scale. This book addresses this interaction between egodocuments, other sources, the society from which they spring, and the variable scholarly approaches in the humanities. I am of the view that egodocuments can provide guidance regarding important debatable issues in the humanities; and that analysis of such sources provides an opportunity to understand the strengths and weaknesses of the academic discourse.

This chapter has addressed a certain paradox relating to self-expression; definitions of egodocuments give rise to endless variants of such interpretation. The overlap between different categories of egodocuments has greatly increased in recent times—and that has undermined a systematic understanding of the phenomenon. At the same time, these categories of sources have become more interesting—and more appealing subjects for scholars and artists. A certain tension has emerged between the desire to have a clear and recognized definition of the manifestations of the self which have been under discussion, and, on the other hand, a confirmation that the variants of the categories are innumerable.

My analysis of the autobiography is based mainly on two studies carried out in the 1990s and at the beginning of the twenty-first century: first, the writing of more than 350 autobiographies of Icelanders, which I used in my doctoral thesis, and I have discussed before. Second, a study based on a database of all autobiographical sources published from the nineteenth century until 2004 of about 1,100 autobiographies, semi-autobiographies, and conversational books. The latter study will be discussed further below.

The 350+ autobiographies that comprised the core of my analysis in my doctoral thesis related to a discussion of popular culture in Iceland 1850–1940. Ultimately, I made focused use of about 240 books that were a good fit for my study of popular culture. To give the reader an idea of the composition of this database, it should be stated that most of the writings had been published individually in book form. Twenty-five of the autobiographies, however, had been published in periodicals; these were from 20 to 200 pages in length. The books included twenty-three conversational books, and three such works were published in periodicals. Of the 240 autobiographies, only 43 were written by women.[35] It is quite clear that far fewer Icelandic women than men have written their autobiographies—or just about 10 percent of the total number of autobiographies published in Iceland. Scholars who use egodocuments in their qualitative research can compensate for the lack of women's autobiographies by using other types of egodocument, in which women are well represented. That is precisely what I did in my doctoral thesis; women were, for instance, prolific letter writers, and were also numerous among the respondents to National Museum questionnaires. The vast majority of autobiographies used in my thesis were written by males who had been brought up in rural Iceland and spent most of their lives there.

From the foregoing it must be obvious that the egodocuments that were published in the first half of the twentieth century and into the second half were predominantly male literature, in which men recounted their lives and experience in their later years. The latter half of the twentieth century saw a change, in that women's general self-expression became far more prominent. That development took place at the same time that people began to write autobiographies at much younger ages, while forms of self-expression grew more diverse.[36]

I made a special study of 179 of the autobiographers, which revealed that only 4 were born before 1850, 10 in 1850–59, 25 in 1860–69, 29 in 1870–79, 35 in 1880–89, 38 in 1890–99, 27 in 1900–09, 6 in 1910–19, and 5 after 1920.[37] That overview provides a fairly clear picture of the constantly rising number of autobiographies published in the early twentieth century by authors born in the nineteenth century. It should be borne in mind that my thesis dealt with the period 1850–1940, so authors born after 1920 were irrelevant. Interestingly, the geographical distribution of the authors' birthplaces is largely equal for all four regions of the country, with the exception of the northern region which accounted for over 40 percent.[38] All these statistics are of interest, especially in the context of the overall total, which will be discussed below.

A database that was compiled almost twenty years ago in connection with my research project on egodocuments identified 1,089 titles published in Iceland between the second half of the nineteenth century and 2004 that can be categorized as autobiographical sources. Of these, about 85 percent were written by men. The principal characters in the books under consideration here were all born after about 1830.[39] The total, 559 autobiographies, represent different social strata as follows: farmers 120, authors 98, clergy 67, mariners 39, teachers 39, politicians 28, and physicians 14. Just 12 percent of these works are by women, and the other 88 percent by men.

Semi-autobiographies comprised 355 of the group. The first work of this nature was published in 1936, followed by many more as the twentieth century progressed. The content of these books was largely contingent on market forces, and a class of writers appeared who specialized in producing such works. The people who were the subjects of these books represented the following social strata: artists 74, mariners 49, politicians 40, farmers 38, clergy 13, physicians 10, and authors 7. The group comprises 20 percent women and 80 percent men.

No attempt has been made to analyze the conversational books, as the number of interviewees was huge, and one book often reported conversations with many individuals. These books probably comply with the same process of development as semi-autobiographies, as the concept of the book forms is similar.[40]

To this material can be added a huge body of other kinds of firsthand sources that can be characterized as egodocuments and that, in some cases, have constituted part of Icelandic popular culture over many centuries—diaries, letters, responses to questionnaires sent out by ethnographic researchers or the National Museum of Iceland, etc. —much of it unpublished and poorly accessible in uncatalogued archives.[41] In these documents, one is more likely to hear the voices of women[42], especially in collections of letters and in the database prepared by the Ethnological Archive of the National Museum of Iceland. All these texts—both from within the egodocument tradition and the other assorted historical sources—bear witness to a lively literary culture among the ordinary people of Iceland and provide a rich source for the historian interested in investigating the relationship between personal writing and people's real-life experience.[43] The very fact that literacy was general at all levels of society during this period was of major significance to both the written and spoken culture in Iceland.

It has often been maintained that women were less likely to learn to write, through much of the nineteenth century. Reading was a requirement for both sexes, while males were more likely than females to learn to write. No doubt, this theory may be supported by good arguments, and this is probably one reason why women are less likely to be authors of autobiographies and most other kinds of egodocument at that period. Davíð Ólafsson points out that studies of literacy have been carried out, all of which indicate widespread literacy in nineteenth-century Iceland—"literacy" being defined as the ability to read. But Davíð also points out the following, in the context of the lack of data about Icelanders' ability to write:

> Important exceptions to this general lack of data are the responses to a 70-item questionnaire on various aspects of Icelandic society, sent by the Copenhagen-based Icelandic Literary Society (Hið íslenzka bókmenntafélag) to every parish minister in the country in the 1840s. Two questions addressed the issue of writing skills directly: no. 59: 'How many in the parish can write?'; and no. 60: 'The age and gender of those who cannot write?' In 1983 Icelandic ethnologist Ögmundur Helgason published a short article where he analyzed the answers to these particular questions from the fourteen parishes of the county of Skagafjarðarsýsla in northern Iceland. Most of the replies are short, ambiguous and worked in general terms, and frequently state how hard it is to define the concept of writing ability and to decide who is able to write and who is not. Even when they provide actual figures, it is hard to see which groups are taken into account and what standards the evaluation is based on.[44]

Despite the rather unreliable data, scholars have drawn the conclusion that women's writing skills were considerably less than those of men around the mid-nineteenth century. And there is no reason, as such, to challenge that deduction.[45]

Jósef Björnsson (b. 1878), quoted above, provides us with insight into this feminine world, as he reports his mother's interest in education. She was not supposed to be permitted to learn to write:

> She got hold of the capital letters from someone, to copy. But she lacked everything else: paper, ink, or a pen, none of which existed in her home. So she faced a conundrum. Then she came up with the brilliant idea of using the ice as her paper—sheets of ice were plentiful around Svarfhóll, and using a nail or a pointed stick she learned to write her letters, and did not stop until she had more-or-less mastered writing, though her schoolroom was a chilly one.[46]

His mother was a keen reader of books, despite being a mother of ten, with a large household to run. "Her reading time was always in the evening when she was in bed; and if she had plenty of reading material she would not go to sleep until 2 or 3 at night. She had an excellent memory for all she read: if it was a novel, or something like that, she would tell us children the story the next day, and all about the people in it. I was often astonished at how well she told the stories, and remembered them well."[47]

Following on from the abovementioned discussion, the primary emphasis is on egodocuments in an analysis of how the self has predominantly been formed in Icelandic culture: mainly in autobiographical material, while other forms of egodocument are also included for comparison. The common factor of all such sources is that they express the author's personal views, often in concise terms. Sources such as private correspondence and diaries are, to some extent, more useful for the scholar than autobiographies, because they are written close in time to the events and also because they were not written for publication.[48]

The strengths of egodocuments are greatly enhanced when they are juxtaposed with other narrative sources. It is possible to assemble a "source group," a data bank of sorts, which can be an effective tool for explaining and analyzing latter-day events (especially in the eighteenth, nineteenth, and twentieth centuries).[49] Hence, one of the objectives of this book is to demonstrate how such resources can constitute a "source bank" that can be used to throw new light on people's personal experience in past times. It will be elucidated how such sources can work together and compensate for possible limitations that characterize some categories of sources. Such a discussion is sure to inspire confidence in the value of egodocuments among historians and others who study societies and the history of past times.

Bíbí in Berlín

The method of analysis of egodocuments, in whatever form, should ultimately aim to demonstrate to the reader the importance of seeing each book on its own terms, in the spirit of the methods of microhistory, and assessing its value for history, society, scholarship, and the general reader. One of the vital aspects of such an analysis is the author's place in the work, and what factors and parties have an impact on their memories—working in the same spirit as Carlo Ginzburg in his recollection of the early years of microhistory in the world.

Chapter 4 ended with Jóhannes Birkiland, who wrote about "why he became a failure." I took him as an example of a person who clearly experienced mental issues for much of his life; and, because his narrative was "unreliable," historians were reluctant to make any real use of its content. Jóhannes' story, however, is of such a nature that it opens up to readers a view of a world that would otherwise be veiled in mist for most. The value of the work lies precisely in its unique perspective.

Finally, I want to take another example of a person on the margins of society, Bjargey Kristjánsdóttir (b. 1927), known as Bíbí. She was generally identified by the name of her parents' croft, Berlín, outside the village of Hofsós in the northwest of Iceland. Bíbí, initially regarded as a fine child, fell ill in her first year, after which she was seen as an "idiot" by her family and the community. Bíbí was born at a time when no assistance was available to people with disabilities and their families, and having a disabled child was a matter of shame. Hence, Bíbí was subjected to demeaning treatment in her childhood home, and hidden from visitors. She did not attend school but was taught at home and learned to read and write. Bíbí's parents were impoverished crofters, whose social position was not strong. Bíbí had one brother, who was favored over her, because he was a boy and she a "disabled girl," as Bíbí herself put it in later years. Bíbí was also the frequent object of taunts regarding her appearance and physical attributes, which she found very hurtful.

Bíbí lived on the farm of Berlín with her parents and brother until she was thirty, when her mother suddenly died in 1958. Efforts were made to persuade her to move to the newly founded home for people with mental disabilities in Kópavogur, outside Reykjavík in southwest Iceland. But Bíbí refused to go and ultimately she prevailed. Instead, a place was provided for her in the geriatric department of the regional hospital/care home in the town of Blönduós. As a young person, she lived there for seventeen years among the aged residents, until 1974. She was forty-seven years old when she started what she called her "independent life" in Blönduós. For the first few years she lived in a room she rented in the home of her friend, who looked out for her. She later moved into a small house which she purchased with her friend's assistance; it is still known as Bíbí's House. She lived there until her health began to decline, and she spent her final years in the care home in Blönduós, until her death in 1999 at the age of seventy-one.

Bíbí left an extensive autobiography, which she had written in solitude and kept secret from her family and others. The autobiography manifests good intelligence, a fine sense of humor, and Bíbí's insight into her own circumstances and those of her neighbors. The text is powerful in parts, the imagery vivid and often incisive. It is safe to say that in her sweeping diatribes she gives no quarter to those with whom she has had dealings. Bíbí clearly wanted her manuscript to

Figure 16 Glaumbær, Skagafjörður.

be published in book form, although she kept her writing a secret and, in fact, few people were even aware that she was literate. Bíbí wrote her autobiography mostly in capital letters in nineteen notebooks, totaling 1,200 pages or about 145,000 words (the average book is about 90,000 words). Bíbí's manuscript is unique. In places, for instance, she traced over each letter multiple times, as if to ensure that her narrative would not fall into oblivion.

Bíbí's autobiography often presents an entirely different picture from that seen in official documents; hence, it is, in a sense, an anti-history that challenges outdated stereotypes about people with disabilities. Bíbí's autobiography is a unique document that contributes to a greater understanding of the position of those who are marginalized in society, not least women and girls with disabilities. In addition, her story provides remarkable insight into the life and experience of a woman who was excluded from society, sidelined, and denied entry to society's mainstream institutions such as the legally compulsory education system, and in effect also the healthcare system. She was, in her own way, alone, especially after the death of her mother; nonetheless, she succeeded in dealing with her role in an admirable manner. The autobiography is not only a unique document in the context of Icelandic egodocuments, but it is also unique internationally. It is extremely rare for an account by a person like Bíbí, told by herself, to be preserved.

This autobiography was published in the spring of 2022 and is a great testament of a book that on its own can tell a remarkable story.[50] Sometimes, one just needs a specific window into society to be able to give a meaningful analysis of past times.

6

Egodocuments and the Environment

Setting the Scene

The egodocument tradition in Iceland in the long nineteenth century is rich, as has been discussed earlier in this book. A good number of men and women of the peasant class, particularly rural smallholders and tenant farmers, set down records of their lives, for example, in the form of autobiographies.[1] The accounts of people and conditions found in these autobiographies raise insistent questions about the general experience and modes of behavior of poor people in Iceland, particularly in comparison with those more favorably placed in society. Popular thought and the authors' relationship with their environment lend a peculiar tone to many of these autobiographies, opening up new ways of interpreting the history of the whole. In this chapter, I further argue that people's ideas about themselves were strengthened and reinforced appreciably by conditions specific to the nineteenth century, and that as a result the autobiography as an Icelandic phenomenon turns out to be an unusual medium for historical and literary expression.

The foundation that was laid in every home in the country for the shaping of the individual promoted the development of the autobiography, and literature in general. As mentioned earlier in the book, the *kvöldvaka* (the winter-eve gathering) provided a powerful focal point for the cultural homogeneity that prevailed throughout the country: popular culture was available to all, in a remarkably similar form.[2] The very fact that literacy was general at all levels of society had a major impact on both the written and spoken language. The education that reached all levels of Icelandic society provided conditions that enabled people of all classes to feel confident about expressing themselves on current issues and preoccupations.[3] Without this foundation, the Icelandic tradition of egodocuments would have stood on far shakier ground.[4]

This part of the book focuses on what was undoubtedly one of the main influences on how people in Iceland, and in particular those who chose to record their memories for posterity, viewed and interpreted their lives. It is arguable that in the Icelandic autobiographies a certain sense of equilibrium or insouciance may be observed: the author may not actually have a great deal to say, but they intend to tell their story nonetheless; the narrative follows the life course according to a fairly standardized pattern, taking on various shades and nuances from the experience as it unfolds. So, it seems natural to ask: What was it that made people who had perhaps spent almost their entire lives within a narrow compass of experience feel impelled to produce formal written records of their memories? Later in this chapter, I suggest that the explanation is perhaps best found in deep-seated psychological longings among those who wrote their autobiographies, longings that also manifested themselves in these people's attempts to broaden their education through informal channels, often under very challenging circumstances. It is also argued that the autobiographers felt themselves in a sense driven to "textualize" their lives, to interpret them in terms of particular forms of narrative, and by such means to "recreate" them and "balance the books," so to speak.

Is there something special about the authors of Icelandic autobiographies born in the latter half of the nineteenth century and the early twentieth century? Here, I seek to demonstrate their unusual qualities by placing them within the community that had nurtured them. For comparison, reference will be made to the historical development that has been recounted in the preceding chapters, which will be cited where appropriate. It made be deemed certain that all the principal characteristics of Western autobiographies are manifested in the Icelandic ones. The difference lies principally in the Icelandic circumstances and culture. An attempt is thus made here to show how egodocuments can be used in a historical context, and the light they can cast on the lives of people who have not, as a rule, attracted much scholarly attention.

Various narratives of people and their conditions of life give rise to compelling questions about the general experience and behavior of poor people in Iceland, as well as the more fortunate. Their way of thinking and their interaction with their environment lend the autobiographies an unusual character. It is argued below that Icelandic conditions in the nineteenth century greatly reinforced people's sense of self, which informed the form and status of the autobiography as literary self-expression.

The foundation that was laid in every Icelandic home for the upbringing and formation of the individual was important for the development of the autobiography and book culture in general. The simple fact of the general literacy of the peasantry had a great impact on discourse in the spoken and written word.

The education of the peasantry was, in fact, a prerequisite for people of all social classes to have the confidence to express themselves on current affairs. Without that essential foundation, Iceland's autobiographical tradition would have stood on a far shakier ground.

But many other factors contributed to the rise of the autobiography in Iceland, and distinguished it from comparable writing in other countries. In this context, it must first be borne in mind that the Icelandic population was very small in the nineteenth century, and that there was little difference between people's habits and conduct in different regions. While some were wealthier than others, their daily lives were similar. The custom of the winter-eve gathering was an important factor in the cultural equality that pervaded the country.[5]

People and Cultural Landscape

The daily lives of members of peasantry were much the same in the nineteenth century and so people recognized the individual aspects of daily life in other people's accounts. The smallness of society entailed *inter alia* that people readily established bonds with individuals and even events far removed from their own immediate environment and experience. They became acquainted, for instance, with "famous" individuals, or established relationships of some kind with them in the course of a lifetime. Those who were seen as "famous" were poets, politicians, officials, and vagabonds. Acquaintanceship with such individuals encouraged people, indirectly, to sit down and tell their own stories. It is, for instance, a striking element of autobiographies that they recount detailed narratives of the ways of vagabonds.

This equivalence in environment and way of life is of great importance when one comes to assess the value of Icelandic autobiographies, as such relationships considerably reduced the likelihood that an author would use poetic license to embellish the truth. The risk would have been too great, for the likelihood was that readers would recognize the fabrication, and hence condemn the author's work. The same applies to the omission of important elements of an autobiography. In such a case, the work risked being judged unreliable by the author's contemporaries and the general readership. In both cases, the response might be of two kinds: on the one hand, as sometimes still occurs, a person would publicly contradict something stated in a certain autobiography.[6] On the other hand, vague rumors could adversely affect the reception of the work. That intangible force, rumor, could prove a remarkably potent tool for rectifying misleading statements. A few lines of improvised verse, or witty repartee, could demolish the inaccuracy and undermine all faith in the author's veracity.

One of the best-known examples of a decisive response to a memoir is the exchanges between farmer Ólafur Sigurðsson and parliamentarian Þorkell Bjarnason, arising from an essay by the latter, *Fyrir 40 árum* (40 Years Ago), in which he wrote about the living conditions in the nineteenth century in the home region of both men: Skagafjörður, northwest Iceland. Þorkell's essay was published at the end of the nineteenth century in *Tímarit hins íslenska bókmenntafélags* (*The Journal of the Literary Society*). In it, he discussed with unusual frankness the living conditions of Skagafjörður people in the past. The long and detailed essay is an excellent documentary source on people's economic status in the mid-nineteenth century.[7] Þorkell describes an impoverished nation in an impoverished country—a country almost devoid of any formal infrastructure: no roads, schools, or public buildings. Each farm or croft was essentially an island of poverty.

Ólafur Sigurðsson, who was from the same region as Þorkell, was gravely displeased by his account of life in Skagafjörður, and he sat down to write an essay in rebuttal, in which he described very different conditions from those reported by Þorkell.

Essentially, Ólafur recognizes right at the start of his essay that the conditions that give rise to the dispute in fact existed, when he states that Þorkell describes "in many ways the lowest of the low—in fact the worst oafishness and squalor, that he may have heard of, or seen, on occasional crofts, when he was young; and there is more like that in the essay, which cannot be deemed to show the parents of us older folk in a favorable light."[8] He takes the view that it would have been preferable to describe the average farmer of the period, going on to remark: "But in addition it would have been blameless to omit the very worst cases of which he may have heard, for this is, after all, an account of his own nation, and especially the people of Skagafjörður, which will not be read by us Icelanders alone."[9] To Ólafur's mind, Þorkell's account is antisocial: it is not supportive of Icelanders' notions of autonomy, which were grounded precisely in the belief that everybody must do their bit, must make an effort to support progress.[10] To admit the existence of poverty and want in people's lives was deemed almost blasphemous.

The editor of the periodical *Þjóðólfur* had, after the first phase of the dispute, drawn the attention of its readers to the ongoing debate. Broadly, he took Ólafur's side, deeming his criticism of Þorkell justified. Þorkell wrote a retort to *Þjóðólfur*:

> I believe that, with respect to my upbringing and conditions of life at that time, I stood considerably closer to the part of the peasantry I describe—in other words

Figure 17 Keflavík, Hegranes.

the poorer of the working class—and thus had just as much opportunity for familiarity with the way of life and thinking of the peasantry as this upper-class gentleman did. He was of wealthy family, and no doubt he grew up in a life of happiness and sunshine.[11]

This debate is most interesting, for a number of reasons: First, it underlines the importance of seeking to understand the attitudes of people who had grown up in different conditions of life from those who never went hungry. In a sense, it might be maintained that a huge gulf might have existed between the perspective of the haves and the have-nots. Hence, the value of the autobiography, and egodocuments of any kind, is reflected in the dispute between Þorkell and Ólafur. Second, the dispute highlights the small size of the society and the proximity between people. If something was incorrectly stated, people did not hesitate to contradict it. These conditions undoubtedly encouraged writers to strive to be truthful, if they wanted to earn respect. But differences of opinion were, nonetheless, inevitable. They were only natural.

Truth

It is entirely reasonable to assume that the interaction between authors and their readers ensured that the vast majority of writers sought to tell their stories in such a way as to establish their trustworthiness. Many authors address precisely this issue in their autobiographies, and some state that a number of people can corroborate their account. Magnús Magnússon (b. 1892) discusses the subject of truth in his book *Syndugur maður segir frá* (*Testimony of a Sinner*). Magnús points out that he is not alone in being able to confirm the veracity of much of what he writes in his autobiography, "for a large number of people mentioned in my memoirs are still alive, and can thus testify to how reliable my account is, from their own memories."[12] It is also clear that the respect and affection felt for the written word placed some restrictions on authors' flights of imagination, as their reputation was at stake. That respect is clearly seen in many autobiographies, which may be attributed to the tradition of the winter-eve gathering with its discussions on the texts and their content. The tradition and its customs tended to bolster faith in the written word. Those who failed the test of truthfulness were instantly dismissed by most readers. It was simply too risky for authors to peddle untruths.

The demand for truth was a concern to some, emerging particularly when an author heard some rumor that their writings or ideas had been criticized. Sigurður Ingjaldsson (b. 1845), for instance, mentions in the foreword to the second volume of his autobiography that he is aware that some people have cast doubt on much of what he wrote in the first volume, deeming it implausible.

Sigurður, taken in by strangers as a child, lived in want during his early years; he recounts his early misfortunes in detail in his autobiography. His descriptions are plainspoken, and no doubt some readers found them unbelievable. Hence, he saw reason to address these skeptics directly: "Hence I challenge them to prove by reasoning that I tell untruths, or that I have been in the habit of telling untruths at home in Iceland or here in America. There are many people still alive, who know me both at home and here, who can bear witness to this."[13] These writings are interesting in light of people's feelings about the written word. For many, it appears to have been paramount to give a true account—it was almost blasphemy to be accused of telling an untruth. The autobiographies of nineteenth-century people may perhaps be said to be marked by this principle, in that many of them are rather formal in presentation and they tend not to be poetic.

As the twentieth century progressed, authors increasingly tended toward a confrontation—or reckoning—with their past, and this often evoked a response from interested parties. Such a reckoning is to be found, for instance, in *Perlur og steinar* (*Pearls and Stones*) by Jóhanna Kristjónsdóttir (b. 1940), cited earlier. The book mostly focuses on the subject of her marriage with Jökull Jakobsson (1933–78), a renowned Icelandic author of the latter half of the twentieth century.¹⁴ Jóhanna wrote a very frank and personal account, which caused offense to members of Jökull's family. Addressing the period of her life when she was married to Jökull, the book inevitably made reference to his friends and relatives, some of whom were judged harshly by the author—such as Jökull's parents, the Rev. Jakob Jónsson and Þóra Einarsdóttir, who were well-known and respected figures in Icelandic society. Jóhanna's censures met with a chilly response from the Rev. Jakob's other children, and attacks on Jóhanna appeared in the press. The book was published before Christmas 1993, and on Thursday January 13, 1994, an article was published in daily *Morgunblaðið* under the headline: "Andmæli gegn óhróðri" (A Rebuttal of Slander). Signed by Jökull's siblings, the article begins:

> It is sometimes the right thing to ignore lies, gossip, slander and innuendo. But so disgracefully has Jóhanna Kristjónsdóttir maligned the memory of our late father and brother and dishonored our mother that we, the surviving children of Þóra Einarsdóttir and Jakob Jónsson, cannot bear to think of our mother, who died on 9 January last, going to her grave without our making our rebuttal known.¹⁵

The siblings point out in their article that they can happily testify, anywhere and at any time, to the kindness and goodness of their parents. They reject Jóhanna's portrayal of her parents-in-law, and accuse her of extensive lies and misrepresentation. "The book is, from first to last, evidence of the mindset and character of the author," the siblings write:

> for it is based on a breach of confidence vis-à-vis deceased people, and personal vilification of those who are no longer able to answer for themselves. We are, however, quite certain that our parents' memory and reputation will not be tarnished in the minds of the many relatives, friends and well-wishers they acquired in their personal and professional lives over many decades, in addition to which the innumerable writings of father and son stand as a truthful monument to them.¹⁶

The family's response arose partly from a TV interview with Jóhanna, in which she emphasized her perceptions of the family. Jökull's siblings made reference to the TV interview: "Those who saw the TV show cannot have failed to notice Jóhanna Kristjónsdóttir's zeal in defamation and gossip. Gleefully laughing, she reiterated her slanders about our family, and was clearly having a wonderful time there, beyond all bounds of decency and morality."¹⁷

Jóhanna's book was reviewed by Einar Falur Ingólfsson, a fellow journalist on daily *Morgunblaðið*, early in December 1993. His judgment of the book, at the start of his review, was as follows: "The narrative is honest and sincere, recounting Jökull's virtues as well as his vices; Jóhanna was probably the person closest to him, who knew him better than anyone else, and this is evident in reading the book: it is a frank book, and arresting."[18] Einar Falur's review is favorable, but toward the end of the review he comments: "She tells the story of their relationship, a story that some may find too explicit, others perhaps painful. But it is a story that readers should hear, depicting a credible picture of her relationship with the artist Jökull Jakobsson."[19]

There is much to agree with in Einar Falur's comments on the book: it is a frank account, and the author does not hesitate to express her views about her life with Jökull Jakobsson. Such an account can be both effective and informative; in addition, the author, with her own strong views, steps into the province of the private lives of people who are not really anything to do with her. This narrative approach evokes various moot points about the status and right of an author to express themself about their circumstances and those of others. A good example of this kind is a private matter concerning meteorologist Þór Jakobsson, Jökull's brother, which features in the book in highly critical terms. The reader, and the critic, must surely ask what gives the author the right to express herself on other people's private lives as emphatically as Jóhanna does in this case. I am of the view that a confrontation requires the author to take a clear stance regarding the deeds recounted, and the reader must understand the terms on which the confrontation takes place, if this literary form is to function properly. Jóhanna may, perhaps, be criticized for not having clarified her position and explained to the reader her motivation for writing the book. Did these people mean nothing to her? Or had they so grossly encroached on her rights that there was no limit to how far she might go in her account?

To return to the nineteenth and early twentieth centuries, it is clear that people of all classes did not hesitate to sit down and write an account of their lives. In addition, it is striking that many of those who wrote about their lives felt that they did not have much to say. They simply wanted to tell their story for the story's sake. The motivation is thus not necessarily personal in nature, or aesthetic, as discussed below. In many cases, it derives from the desire to tell people a story: to "pay forward" the childhood entertainment of listening to stories—to repay a story with another story.

In his autobiography *Á tveimur jafnfljótum* (*Shanks' Pony*), Ólafur Jónsson (b. 1895) maintains that he is not writing a story that may be seen as entertaining:

> For that to be the case the narrative must either deal with significant, unusual or tragic events, or be buttressed by a special narrative skill; but I fear that both are

lacking here. Few of what are generally termed great events have taken place in my life, but that is not the crucial matter. The field of memoirs is so narrow and personal that one's judgement of the events must surely also be personal, and quite different from when histories of peoples and nations are written. An event which in that context is small and not worth recounting may be huge and highly significant in the life of an individual.[20]

It is important to realize that many Icelandic autobiographies are characterized by a certain modest or self-effacing quality in the writers. The vast majority of such writings display a certain equilibrium between the author's psyche and their desire to write about their life course. It is for that very reason that Ólafur Jónsson addresses the personal tone of the autobiography, which many readers may not notice: initially specific events may be deemed insignificant, serving only to fill up the narrative; however, in due course, it transpires that these events in the author's life are appropriate ways to shed light on their character and disposition. In other words, autobiographies are a phenomenon whose standards are variable and may prove difficult to identify. Thus, one may "wander" almost endlessly within each text, in each work, and approach it from different perspectives. Hence, a reader or a scholar working with narratives in egodocuments must bear in mind that understanding is a function of their own mindset. But that makes no difference to the phenomenon of egodocuments and their origin as a medium for personal expression. For that reason, it is questionable to enumerate at length the *attributes* of egodocuments; these are works that stand alone and can be molded almost at will to the subject researched by the scholar—just like any other source used within the humanities and social sciences. It is, to say the least, questionable to take definitions over-literally and put them forward as a guiding light.

In his autobiography *Ljúfa vor* (*A Lovely Spring*), Magnús H. Árnason (b. 1891) addresses the matter of his writing specifically. This discussion gives an excellent impression of what motivated many autobiographers:

> And while I feel, and am well aware, that I have not succeeded in writing any work of art, I shall continue to write down some of the memories that constantly gather in my mind. I have generally followed the rule of recounting specific events and describing them as they happened, giving in that manner an account of the life of a country boy, but without any continuous narrative.
>
> In many cases I state the year in which an event took place, and those dates are certainly correct, as these are major events; but in the case of more minor events a date may be inaccurate by one year. I have striven to write my account

in few words. But I know there are many defects in my narrative, for I have never attended school but for one year in evening school in Akureyri. This is thus the work of an unschooled farmer, not the polished work of an educated man who has sat at his studies for 10–18 years.[21]

Clearly, the approaches of different autobiographers vary widely. Readers will observe, however, certain common factors in the work of many writers, which will be discussed further below. But I want to state clearly that this discussion is not intended to be a comprehensive survey of Icelandic autobiographies—such a task would be impossible, as I have sought to explain in this volume. Each book is a world of its own, and any attempt to fit it into a specific model undermines the potential for enjoyment of such literature. I have sought to inform the reader about the important attributes of autobiographies, which may prove helpful in reading and using sources of this nature.[22] An important factor in this context is how egodocuments have been used in research on women, when so fewer women have left writings, in both Iceland and elsewhere. The fact is that scholars have worked inventively with rather limited material in order to connect egodocuments with women's history, as will be discussed later in this chapter. But first, a few comments about the nature of semi-autobiographies.

The Author's Responsibility

The above discussion of Jóhanna Kristjánsdóttir's autobiography raises questions about the responsibility of the authors of such works. It is safe to say that the relationship between the author of a semi-autobiography and its protagonist is often complex, and is manifested in various ways. A well-known case in Iceland was a controversy that arose from the semi-autobiography of psychiatrist Esra Pétursson, written by journalist Ingólfur Margeirsson.[23] Esra's candid account of his relationship with a patient proved contentious. Clearly, Esra had violated all medical ethics, both by embarking on a relationship with the patient and then by discussing her medical history and their sexual relationship. Esra may be said to have rubbed salt into the wound when he bluntly recounted this tragic tale in his semi-autobiography, after the patient had died by suicide. Esra added insult to injury by alleging that the woman's parents were responsible for her misfortunes. That account, together with Esra's high opinion of himself, led to extensive debate on narratives of this kind. It sparked a hostile response from the woman's family, from Esra's fellow-physicians (he was later expelled from the Medical

Association), and from the public. There was near-universal agreement that Esra had gone too far in his account—so far that living people with a connection to the case would be substantially affected.

Esra was not alone in being criticized for his story. The author of the book, Ingólfur Margeirsson, was also censured for his part in the work. Ingólfur, however, was undismayed; he felt he had been fortunate to have the opportunity to work on Esra's story. And Ingólfur had high ideas for the book: to apply to his subject the theories of no less a person than Sigmund Freud. "If the author and narrator are aware of Freud's theories and the techniques of psychoanalysis," writes Ingólfur in his foreword to the book, "there is little to prevent application of the unique technique created by Freud in order to understand a person's life with more depth than has generally been the case in biographies."[24] Ingólfur would appear to have failed in his attempt at psychoanalysis on Freudian principles, since, as mentioned above, the book and Ingólfur's role in it sparked a scandal shortly after publication; in due course, legal proceedings in the case led to both Ingólfur and Esra being convicted in the Supreme Court.[25]

The case of the psychiatrist's book raises various questions about the author's responsibility in writing of this kind: How far should they go in their account? When should they step in and stop a protagonist who is clearly on the wrong path, and convince them to change direction? These are matters of conscience that all authors face in writing about their subjects. Authors of books of all kinds face such questions in their daily work and must make up their minds whether they wish their name to be connected with such deeds as Esra recounts. Authors are aware that it is possible to report events factually, without violating confidentiality or encroaching on people's privacy as decisively as Ingólfur's book did. Perhaps the writing of this book was not guided by the quest for truth but by other ideas.

Ingólfur Margeirsson opted to regard Esra's account as credible, and no doubt he had good reasons to do so: "There was quite a commotion last Christmas over the biography of Dr. Esra Pétursson, as many people felt that it violated the privacy of a deceased person in an inconsiderate and shameless manner," wrote Matthías Viðar Sæmundsson, who taught Icelandic literature at the University of Iceland, in an article in daily *DV* in 1998. He continues:

> Family members thus called for an investigation, legal proceedings commenced, writs were issued, and now a verdict has been reached in the case, while author Ingólfur Margeirsson deplores his predicament and that of free speech in Iceland. Hence this appears to be a classic example of the battle of the individual

against the system, the never-ending tale of good (Ingólfur/Esra) and evil (family members/law courts).[26]

In his article, Matthías Viðar discusses a resolution by the Writers' Union of Iceland on what he terms "Ingólfur's problems": this resolution, says Matthías, "conflates old clichés on the roles of authors and journalists—that information may offend and shock people and disrupt peace of mind, that the messenger should not be blamed, as in olden times." Matthías goes on to criticize the Writers' Union for its bizarre conclusion that the sanctity of private life is of small importance, at least by comparison with the importance of authors and journalists being able to report on people's most private affairs without any intervention by the legislature. Matthías Viðar expresses the view that in many cases freedom of speech is "a synonym for unbridled presumption, even a sales device, a tool in the media's marketing efforts." Here, Matthías is probably referring to the fact that Ingólfur was not only the author of the book, but also its publisher, who had direct financial interests at stake. Matthías Viðar reaches the following conclusion: "Authors are not immune from the trials and rights of others, as the Writers' Union resolution implies; they must surely bear responsibility for their words, whether in fiction, journalism or biography; for otherwise freedom of speech may become warped into its distasteful opposite."

In 1995, two years before Esra's book, *A Sinner's Requiem*, was published, Ingólfur Margeirsson had written an article in *Morgunblaðið* about the activity he called the writing of "life stories."[27] Here, Ingólfur clearly refers to semi-autobiographies, as he makes frequent reference to the relationship between the author and the subject (interviewee).[28] The article has just one intention, that is, to draw attention to the role of the author of a semi-autobiography in the process of creating the work. Ingólfur argues so convincingly that he succeeded in persuading me, and no doubt others, of the importance of the author in the production of books of this kind.

> Wise men sometimes say: the novelist is the novel; the poet is the poem; the playwright is the play. So, we may ask: is the biographer the biography? Can another person's biography reflect its author? The answer is yes: the biography always reflects the author, good or bad. A true biographer writes himself into the biography of another person. [. . .] It is the biographer who listens to the interviewee and evaluates them, selects what is to be included in the book, and what omitted.

Ingólfur speaks very clearly here, and hence the conclusion to his article comes as no surprise:

People must understand that the writing of biography is both delicate and humanitarian. Delicate, because the author must recreate an individual's journey on earth. So, the author's responsibility is great; it is he who must present the subject's events, achievements, emotions and thinking. Humanitarian, because honest biographical writing is by nature cathartic for the life of the person in question—a kind of spiritual therapy, a reckoning and rethinking, a mental stocktaking. [. . .] The core of the biography is humanism, for true biographical writing is in its nature a deep and sincere interest in humanity and its life on earth.

The "humanism" behind the book *A Sinner's Requiem* is certainly of a strange nature. The verdict of the district court on May 8, 1998, states, in expounding the facts of the case: "The accused [Ingólfur Margeirsson] states that he was bound by confidentiality to the co-accused, and that he saw it as his duty to record his account of his life so that it should be correctly reported in the book. *He says that he saw himself as the editor of the work, first and foremost.*"[29] The role of the author has here become insignificant, as compared with Ingólfur's declarations in *Morgunblaðið* in 1995. All of a sudden, he is unwilling to admit that he made much contribution to the book.

In the end, the story of Esra Pétursson's semi-autobiography and the court case that arose from it demonstrate the truth of what Ingólfur Margeirsson had maintained in 1995, that in the writing of such books the author has a great responsibility. It is hard to say what made Ingólfur change his mind. Perhaps Esra contrived to mesmerize Ingólfur: this is precisely one of the risks that Ingólfur sees biographers as running: "that [. . .] the biographer becomes too enamored of the subject, is captivated by the character and their life, so that the subject gains too much control over the author." The implication of Ingólfur's argument is that he takes the view that the author creates the person who is the subject of the book, conjuring order from chaos.

Ingólfur stresses that the author may not invent—that is a deadly sin. Here, he addresses a vital question regarding the attempt to create a unified narrative from a person's life, without inventing anything. The question is: How is that possible? One cannot expect an author to recreate the life of the person in question precisely as it was; hence, the author must make or create a narrative that resembles the person's life to some extent. Otherwise, the argument for the importance of the author is fallacious. It almost seems that Ingólfur is unaware of the dilemma that faces every author of a creative work—the implications of the choice between what is important and unimportant. The composition of any semi-autobiography is based on such a choice between elements of the protagonist's life. The responsibility of the author of a semi-autobiography consists *inter alia* of an evaluation of the entire life story of the protagonist and that person's personal attributes. Ingólfur fails in working systematically with his source material in the manner he described as necessary in his article in *Morgunblaðið* in 1995. As a result, the reader is greatly disappointed. The position in which the reader finds themself is the more striking because Ingólfur had previously done such excellent work with his memorable book on the life of mezzo-soprano Guðmunda Elíasdóttir.[30]

Many years later, Ingólfur looked back on these events in an interview in daily *Fréttablaðið*. He recalled the moment when he stood before the Supreme Court, awaiting the verdict: "All the judges were on the bench, and when I saw seven judges, in their splendid blue robes, everyone holding a copy of the book, I said: *Well, I have gone as far as I can as an author. This is the peak*."[31]

Women Under the Magnifying Glass

One may ask: What influence has this development of both autobiographies and semi-autobiographies had on research into the position of the sexes within the scholarly world? The status and value of women's accounts are summed up in the introduction to the collection of articles *Interpreting Women's Lives* as follows: "Traditionally, knowledge, truth, and reality have been constructed as if men's experiences were normative, as if being human meant being male."[32] The volume sets out to show how that perspective distorts all scholarly attempts to discuss life and existence, for the simple reason that women are a significant part of the social structure. Here, the standardized picture of the world is rejected, a picture that was in large part white and masculine, and replaced by the viewpoints of both genders, different classes, ethnic groups, and races. The entire purpose is to break down people's older ideas of the position of the sexes and the workings of society. It is a well-known story: feminist commentators started to conduct their work on the basis that all history was based on conflict between the sexes and that the gender perspective must inform all scholarly research. "Since feminist theory is grounded in women's lives and aims to analyze the role and meaning of gender in those lives and in society, women's personal narratives are essential primary documents for feminist research."[33] The self became the key component in the academic approaches of many feminists in the second half of the twentieth century, and this approach has had a major influence on scholarly thinking, among other reasons because it has encouraged incisive criticism of the importance of the grand narrative.

A call was raised for women's accounts to be heard. But how was this put into practice? Because those who had collected sources in earlier times were men, personal sources by women—sources in which they found the opportunity to express themselves on life and existence—could prove hard to come by. So purposeful measures needed to be taken.

First, moves were set in train to interview women who had been active in human life through most of the nineteenth and twentieth centuries, giving them the opportunity to describe their varied experiences (semi-autobiographies and conversational books). The group behind the publication of *Interpreting Women's Lives*, for instance, has collected large numbers of accounts by women and has sought to produce material from them in a highly interesting manner. The results have been quite impressive.

Second, historians adopted the course of applying new methods to traditional sources in cases where their research was directed to periods in the distant past in order to recreate the various viewpoints of those involved and try to bring out voices that have been suppressed. The methods of microhistory have been crucial to the work of many historians here by providing the means of reading from the sources signs and clues that were not immediately obvious when they were studied. A celebrated example is Nathalie Zemon Davis' treatment of the story of Martin Guerre: instead of concentrating on the "main event" of the story, the return of Martin Guerre, she directed her attention to his wife, Bertrande de Rols, and deconstructed her role in the narrative as an active agent.[34]

Third, these movements within the world of scholarship gave an impetus to considerably more determined attempts to examine the basis of the collection of sources, their archival preservation, and their recording. The results have been particularly instructive, since they have shown that many more egodocuments were produced by women than was previously believed. In her master's dissertation, Icelandic historian Guðný Hallgrímsdóttir demonstrated that large amounts of material that were in fact written by women had been entered in the archives unascribed or under the names of their fathers/husbands/sons—as if it had simply not been considered worthwhile noting the true details of who had actually produced them.[35] Guðný's identification of this "new" material, and similar results produced by Icelandic colleagues who use the methods of microhistory, have revolutionized the ideas of Icelandic historians on the position of the individual in history and the approaches available to historians in researching such matters.[36] Again, this work in Iceland may be compared with the "Perdita Project: Early Modern Women's Manuscript Compilations," conducted by a team of scholars based at

Nottingham Trent University and Warwick University in England with the aim of building up a database of women's manuscripts from various parts of the world, as mentioned before.[37]

Research on autobiographies has taken account of these changing attitudes in recent years. New ideas in the humanities and the social sciences have led scholars to start doubting whether it is possible to produce a coherent and integrated picture of a life, and have shown that individuals' accounts of their own life courses must always be a fabrication, an improvisation raised on the blurred boundaries between reality and imagination.[38] The reality that appears in autobiographies is, however, always "true" on its own terms, and interesting as such. Scholars have, in fact, started to talk more about the sources on the basis of such ideas. Our explanations of the world are "constructs" that follow certain scientific laws, and I believe that it is a fundamental issue for scholarship that people should be clear about the presuppositions that lie behind these constructs. Research on egodocuments thus provides significant information about the material that scholars are currently searching for in ever-increasing measure. At the same time, it is important to understand the motives that are at work in any given society that influence both men and women alike in their attempt to express themselves.

It is notable that women born in Iceland around or after 1920, into a tradition that was marked by male perspectives, who wanted to express themselves within the boundaries of the autobiography, in some cases succeeded in breaking free from the conventional form of expression that such literature had bequeathed to them (and in fact to men too). As an example, here we may take the writer Jakobína Sigurðardóttir (b. 1918) and her autobiography *Í barndómi* (*In Childhood*), published in 1994.[39] Initially, Jakobína set out to write an ethnographic description of her childhood home in Strandir in northwest Iceland, as a kind of answer to another well-known book, *Hornstrendingabók* (*Book of the People of Hornstrandir*) by Þorleifur Bjarnason, published in 1983, which mainly dealt with the life and topography of the region in question.[40] Jakobína seems to have been very unhappy with Þorleifur's presentation. But her attempt misfired because she eventually felt herself compelled to step into the narrative, to abandon the form of ethnographic description and tell the story as she had experienced it. In a certain sense, her own self became the focus of the narrative. Here, a new type of autobiography was taking shape which had the self of the central character as its main subject, which I call "the culture of confession" (see later discussions). Jakobína underscores her position in the work by ruminating on how memory works, how and whether it is possible to tell one's own story, and what such narratives are worth. All of this is an indication of her consciousness of the limits of form and text.

This train of events completely alters the position of history with respect to the past. One might say that the centralized connection of history, as it appears for example in the historical memory, loses its foothold and multiple versions of the past emerge—many histories, miscellaneous and multifaceted. And as the compartments that the individual memory has relied on disintegrate, so the central existence on which "the memory of the nation" rests falls apart. At this point, everything coalesces—the self, the idea of history, and memory—and areas of learning come into existence that are more difficult to demarcate according to the traditional laws of the sciences. Women's right to exist is acknowledged, and academic study has had to change its emphases, due to the demand that they and others who have hitherto had no "currency" in history now achieve their place, just as was described previously in connection with the history of women's and gender studies.

Ancient Sagas and Living Tradition

The "sagas of Icelanders" comprise about forty texts, the longest being of similar length to a modern medium-size novel.[41] Most of the best appear to have been written during the thirteenth century but are clearly based on older material, both written and oral. They deal with Icelanders who lived in "the Saga Age"— the generations after the settlements, up to around 1030—and in particular their feuds and disputes. There is clearly some kind of factual basis behind the events recorded. Equally clearly, the sagas are not to be treated as purely historical records; the people and events are clothed in an epic grandeur whose roots lie in the common Germanic heroic heritage. There are certain similarities in construction to chronicles, but the sagas are tightly and consciously plotted so as to come to aesthetically satisfying conclusions.

While most of the events described take place in Iceland, Icelanders of the Saga Age travelled widely and there are many scenes set in other parts of the Viking world—Norway, the British Isles, Greenland, and even farther afield. There are strong elements of popular superstition (ghosts, portents, etc.) and in places we find themes and motifs that can be traced back to religious or mythological material, both Christian and pre-Christian. In general, though, the world of the sagas is firmly secular: the impression is very much of real people in real settings, heightened by powerful moral considerations, such as the sense of honor, and social themes, such as the struggle for resources in a harsh environment. Another element in this realism is the central part played by the political and legal background of the Saga Age, that is, a loose federation of competing local chieftaincies bound together by a single law. This political structure, called the *þjóðveldi* or, in English, the Icelandic Commonwealth, is discussed later in this chapter.

The sagas are noted particularly for their style, their narrative technique, and their characters. Stylistically, the prose gives an impression of naive simplicity, using concrete vocabulary and short, compact sentences. This, however, is a very calculated simplicity, the mark of a high literary sophistication on the part of the authors. Events are always presented externally, with the appearance of detachment and objectivity. Things are reported but never explained. The author "pretends" to be impartial between the protagonists, and the characters are allowed to reveal themselves only indirectly through what they do or say. Exceptional in this respect are the verses with which many of the sagas are studded and which purport to come from the characters concerned; here, we are sometimes allowed direct insights into personal feelings and attitudes.

The debt owed by the autobiographers of the nineteenth and early twentieth centuries to the story-reading tradition at the winter-eve gatherings in Iceland is considerable and hardly open to dispute.[42] The sagas and other ancient writings exercised a considerable influence on children in their formative years. With their support, young people were able to face up to and endure the hardships that were an ever-present part of rural life in Iceland.[43] The sagas provided children in farming communities with the models and examples they lacked due to the heavy workloads placed on their parents and guardians. They taught them to fulfill their roles with stoicism and accept whatever circumstances threw at them, just as the ancient heroes had done.[44] But, as argued below, the sagas provided them with many other motifs that they were able to seize and adapt to their personal needs.

According to literary historian Vésteinn Ólason, professor emeritus, the ancient literature fortified people in their struggles with daily life. Men needed courage as they ventured out to sea in open boats in deepest winter or across mountain tracks in uncertain weather, and endurance and tenacity were an ever-present necessity, even when not in the face of imminent mortal danger: heroes who show no fear and triumph against all the odds were naturally salutary models: "It was without doubt this more than almost anything that made the sagas dear to the farmers who chose them as material to read out to their households: they fostered courage in the menfolk and inculcated in the womenfolk an appropriate respect for their achievements."[45]

Vésteinn's comments on the influence of the ancient literature on the conceptual world of people in modern times (1500 to the present) and possibly earlier are fully in line with what emerges from the vast majority of the autobiographies. From the autobiographies, however, we can cite much more direct evidence of the influence of the sagas on the mental world of children and, indeed, all cultural life in the nineteenth century. Autobiographer Sæmundur Dúason (b. 1889), for example, has this to say about his childhood response to the ancient literature in his book *Einu sinni var* (*Once Upon a Time*):

> It might well be that all this reading and *rímur* poetry[46] shaped my character and attitudes to the present in various ways. This was at a time before people started casting doubt on the veracity of the sagas, though not everyone took the most flagrant exaggerations in them seriously. To me, at least, much of what I read was unadorned reality.[47]

Following on from this sweeping statement of attitude, Sæmundur attempts to assess precisely how the sagas influenced him and what kinds of models they provided: "There was no shortage of examples for anyone who wished to model himself on the conduct of the great men. Conversely, neither was there any dearth of bad examples to shun."[48] He goes on:

> Though I do not recall attempting explicitly to ape the saga heroes, it is quite certain that I admired those heroes who displayed the greatest manliness in all they did. Similarly, I felt a deep aversion to those who were the meanest scoundrels and wretches, men you could never trust and who left a trail of mischief wherever they went. The ethics of the sagas were more often than not absolute and categorical.[49]

From this and many similar examples it is clear that the world of the sagas permeated the lives and attitudes of children and young people in the nineteenth century—and indeed of the vast majority of the peasantry of Iceland, as Vésteinn Ólason points out.

Magnús H. Árnason gives a picturesque account of his quickening interest in the sagas as a child:

> I found learning to read fairly easy. But I was a bit lazy. I started reading the sagas when I was ten. And once I had managed to pick my way through *Egils saga* there was nothing I wanted to read more than the sagas. My father had *Víga-Glúms saga* in Gothic lettering and I learned this script so as to be able to read the saga. When I had got hold of and read most of the sagas, there was still *Grettir's saga* that I had not read. I got word that Ólafur of Melgerði had a copy, but the story went that *Grettir's saga* was such a favorite of his that he would not

lend it to anyone. But I wanted that saga very much, because I had heard Grettir talked about so much."⁵⁰

Magnús plucked up his courage and went to visit the farmer. "I broached the matter with some trepidation but Ólafur took my request well and said he felt he had to lend me the saga, since I had gone to all the effort of coming out in a snowstorm to ask for it."⁵¹ Children like Magnús appear to have been driven by an unquenchable desire to devour these ancient tales; as he himself tells us, he had grown up among animated discussions of the qualities of the principal characters.

We find a similar picture in the autobiography of Hafsteinn Sigurbjarnarson (b. 1895), where he describes the winter-eve gatherings on the farm where he lived as a child:

> When the light had been lit in the evening it was an established custom for sagas to be read all night until half past eleven, except for the time when people went to attend to the cowsheds or to eat. This reading fell to the boys from Syðsti-Hvammur. The sagas were passed on loan from person to person and everything was read that could be obtained, often the same books winter after winter, the sagas and whatever else.⁵²

The sagas were discussed with animation and in minute detail in many households: "The reading was almost always followed with interest by young and old, and when there was a break in the reading the material was discussed. Very often opinions were divided," said a male respondent (b. 1861) from Austur-Húnavatnssýsla, interviewed in 1930 by Danish folk high school teacher Holger Kjær on his journey around Iceland surveying attitudes to education. Kjær's informant went on:

> When talking about sagas, different men had different heroes. Some even pleaded extenuation for character defects and wrongdoings that came up in the story and tried to argue that such and such had to be that way; others made counter-arguments, and the discussions at times became quite heated. These discussions served to quicken and sharpen the understanding of us children of the characters of the people in the sagas and how they wove the thread of their fate to achieve fame and renown, prestige and success, or infamy and shame, downfall and disgrace, life or death. My heart often burned in my chest and my eyes filled with tears, either of happiness or sorrow.⁵³

Literary historian Viðar Hreinsson cites a passionate example of this empathetic involvement in the ancient sagas in the poet Kristín Sigfúsdóttir's (b. 1876) description of a saga reading in the house where she grew up:

> An old woman told me that at one time in her childhood she had heard *Laxdæla saga* being read in the house where she lived. When they got to slaying of Kjartan, an old man, half in tears, called in from out in the living room (*baðstofa*): 'Oh, stop reading, stop reading. What a damned accursed villain that Bolli was to kill Kjartan!' The man who was reading fell silent and put down the book. But after a little while another sound came from the same direction: 'Oh well, maybe you can carry on just a bit further.' And so the reading was resumed.[54]

It is important now to consider to what extent and in what ways this influence of the ancient sagas was passed through to the writing and form of autobiographies. It seems reasonable to hypothesize at this stage that the influence went deep, pervading all aspects of their writers' literary activities. If so, this has fundamental repercussions for our treatment of autobiographies as historical sources. We must therefore now turn in greater detail to the relationship between form and content in autobiographies.

Literary Motifs

The fact that a single literary form can have so dominant a place within a culture as we find in Iceland can bring various problems of interpretation when sources such as egodocuments are used in sociohistorical analysis. The problems can affect both the literary and the historical value of such sources. A chain reaction of mutual influence is liable to arise, leading to circular argumentation—"sites of memory" in the life course, such as confirmation in the nineteenth century, had a decisive effect on people's social formation; the values associated with them may result in those who looked back over their lives "reshaping" their experience in accordance with a predetermined structure in which the event itself had a specific place, assigned to it by the institution responsible. In the case of confirmation, it was, of course, the church that determined how the event was interpreted. To take another example, when considering childhood the autobiographers offer two principal interpretations: their younger years are seen either as a road that eventually brought the individual to happiness and fulfillment, or as one that led to ruin and consigned people to the stony path of poverty and hardship.[55] The choice taken by individual autobiographers when interpreting their own lives was determined by what the person in question believed to be the actual experience in their own particular case.

It rarely occurs to people to view the interpretative route they select as part of the process involved in each person's reevaluation of their own self: it is regarded rather as a genuine reflection of their life as it actually unfolded. The way people present and explain their life course is, of course, based on their experiential observations of life as a whole, but it is also colored by the narrative approaches on offer, by new insights into the self, and by the very process of retelling personal life and experience. The narrative methods thus create a circle of mutual influence, taking in the individual, the literary form, the environment and experience, all coming together to determine how authors of autobiographical writings present their formation in written language.

It is worth asking what significance this has for the use of autobiographical literature and the shaping of memories. As I see it, there are two aspects in particular that need to be addressed here. First, the influence of the sagas on children's upbringing and early experience of life—and the sagas continued to be a central part of people's lives throughout their adult years. These people had no problem putting themselves in the shoes of the saga heroes and many thus came to the conclusion that their own everyday lives were special and remarkable in the same way as those of the early settlers of Iceland.

Second, the unique regard in which the sagas were held—a status that still in a sense hangs over all cultural activity in Iceland and was until very recently instrumental in shaping people's modes of living and thinking—extended, unsurprisingly, to their literary form, making the sagas the obvious pattern from which most autobiographies were cut until well into the twentieth century. The dominance of the received forms, we can imagine, led people to see their own life experience, for instance from their childhood years, in terms of precepts and patterns found in these texts. We see this most obviously in the use of certain motifs. A striking case in point is the repeated occurrence of the "coal-biter" or "male Cinderella" motif, in which a person who shows no promise as a youngster eventually blossoms to display unexpected talents. This was a familiar motif to all Icelanders—from the Bible, in the story of Jacob and Esau, but especially from saga literature, especially *Grettir's saga* and the *Tale of Þorvaldur the Far-Traveled*. Motifs of this kind were a part of people's lives and could shape and color how they interpreted the world and, by extension, how they remembered their own childhoods and so how they came to present their lives in text. In this sense, the sagas were a completely natural and integral part of the authors' relation of the events of their own lives.

In recent years, Viðar Hreinsson has drawn attention to the prevalence of the coal-biter motif in Icelandic culture in a series of articles and lectures.[56] For instance, in relation to the poem "Fíflið" (The Idiot, 1895) by the Canadian-Icelandic poet Stephan G. Stephansson, he notes:

> In the poem Stephan brings together the main features of this narrative motif. In his youth the coal-biter is a simpleton, a child who is generally on the outside but who enjoys the love and favor of his mother. He pays scant regard to the conventional rules of social intercourse but turns out well in the end. This is originally a folktale motif, related to the Cinderella story and familiar to Icelanders from the tales about the youngest sister Helga, also known under the name Kolrassa Krókríðandi [Coal-Bottom Corner-Lurker], and from tales about the farmer's youngest son. However, the coal-biter emerges fully naturalized and individualized in the ancient sagas.

Viðar notes that many coal-biters were endowed with "big" personality traits that drew attention to them. They flouted social conventions, had a will of their own, and were determined to get their own way. Moreover, the coal-biter motif "can accommodate endless variation, for instance inner conflicts and serious flaws of character." Viðar goes on to analyze the attributes of two of the best-known saga heroes, Egill Skallagrímsson and Grettir Ásmundsson, and points out that in *Grettir's saga* "we see a constant tension and interplay between, on the one hand, pain, loneliness and fear of the dark and, on the other, teasing, provocation and tomfoolery." All the features mentioned here leap out at us from many of the autobiographies and point the way to how many of the authors interpreted themselves and how they intended to be seen by others.

The image of the "great hero" that gained currency with the majority of saga readers early in the twentieth century superseded the interest in and identification with the coal-biter. Heroic motifs became more sharply defined and more influential around and after the time of the movement for self-determination in the second half of the nineteenth century, and were underscored by constant appeals to the "Golden Age" of ancient Iceland. "At times there is a noticeable tendency to idealize and glorify beyond all restraint," says Viðar in the lecture quoted above. Reflections of the coal-biter motif in autobiographies can be seen as evidence that the sagas had a much deeper resonance for their readers than we find in subsequent periods: to the autobiographers and their peers the sagas were an integral part of their lives, their position unquestioned, offering endless possibilities of approach and analysis. What Viðar calls "the glossy image of the Golden Age" was largely a construct of the middle classes, a weapon to be deployed in the service of national autonomy, and it is this image that has dominated to the present day. But among the rural peasantry—the people who read the sagas constantly and whose lives were fully immersed in them—this idolization of the sagas did not preclude a continuing creative response to their material. The sagas remained a fixed and reliable reference point in their psychological as well as cultural (spiritual) beings, living examples to people in their daily toils; and their leading motifs found their way into the self-image of rural Icelanders when they came to set down their own lives in writing.

One thing is certain, the sagas were a living part of the mental world of many of their peasant readers; for this we have the evidence of autobiography after autobiography. To these people the saga world was at times so real and potent, so "true," that ordinary laboring Icelanders with only the most rudimentary formal education had no hesitation in coming forward to argue the toss with any academic scholar who was so bold as to cast doubt on the veracity of the sagas. Helgi Haraldsson (b. 1891), a farmer from Hrafnkelsstaðir in the southern lowlands, achieved national celebrity for the vehemence with which he participated in a number of scholarly disputes in the middle years of the twentieth century, for instance over the identity of the author of *Njáls saga*.[57] And he was not alone. In 1979, Kristín Geirsdóttir (b. 1908) from the remote farm of Hringver in Tjörnes in the north wrote to the prestigious literary journal *Skírnir* expounding her views on the theories of ancient academic saga scholars:

> I have to acknowledge that for all my interest in the ancient writings of Iceland my knowledge of them is not cast in steel. Far from it. I have neither had the stamina nor the circumstances to delve into them as I would have wished. But these books have been enormously precious to me from as far back as I remember, and if anything is to excuse me for trying to write as I do now it is my heartfelt love for the ancient literature of Iceland.—This may probably be called 'sentimentality', and I have noticed that this kind of thing is not in favor among modern literary commentators. But there are also various things in these matters that I have difficulty understanding, because it is hard to reconcile them with my ordinary native common sense.[58]

Kristín goes on undeterred to shred to pieces the arguments of academic scholars, using as her weapon her "feeling" for the story world of the sagas as acquired in the setting of her childhood living room. Her 1979 article was followed by two more in 1990 and 1995, also published in *Skírnir*.[59] Kristín had something to say about the work of just about every other critic of the sagas. The youngest object of her disapproval was Professor Guðrún Nordal, now director of the prestigious Árni Magnússon Institute for Icelandic Studies, about whose research Kristín writes:

A recent edition of *Skírnir* (Autumn 1992) contains much of enormous interest. My attention was first drawn to an essay by Dr Guðrún Nordal, 'Freyr fífldur' [The Cuckolding of Freyr]. What interested me in this article was, in part, that ever since I was a child Sturla Sighvatsson has left an indelible impression on my mind, both for his complex personality and for his tragic fate. Also lasting in my memory has been the strange story of Hallbjörn of Kiðjaberg and his wife Hallgerður, and his verse 'Ölkarma lætr arma,'[60] the unforgettable cry of a man at the end of his tether, has affected me more powerfully than just about anything else I know in Norse verse. But never had it occurred to me that there was any connection between the two, the story of Sturla and the one about Hallbjörn and Hallgerður.[61]

Kristín then goes through the saga against the background of Guðrún Nordal's ideas: "From what I could gather, Dr Guðrún considers that in Sturla's nickname lies an imputation of unmanliness, but this was entirely beyond my comprehension."[62] What is notable here is this extraordinary "feeling" for the material that we find in Kristín's presentation of her case, the intuitions of an uneducated working woman from the north of Iceland.

To explain this personal response, we need to look in greater depth at the various motifs we find in the sagas and the power they exerted over ordinary people. Possibly the best way to do this is to analyze precisely how these different motifs are reflected in autobiographies. Such an analysis increases appreciably our understanding of the independent status of the sagas and serves to identify the particular parameters within which the authors operated, thereby helping us

Figure 18 Ormarsstaðir, Fellum.

to explain how they understood specific events or relationships, for example with parents and friends. Above all else, this interrelationship between form, motifs like the coal-biter, and general individual experience demonstrates clearly that the literary form of the sagas lies at a much deeper level within the psychology of people brought up in nineteenth-century society and well into the twentieth century than we might at first suppose. This striking linkage of form and reality makes the autobiography a particularly significant point of contact between the mental constructs and the experience of people at all levels of Icelandic society.[63]

7

The Autobiography and the Life Course

Childhood and Death

All autobiographies comprise several elements that are determined by the life course. This is one of the major attributes of autobiography, but it is manifested more clearly in some books than others. The vast majority of autobiographers discuss their childhood in detail. This is the life stage that most writers feel compelled to examine in extraordinary detail—so much so that it can often prove too much for the reader. Many authors, for instance, report whole conversations and describe events, people, or objects in minute detail—all presented in such a way that the events might have taken place yesterday. And the writers make judgments grounded in their own experience: "People were not always sympathetic to poor parents who were struggling," writes Kristján Sigurðsson (b. 1883) in his book *Þegar veðri slotar* (*When the Weather Dies Down*), "even when they had to send their children away to work, as soon as they were able to do small tasks and watch over livestock—and even less, if someone offered to take the children in and foster them. But one could not rely upon the children being treated well. And nobody asked whether their parents missed them."[1] Kristján goes on to recount how his siblings were sent away, one after the other, around the age of ten, and then describes his own experience: "And now was the last chance to look over my shoulder, hoping to see Mama, and she was still standing on Snösin. I was twelve years old, the fifth child she had sent away into the unknown."[2]

Not only do autobiographers write extensively about the value of childhood, but ideas about child-raising and the status of children and youngsters are also a common feature of this form of egodocument. Many looked back with affection on their early years, and part of the motivation for autobiographical writing was precisely to memorialize people—parents or others—who had been kind to the author at this vulnerable stage of life. Others had less happy stories to tell; many of the autobiographers reach some judgment on this period, in one way or another. Björn Jóhannsson (b. 1891), the son of casual laborers with no fixed master, recounts his family's tribulations in his youth: "and it is true to say that I never had a settled home for as long as I can remember until I reached confirmation age [around 14]."[3] Matthías Jochumsson (b. 1835), another autobiographer, cited before, tells of being sent to a foster family at the age of ten, and recounts that his move to a new home affected him badly:

> Yet I have nothing to report to prove conclusively that I was treated worse than youngsters of my age away from their families were generally treated when they were supposed to work for their keep and clothing.
>
> It is another matter, whether that treatment would be deemed entirely fair or just in these times. Nor can I praise my progress in those years, for it was precisely that first chapter of that period that acutely stunted my growth and development in various ways. But that may be attributable to my youth, strange character and timidity, as much as to any external influences. Overall, due to what I call those travails, my development was very slow. But however, that upheaval that then faced me is examined, I stood, as a child of ten, at the first crossroads of my life.[4]

It is a striking feature of autobiographies that so many authors apparently stand at some crossroads in their lives at this stage in their life course. I have seen this as a function of the fact that from the age of five or six, children were allotted tasks which they were expected to perform conscientiously, often without supervision. They were assigned to herd and watch over livestock far from the farmstead, and under such circumstances it was essential for children to learn to keep their heads—note that these were children who had generally been brought up on stories of ghosts and supernatural phenomena. Matthías Jochumsson describes his mental anguish under such circumstances:

> And it was no better when the tales of elves and ghosts began to be told—and that was at an early age. They were told to us by an old woman named Solveig, without our mother's knowledge, for she had forbidden her from filling our minds with stories of mythical creatures. Before long I was imagining ghosts and specters, especially at night and in twilight, when I was sometimes out in open country. My mother had firmly inculcated into us that children had nothing to fear from anything of that kind, provided that they remembered to say their prayers [. . .] What I found worst was how little good my prayers did me, for the hallucinations continued during the hours of darkness, even though I recited three times what I knew of my Bible verses.[5]

Many autobiographers report having had similar feelings to those described by Matthías. Elías Halldórsson (b. 1877) discusses the significance of an environment of religious belief and folklore for children's mental well-being, and the background to that culture:

> But they had two sides. One was to inculcate into children belief in God and faith in divine protection. The other was that through saying of prayers, ideas were insinuated into children's minds about evil spirits and devils that would strive to harm them. In order to keep children compliant, they were unceasingly intimidated with tales of [ogres] Boli, Grýla and the Yuletide Lads, and darkness, etc. Then when they were older they got to hear tales of ghosts of infants exposed and left to die, hidden people [elves], fetches, kelpies and monsters.[6]

Children were thus under some stress at this period of their lives—in addition to which was an aspect of their lived experience that was far from cheering: death. Death was a constant presence, and in my view, it had a permanent impact on children's lives. All saw close relatives—siblings, parents, grandparents—die, some long before their time. In the mid-nineteenth century, more than 35 percent of infants died before reaching their first birthday, while infant mortality declined toward the end of the century.[7] A large proportion of children aged one to five years also died of diseases for which no treatment existed. Thus, many children saw two to four of their siblings buried.[8]

In his autobiography, Indriði Einarsson (b. 1851) gives a moving account of the deaths of his siblings. Of the fifteen children, six lived to the age of eighteen; one of these died of typhoid when he was working as a fisherman. The rest lost their lives to diphtheria, and that loss made its mark on the whole family:

> All that loss was a grave mental trial for the parents, and instilled fear in all us children. When we heard about the diphtheria, we would exchange glances, silently asking: which of us will die this time? Time generally revealed which of us it was. For some time during my childhood I could hardly imagine that I would survive the age for diphtheria and reach the age of 14.[9]

Descriptions of this kind are put forward in quite an outspoken manner, without wallowing in the circumstances. "Sufficient unto the day is the evil thereof," was the watchword that defined how children were raised. "I was my parents' first child," writes Jón Kr. Lárusson (b. 1878) in his autobiography, going on to say: "They had three children in all; two died young, and my mother died giving birth to the last, when I was three years old. My father then gave up the farm and became a casual laborer."[10] And so life continued: the rhythm of the seasons and of work went on, regardless of people's health and life expectancy.

Another autobiographer, Guðrún Guðmundsdóttir (b. 1860), described the impact of the deaths of her siblings on family life. She was one of ten siblings, five of whom died young. The account begins when her eight-year-old brother died suddenly at home in his bed. Once she understood what had happened, she broke down:

> I was charging around the room with the baby in my arms, sobbing over and over again:
>
> 'I want to die too. I want to die too.'
>
> 'You may get your wish,' replied my mother. She gave me no other words of comfort.
>
> My father was sent for, and Bergur was laid out. I didn't see my parents cry, and I wasn't crying any more myself.
>
> After that my parents went out to sow the cabbage patch. I was left inside with the baby and the dead body.[11]

That same year, just before Christmas, the family lost another child, aged six, to diphtheria:

> Now the loss was greatly felt and Christmas was a dismal time with no candles or games or fun. I never heard any reference to these ordeals but once, when farmer Kjartan of Brattagerði came to my father to commission him to make something. And he said to him:
>
> 'Well, you had a bit of luck. It lightens your burden.'
>
> My father said:
>
> 'Were you lucky when your children died?'
>
> 'Well, I've accompanied nine of them to their graves with my wife, and I've never shed a tear.'[12]

Children's constant exposure to death, watching significant people in their lives die in front of their eyes, and the lack of emotional support left them with the sense that they really could not count on anyone in their immediate environment. Málfríður Einarsdóttir (b. 1899) expressed her sense of helplessness in a bitingly cold description of her surroundings. She lost her mother at birth along with her twin brother, and her first memory was connected to the death of a small child. "How is it that I was not dead a long time ago? From boredom and fear, if not something else."[13] Even those who received some emotional support very soon understood that they would have to rely on themselves. This might not have been a conscious realization, but rather an underlying message that was felt and expressed all around them. They sensed all the death traps which people had to live with and overcome on a day-to-day basis and the fear of losing their relatives ultimately shaped their worldview.

Sigurður Jón Guðmundsson (b. 1895) expressed this feeling in his autobiography following his mother's death at their home after giving birth to his baby sister: "Everything was done to comfort me but unsuccessfully. I was introverted, reserved and carried my grief in silence."[14] When he saw his mother's coffin in the grave, he totally lost control of himself and nothing seemed to be able to comfort him. When he finally stopped crying, he grew introverted again and withdrew into himself. "I had aged many years, and did not speak, just as though I was mute. My sister Susanna cried a lot, but she only had to look into my face to stop crying. When she saw that I did not cry she then did not want to cry either. In this sense we were indirectly a comfort to each other."[15]

Tryggvi Pálsson (b. 1869), who lost both his parents very young, discussed in his autobiography that he always felt that he was somehow less worthy than the rest of his kin, who were considered of almost noble origin.

> Even though I lived with my relatives I often felt very lonely and that I was missing both shelter and protection. I was an eleven year old boy who did not have either a father or mother. Therefore I soon became—as a child and a youngster—unusually sensitive, dreaming and weak in many ways. I could not bear reproofs and was often full of fear and apprehension. This character of mine made me soon very depressed and rather introverted. And normal children's laughter and child play I never really experienced. My life in my childhood was therefore marked with indifferent loneliness.[16]

In other words, the whole experience was so traumatic that children often had a very hard time getting back on track.

Sæmundur Dúason, cited above, recounts that he would often dream portents of future events. One such dream presaged his sister's death and that of children on neighboring farms:

> Some weeks later the diphtheria came to the Fljót district. That illness swept away many a child. At Laughús, all of us children who were at home fell ill. ... When it was all over, the illness and the deaths of the children were seen as resembling my dream of the ordeal in the Laxósar estuary. The lads who, in my dream, were the first to get out of the river—Grímur Þorlákur and Grímur Jósef, died almost at the same moment. After that Katrín and I started to get better. That was shortly before Christmas. We had been promised that we could get up and get dressed on Christmas Eve.[17]

They were asked how they were feeling; he said he was better, while Katrín was worse:

> That was, as I mentioned above, towards evening on Christmas Eve. Katrín died on the day after Christmas. The body was wrapped in a shroud. The day that Katrín was wrapped for her coffin, I was allowed to get up. We had been promised that we could get dressed at the same time. And that promise was kept. And our paths parted.
>
> Dad made coffins for all the bodies. Later they were taken on a sledge up to Barð, and laid in one grave in front of the church entrance. I still wasn't quite well. The disease had me by the throat. I had difficulty breathing. And I sometimes felt sad. I was the only child left in the home. It was a huge change. Sometimes I saw hallucinations and was frightened.[18]

In addition to the loss of a family member, children often had to face other kinds of adversity. Valdimar J. Eydal (b. 1901) fought an uphill battle from a young age, and a series of events shaped his emotional outlook. He lost his mother at the age of five, which left him with a sense of emptiness; and in an accident he also lost a foal which had been given to him. In addition, a lamb which belonged to him was slaughtered, and the money which had been given to him was used for the home; and then he experienced the deaths of some friends. "All this misfortune made me early on unsociable and bitter. Why dream when all the dreams turned out to be illusions? Why work around the clock, but still never manage to be able to provide for oneself, and never own anything, and what little people owned was then finally taken from them?"[19] These feelings which Valdimar expressed were far from being the exception. What most characterized young children during this life stage was helplessness and fear.

For example, for the families who depended on catching fish, reality could often be harsh. Lárus J. Rist (b. 1879), a son of a single father who was a cottar in the small town of Akranes on the west coast, illustrated this feeling in his autobiography. At the age of three, Lárus lost his mother and an infant sister. One of his first memories was of his mother as she rested peacefully in her coffin. His father was extremely poor but hardworking as an agricultural worker and a fisherman:

> My father approached fishing with great enthusiasm, even though the catch was poor during these years and he much preferred land work. Sometimes when I woke up in the morning I was caught by the feeling, when I saw that my father was not in bed and I learned that he had gone fishing, that he would drown. Accidents and drownings were so common, that grief totally occupied people's

thoughts, to the extent that people did not talk about anything but accidents and their consequences. Of course the most able men went fishing, while the wives stayed at home with the children and the elderly.[20]

Jón Þórbergsson (b. 1882) expressed the impact that the death of his brother had on him and his family. His brother was the eldest of four and died when he was nine years old. This is how he recalled the memories from this event: "He got sick in the evening and choked to death in my father's arms the next evening. It is still so drastically clear in my mind how my parents' grief was deep as it was with all of us, when this happened.... On the next farm four children died from the same disease."[21] Jón points out that the grief lasted for a long time and was later stirred up when his mother died a few years later. His brother Jónas also addressed the enormous grief which he and his brothers went through when their mother was dying. Their whole existence totally collapsed at the funeral.[22] "Our sorrow had been silent from our mother's death up to this moment. Now the grief took over. We held each other's hands shaking and gave this enormous cry, which is like the end of all, where the fear of a child's desperation alone leads."[23] Parental involvement with their children was a topic of discussion during the nineteenth century. Arnljótur Ólafsson, a nineteenth-century theologian and demographer, mentioned in his article written in 1858 on population development in Iceland that parents did not pay enough attention to the well-being of their children and "congratulate each other if God had taken their children away, and by that used

Figure 19 In Raufarhöfn.

the name of God as a cover for their sinful negligence."[24] This is, in fact, implied by the above quotation, when the neighboring farmer says to the grieving father: "Well, you had a bit of luck. It lightens your burden."

In other words, you were better off losing this child, and should now just try to get on with your life, as I did when I lost mine. The father's response, though, indicates that he was not exactly in the mood to celebrate, but the overall account of these events does indicate a certain indifference.

Emotional Communities

We have now reached a crucial point in identifying the nature of the emotional relationship between parents and children.[25] There was obvious care and affection between parents and children but the outlet to express them hardly existed. Therefore, the reaction to the death of a family member could often be cold and sometimes met with an air of indifference. To give a further example of this calmness and distance that parents created between themselves and the outside world, the story of Ásmundur Helgason (b. 1872) sheds some light on these emotions. In his autobiography, Ásmundur describes his reaction when he was told of the death of his son. He was shocked by the news but kept on working in his vegetable garden before he went to his farm to break the news to the rest of the family: "I think it is true that I have never worked as hard in the garden, but afterwards I felt stronger and more able to relate the news of the passing of our son. For the first time I thought that I understood the spirit in Egill's *Sonatorrek*."[26] In other words, the emotions of grief and care ran through the parent's mind, in the overwhelming majority of cases of the loss of a close family member. However, at the same time, their life had treated them harshly and they realized that they had to continue with daily affairs as if nothing had happened. Any delay in the work ahead could jeopardize their own existence and that of their dependents. Thus, the period of grief was short and death often appeared to be met with indifference.

Just to give an example of the kind of hardship some parents had to go through, let us take a look at the case of Guðrún Björnsdóttir (b. 1832). She was raised under extremely harsh circumstances. She lost a brother at the age of three and her mother when she was fourteen. She spent her life in service, and she had a baby out of wedlock. She had literally been on the road from an early age and worked on twenty-five farms when she moved to America at the age of fifty-four in 1883. After she had the baby, she was transported back to her home community, as was the norm in those days, and the child was fostered there. Her daughter died a few years after she had given her up for adoption. In describing her death, the following was all she had to say: "My daughter Baldvina went from farm to farm after this and died finally in her home community in Eyjafjörður. Our moments together had been short and infrequent and finally a total separation."[27]

The nature of the work on farms meant that children saw animals which they had befriended go to the slaughter, and they also lost contact with farm workers who often moved from one master to another from year to year. *Loss* was thus a permanent feature of farming life, which children regularly faced. This is recounted in many autobiographies—the first tasks, and the autobiographers' first conflicts with their work and themselves. Such accounts are a striking feature of all types of egodocuments from the nineteenth and early twentieth centuries.

On the other hand, at around the same time that they were expected to begin taking part in the farm work, children started learning to read and write. And for most of them that study was a source of pleasure. I have maintained that literacy skills enabled children to get to know who they were. It is striking that so many learned to read so quickly, often with little instruction.[28] In addition, they had considerable freedom to read what they wanted (and in many cases they would read everything they could get hold of).

Around the age of ten, this tendency was reversed. Learning became a chore, while work was the path to achievement. By this age, children were working alongside their parents or guardians while preparing for confirmation (at the age of about fourteen), and they did not look forward to those studies. Every confirmand had to learn Luther's *Minor Catechism* by heart, and that proved a difficult task for many.[29] There were exceptions, however, such as Sigurður Árnason (b. 1877): "I was probably one of the few who did not dislike the *Minor Catechism*. I quite enjoyed it, and I quickly learned it by heart. Long before I was confirmed I could recite all the first half of it by heart, in order, word for word."[30] This change is noticeable in many autobiographies, but in my view it is not sufficiently crucial to be deemed a turning point in the child's life. The big change in the lives of all children in Iceland followed their confirmation.

The Future

Childhood and accounts of childhood generally end with the autobiographer's confirmation. This was indeed a turning point in a child's life. Sveinn Víkingur (b. 1896) recalls the powerful emotions he experienced at that time:

> Some spectacular and incomprehensible change had taken place. And that change was mainly to me, and within me. I found myself in some strange wasteland, having lost all the world, without having any clear understanding of how it had happened. And even more extraordinary was that I did not exactly regret what I had lost.
>
> The Paradise of my childhood was closed to me for ever. I felt that there was no way back, and in a way I accepted it. But the world that was now opening up before me was strange and unknown. I wasn't at ease there, I didn't yet feel that I belonged there, didn't know how to deal with it—I was, all at the same time, uncertain, hesitant and shy.[31]

Many autobiographers give highly dramatic accounts of the way that confirmation changed their way of thinking—reflecting the momentousness of the occasion. Gunnar Benediktsson describes the mental turmoil arising from his confirmation:

> Fermenting in my psyche was some spectacular turning-point. I was no longer a child; I had reached the age of manhood with the right to autonomy, and duties, and responsibility for myself and my actions. This burst out immediately after the confirmation ceremony.... The following day I was still possessed by the desire for the maturity to undertake great things, and the sense that that maturity was now flooding over me. I was alone, digging dung out of the shack that was the easternmost building in the farmstead. I have no recollection of how I came to be alone at that task—but one thing is certain: I relished it. I think it likely that Dad may have been away, and that I had spotted a task that needed doing, and did it on my own initiative.... I can still feel the sensation of joy that I experienced, as I was one with my work—the effort of it, and my own judgment of my competence to perform the task.[32]

After confirmation, the future held three main prospects for youngsters: first, to remain at home with their parents for the time being and continue to perform much of the same tasks as before; second, many children went into service in the homes of strangers, where they were treated as adults with very limited rights.

Some, however, had to leave home at a far earlier age, due to their parents' poverty or because their household was dispersed, for instance on the death of a parent, as mentioned above. Orphans often received little care and might be subjected to slanderous talk and abuse. Hafsteinn Sigurbjarnarson (b. 1895), cited above, had to stand on his own two feet from an early age, although nominally he remained with his widowed mother in her penury. Before her husband's death, the couple had received poor relief, and on his death she lost everything, as a matter of course, but was permitted to keep her children with her, by the grace and favor of the authorities. Hafsteinn's mother had striven to work to pay off the debt to the authorities for the poor relief. He writes about the time when the debt had been paid off:

> When Mama had heard my account, she said: 'I'm well aware that your upbringing has been different from what I would have wished. And I can never make it up to you. Now you are over the most difficult part, and I hope that the future will make up to you for what was lacking in your upbringing. The reason why I asked Jóhannes to allow you to walk up to Kothvammur with me was that you told me once that you were sometimes teased for being brought up on poor relief. Now you are a witness, both with your eyes and ears, that the debt to the local authority is paid off, and I am now as free as if I had never received poor relief. So henceforth you can point to the accounts of the local authority, if anyone shames you for being a pauper.'[33]

Hafsteinn's story is engraved on his memory, and it is perhaps all the more poignant because he recalls it so well.

Third, a small number of Icelanders in the nineteenth and early twentieth centuries were able to go to school and continue their preparations for life ahead. These were sons of officials and prosperous farmers, headed for secondary education at the Latin School in Reykjavík, and some even to university in Copenhagen. This was a very select group, and youngsters of poorer families had hardly any chance of taking this path.[34]

Accounts of the teenage years are sometimes quite detailed, but rarely anything like the childhood memories. Narratives of this stage of the individual's life—a time when they were on their own and had little say in their own lives—tend to be quite personal, as the autobiographer devotes considerable attention to their relationship with their surroundings during this period of flux. The author is the focus of the narrative, both during childhood and in the teenage years. And many of them refer to this period of life as *the formative years*, invoking their personal experience.

The formative influence on the memories of children and youngsters at this stage of life was primarily the attitude to work. Friðrik Hallgrímsson (b. 1895) was the youngest of six children. Although poor, the family lived on quite a good farm:

> From confirmation age, and in fact earlier, I worked in the household as much as my powers permitted, and in fact more than that. My father was rheumatic, and sometimes he suffered such severe pangs in his back and muscles that he was confined to bed for variable amounts of time. And as I was the only son in

the house in the absence of my brother, I had to undertake demanding work from an early age. For instance in caring for the beasts in winter in all weathers. I remember that sometimes I was on the point of giving up—I felt that all possibilities for enjoying life like other people had been snatched from me. On occasion I burst out crying because of my adversities—but I had no-one to turn to with my sorrows.[35]

Guðmundur J. Einarsson (b. 1893) was the son of a couple who were "poor, but diligent and self-sacrificing." He described that period of his life as follows:

To tell the truth, I felt I had never had a real youth—at least not a youth like those which have been glorified by many in stories and poetry. Domestic economy in those days required every person in the household to contribute all the energies he or she had. Many became old and broken-down before their time. Even the atmosphere was fraught with worries about the farm and anxiety about the future. Few people could sustain that burden without being molded by it, both mentally and physically. It was before my time that the fear of Hell and damnation lay over people's minds like freezing fog; yet poverty turned people a frosty grey, and their feeling of helplessness and stagnation destroyed them.[36]

The characteristic feature of accounts of the next life stages is that the autobiographer steps out of the narrative, and the action tells the story, so to speak. Little space is given to the narrator's personal or emotional life. Family life features, often with a statement along the lines that the author married on such a day, and that their spouse was the greatest good fortune in their life. Those who go farthest in discussing emotions and marriage are people such as Þorbjörn Björnsson (b. 1886), author of *Skyggnzt um af heimahlaði* (*The View from the Home Farm*). Þorbjörn had noticed a fine young woman on a nearby farm, but he felt he had little chance of attracting her attention, as there was so much competition from other lads. Þorbjörn reports how the two finally got together: "After enjoying good hospitality in the evening, Sigríður the farmer's daughter and I got talking. We talked far into the night, and that conversation ended with our promising to stay together for the rest of our lives."[37] Their engagement met with approval and was formalized. The author adds:

I say quite a lot about this, because I feel there is nothing wrong with me, and others who write about their lives, writing with some clarity about the most momentous contracts they have made in their lives—which I deem the contract of marriage to be. And it is also quite enjoyable to recall it all, from the first times I spent with my wife until the present day.[38]

The author here discusses the subject of his marriage like any other farming business, so to speak. He needed to acquire more land and livestock, and find a wife: all necessary tasks based on "contracts" negotiated with others!

It is hard to imagine the emotional and intimate life of married couples at the time. Autobiographies generally have little to say on the matter—just as in the case of courtship. There are, however, sometimes indirect clues in autobiographical accounts. Hafsteinn Sigurbjarnarson (b. 1895), for instance, recounts events in a household where he stayed after his father's death. He describes the illness of the farmwife in the home where he was living with his mother:

> One day I was alone in the house with Guðmann's wife, and she started to clean a wound on one breast. I had seen her clean the wound before, and she did not try to hide it from me when she cleaned the wound, which was large and horrible. I think that the hollow in her breast was about half the size of a cup. The smell from the wound was awful when she was dressing it. When I was in bed that evening I asked Mama: 'What's wrong with Helga's breast?' She didn't know what I was talking about, and got me to describe what I meant. I told her what I had seen, and she scarcely believed me. The next day Mama asked Helga what was wrong with her breast. She made light of it, but she eventually agreed to show Mama the wound, which horrified her. As a result Mama had a private word with Guðmann, and asked him whether he didn't know about his wife's problem with her breast. It transpired that he had no idea, and had not noticed the smell of the wound.[39]

Helga the farmwife was subsequently taken to Reykjavík for medical treatment, and died there shortly afterward. This small story tells us so much about people's relationships and the emotional life of married couples in the old rural society.

Most of the autobiographers (predominantly male) pay about as much (or little) attention to their children as to their spouses. They are mentioned as part of the process of achievements in life. This is the subject of later life stages—after the autobiographer has settled down in marriage: their life's work is recounted in terms of victories and defeats. Many autobiographers term this life stage the *productive years*—when they expatiate on how they succeeded in expanding their enterprises, extending the farm, and cultivating the land. Progress, whether in the public or private sphere, is a classic theme of autobiography: the author writes about their role in advancements in the country and the ongoing campaign for national autonomy. The nature of that campaign was that each man played his part and did his best to work for the good of his country. The tone of the autobiographies tends to be much the same, expressing the writer's desire to explain their contribution to their own and the nation's struggle for autonomy.[40]

It goes without saying that this analysis is far from applying to all autobiographies. In some, the author remains in the background throughout the narrative; in these cases, the emphasis is more on the way of life, working methods, and events. In other cases, the "productive years" are recounted in a highly personal manner. But the general tendencies described above need come as no surprise. The early and teenage years are, naturally enough, the time when each individual goes through major changes, which inform the rest of their life. So, it must be deemed natural that the most space is devoted to describing the formative process that takes place. This is the life stage that, for most people, lays the foundations for what is to come.

In this context, it is worth reiterating that the structure of Icelandic society in the nineteenth and twentieth centuries served to reinforce childhood memories as they are manifested in egodocuments. Most Icelandic autobiographers grew up in a simple, closed community. The fact that the lives of the majority ran along fixed lines—largely untouched by outside stimuli, year after year—meant that it was easy to fix in memory all the major aspects of daily life. There were important exceptions to this rule—families who found themselves outside the bounds of society. Such people often experienced appalling hardships in their vagrant lives. But even for this marginalized group the regular repetition of annual tasks was part of their lives. And for children it was essential to be on the alert, as they were expected to observe and then perform tasks from an early age. They had to be able to concentrate, and daily life may be seen as the "syllabus" they studied—a reality they had to learn and understand in order to play their part in family life. Unexpected events, exceptions from the daily round, immediately caught the child's attention and were stored up in memory. Þórir Bergsson (b. 1885) explains this in his autobiography: "Life went so slowly in those days that there was plenty of time to commit to memory what one saw and heard, depending upon how one's wits and power of observation gave one the ability to see, hear and grasp. There was no rush about anything; a whole week was a long time."[41] The rhythm of life would change, and that entailed a transformation of self-expression.

By the same token, the years that followed were ingrained in the psyche due to unending labor and toil; for most, everything else was irrelevant when they looked back. The *productive years* was thus an accurate term. Discussion of the personal aspects of human life, including the family, was in direct proportion with the heavy burden of work in daily life.

Emotional Outlook

Examined from the viewpoint of a child growing up in rural Iceland during the nineteenth century, it can be argued that this love for the written word was no coincidence in Iceland, even though the opposite might be assumed in a peasant society. Given the lack of emotional support that children experienced at an early age and the confusing signals that children received when they saw the world tremble under their feet on a regular basis, it is not surprising that they turned to the literary world for what might be called moral authority. This outlet provided an escape from the harsh reality of Icelandic life and allowed children to drift into an imaginative world of literature. They knew this world intimately and connected with it because it was rooted in their culture and their society. This ideal picture, which was traditionally painted in this literature of the former glory of the Saga Age or brave stories of people and how they stood up against foreign domination, gave children some sense of moral authority.

In his doctoral dissertation, Icelandic historian Guðmundur Hálfdanarson has a different interpretation for why the Icelandic saga was so important in the Icelandic peasant culture:

> For one thing, backwardness and isolation prompted a strong nostalgia for the past, at the same time that it bred a pessimism about the future. As a consolation in the bleakness of the present, people read and recited the sagas; these medieval literary texts were the only national treasures the country had. In them the Icelanders found their golden age, in the period following the settlement, when the nation was free and the country virginal and generous. At the time, Icelanders had an international reputation as bards and hired hands in the service of foreign kings. Since then, everything had deteriorated. . . . Consequently, Icelanders cultivated a strong and intense historical sense through an unending glorification of the past.[42]

When I refer to a moral authority in this context, I mean something that one can look up to and on which to structure one's life. Icelandic literature filled a void in the lives of children and appropriated roles where society in general and the church and their parents in particular had failed. The message given to children was to walk toward their destiny with calmness and dignity and take on the world at any cost. Sigurður Nordal, an Oxford University professor of Scandinavian literature, summarized the kinds of impressions the sagas left with readers: "True, the authors of the sagas of Icelanders are not much interested in politics as such: they focus on the individual, not on society or the state. Above all, they wish to praise and preserve the ancient vision of manhood, ideals of liberty, courage, pride and honour."[43] It is clearly evident from the sagas, according to Sigurður Nordal, that "the heroic attitude and the unemotional self-control it fostered, fully realized in the style and approach to their subject of the best saga writers," did have a major impact on children and adults who were exposed to this literature. These fundamental characteristics of the Icelandic sagas guided children, in my opinion, as they learned how to react to the expectations which they had to shoulder.

Hannes J. Magnússon (b. 1899) explained the poignancy of this literature.

> Yes, there was a great deal read aloud in the winter-eve gatherings at my home from the time I first remember. Of course, some of it was not worth very much, but this book reading was the spice of life. It was just as if we were taken to another level, away from daily hardship, and prevented from intellectual death. It is no misfortune to be poor, to have to fight for your life and work hard, but it is a misfortune to let that poverty and that hardship kill every dream of yours, every thought which takes you away from everyday life.[44]

It is very easy to see how children were drawn to this literature, both because of the message it carried and also because the stories were exciting and situated in the Icelandic landscape, both social and geographical. The same could be said about the Scandinavian sagas written by Icelanders in the Middle Ages, which had some of the same characteristics as the Icelandic sagas. Those stories were also read in Iceland with great enthusiasm. Jónas Jónasson (b. 1879) pointed out that the Scandinavian sagas were his father's favorites:

> I admired my father most when he read aloud the sagas. He read mostly the Scandinavian sagas, which he read aloud during the winter-eve gatherings when he was in a good mood. Vibrations of admiration and bliss went through my body when I listened to it, because my father was a great reader. Everything he read became alive, and I felt that I was witnessing these events or even that I was a part of the whole ordeal.[45]

Hannes confirms among Icelandic children a strategy for survival by relating to what was read during the winter-eve gatherings. One autobiographer mentioned that he did not necessarily believe every episode in the sagas especially when there were obvious exaggerations, but still they took him by storm:

> It is very possible that all this reading and poetry might have had some influence on my personality and attitude to the present times. . . . At least many things I read were a living reality for me. There were no shortages of opinions from the

adults to make judgments about these literary heroes. A lot of heroism took place there and a lot of different kinds of noble-mindedness were performed there.[46]

Another autobiographer expresses similar feelings when he discusses the importance of the winter-eve gatherings: "I think that the winter-eve gathering was seen as the main entertainment for the household, with story-telling and reciting poetry being both educational and most likely refreshing entertainment. Then everybody was in a good mood and paid great attention to the story which was read."[47] The constant hardship in the country fueled the children's desire to seek more education. Education became a release from daily burdens and the substance of the literature buffered them from reality.

It is difficult to draw sharp distinctions between religious and secular literature, and children often encountered both forms in the same reading. In many instances, the forms melded and religious poems and psalms combined to produce secular poetry. Furthermore, the Bible could be read as either a religious tract or an exciting narrative. A belief in God mingled freely with superstition. Children listened as the family read the sagas aloud and when they could they read them and other literature, sometimes as a reward for focusing on the *Minor Catechism*. This comes as no surprise since the traditional culture interwove religious and folk beliefs. In more than one sense, formal and informal education went hand in hand. This interaction between the work process and formal and informal education created both a foundation for the high literacy rate in the country and an emotional refuge for children in an otherwise hostile world.

Even though most autobiographers specifically mention that their parents supported their education, especially the religious portion, instances existed when informal education became a source of tension between children and parents. Parents argued that work took priority over all else; education could not interfere with a child's work obligations, or all hell would break loose. Those children who valued education above work had to fight negative attitudes and counteract unfavorable conditions. In his autobiography, Valdimar J. Eyland (b. 1901) describes how his father's worldview affected their relationship:

> There was no question that my father loved me in his own peculiar way and he hoped that eventually I would grow up and become a man; that is to say, if I did not die first of laziness one of these days. According to his world view laziness was the only unforgivable sin and the mother of all vices.
>
> If I or my older brothers and sisters hesitated to follow his orders or restrictions, then it was because we were lazy. Illness he had a hard time understanding,

because all his life he never had a pain in his body except for the last months of his life. According to a view that he shared with many other older people then, a young people's book reading was no road to happiness. It more than likely made the children of the general public spiritually inferior and unsuccessful.[48]

Later, the author mentions that learning came easily for him and when he received good recommendations from his teacher he saw that his father was proud of him.[49]

Ólína Jónsdóttir (b. 1885), who was a foster child, had a similar story. When she wanted to read some newly published books which were brought to her home, her foster mother "had another opinion and thought that reading them would not spark my interest in the work. I was allowed to take a peek at the *Minor Catechism* if I had free time."[50]

For most children, education became a fight worth fighting because it gave them the strength to face reality and continue their lives. It is interesting how the author characterizes his relationship with his father. While Valdimar points out that his father loved him in his own particular way, we see later, when children started to work side by side with their parents, how the relationship was measured through the work process. Tensions could surface, especially when children showed an interest in education.

We have given some indication of how this intense educational interest was possible by pointing out, for example, that pressure from society—mostly from the church—forced parents to give their children some education at home and prepare them for their official entrance into adult society. Additionally, children found moral authority in the secular literature, managing to escape into a world of national honor where they could imagine their lives according to patriotic ideals. It is important to realize that this intense feeling for education promoted basic literacy, that is, reading and writing which came with religious teaching, but it created a much more qualitative level of literacy among children and adults alike. In other words, this educational fervor gave Icelandic children the ability to understand what they read and comprehend the social reality they faced.

In an essay, the legendary Swedish historian Egil Johansson explains what the qualitative level of literacy actually meant. He puts the unusually high rate of literacy in preindustrial Sweden into a wider perspective: "But this also contradicts the modern opinion that literacy is primarily (and solely) part of the so-called modernization process, where industrialization, urbanization, political participation, etc., make up the inevitable framework."[51] Exactly the same is true of Iceland. High-quality literacy, most often associated with modern societies, could be found in Icelandic peasant society and is testimony to the importance of literature for a child's well-being.

One way of verifying this is by looking at political participation. Indirect participation in the political process was frequent in Iceland, as witnessed by the general interest in the struggle for independence and various other political issues.[52] Political articles in magazines and newspapers were read and discussed during winter-eve gatherings throughout the country. People took firm positions on the issues presented in these articles. Guðmundur Jónsson (b. 1873), who was raised on several farms in the southern part of the country, describes what was read at his home: "All newspapers were bought which were published, magazines and most books also. All this was read aloud for the people, also the debates from the Parliamentary Gazette."[53] The *Parliamentary Gazette* (*Alþingistíðindi*), a publication of parliamentary debates, enjoyed a wide circulation and was read aloud during the winter-eve gatherings, as Guðmundur states.[54] This general interest in political issues undoubtedly contributed to the high level of literacy in Iceland, that is, when literacy is defined not only as people's capacity to read but also to understand what is read. That ability did not emerge because of some forced arrangement between the church and the state, but rather served an emotional need for structure and positive moral authority at an early age.

In her autobiography, Guðbjörg Jónsdóttir (b. 1871) mentioned specifically that her parents subscribed to the *Parliamentary Gazette* and that it was read aloud from cover to cover.[55] A lot of autobiographers go into great detail about what was read and how the reading material gave rise to often heated discussions about poetry, literature in general, and politics.[56] In his autobiography, Einar Jónsson (b. 1874) described this activity at his home:

> When the reader took a break, people started to discuss the material and the main characters in it, and made judgments about it from different angles, often with great insight and intelligence, both men and women. These were sensible people and mentally rested, and they often managed to put themselves into the shoes of the protagonists with great sensitivity and insight. Still, their life was constant slavery from the morning into the evening. But these few moments between work and sleep, the winter-eve gatherings, became their strength and nourished their spiritual life.[57]

Indriði Einarsson gives an interesting example of what was discussed in these farmsteads in the nineteenth century. He points out that people at his home once discussed at some length a sentence that came up in a book which had just been read, that evil "was a lack of material and spiritual values."[58] It goes without saying that this is a relatively abstract discussion about a highly philosophical issue, and remarkable considering the fact that the participants had not even minimal formal education.

Another autobiographer, Viktoría Bjarnadóttir (b. 1888), elaborates on the importance of the main newspapers published in the country which carried political news: "Ísafold and Þjóðviljinn were the main newspapers which came to our farm during this period. There was a great celebration when we got them, and a lot of the news which they carried was discussed. Guests who visited farms where newspapers were not bought recited the news from them."[59] Many autobiographers, influenced by the Icelandic sagas, emphasize how these sagas provided them with a strong foundation for a deeper understanding of the debate over Icelandic independence carried out in magazines and newspapers.

It is safe to say that most people did comprehend how important this discussion was for the future of Iceland. Moreover, while most of these people lived in a traditional peasant society, they were nonetheless able to grasp complex political arguments and abstract thinking because they had acquired the necessary analytic skills through literature and poetry. In other words, this traditional culture not only provided a structure for people to learn to read and write, but it also created a context for understanding and analyzing the

Figure 20 In Djúpavogi.

texts they read. Icelanders could understand the material because it reflected their personal situations, history, and culture. For children, it was a relief to be able to identify with literary figures who had taken on a harsh world and survived, a world children knew and had a hard time understanding. This illustrates the depth of the impression this literature left in the minds of Icelandic children. Additionally, literary figures taken from the sagas got new wings in the contemporary atmosphere as current political debates in newspapers and magazines reaffirmed the nation's former glory and gave children a sense of how real these fables were. For children, the sagas were part of both their imaginative world and the contemporary political one.

In the last two chapters, we have dealt exclusively with work and education in nineteenth-century peasant society and how these two issues shaped children's outlooks on life after their first transition. The burden of work could be totally overwhelming for many children, especially when it came with an emotional strain that continued day after day. Under these circumstances, education became for many children an extremely important tool for their mental and spiritual survival. It created conditions where they could retire to and disappear into an imaginative world of their own.

Part IV

Conclusion

Figure 21 In Grímsey.

Face 2 Face with the General Public

Work and Education

In the final analysis, two elements stand out in autobiographers' telling of their stories: on the one hand, discussion of work, and on the other education. People's daily lives were so strongly defined by these two elements, which occupied their time as well as bringing pleasure, that there was scarcely time for anything else. Children started to take part in household tasks from the age of five or six, and their participation gradually increased until they were working alongside adults in the years before confirmation at the age of about fourteen. At that turning point in their lives, their destiny was clear—and in most cases that meant work. The value of the autobiography lies precisely in the way that authors identify themselves so closely with their participation in the work of the household, and some even imply in this way how the work affected them during this period in their life. Jón Gísli Högnason (b. 1908) felt that his father had been a harsh taskmaster. He described his participation at the age of ten in the work of the household: "The extensive and mountainous terrain of the farm meant that there was little time for play or rest—one hardly had time to look forward to anything, only to work."[1]

Fathers often played a crucial role in the well-being of youngsters in their outdoor tasks. Jósef Bjarnason (b. 1878) writes of his father and his views on work:

> Though my father took a keen interest in his work, I think that he would have preferred to work less than he did. His physical build was not such as to tolerate the unending toil and labor he undertook. But a crucial element here was his inherent tendency to demand a lot of himself, and his self-sacrifice—for what he could not bear to see was a slacker at work, though he rarely said much about it. . . . It sometimes happened that we children found him rather strict in governing us, and no doubt he had good reason to be. But he never used strong language or displayed anger. It was mainly if we were lazy or idle in our work; I believe he wanted to train us not to be selfish—for he said to me once, in his old age, that he had wanted us to be something other than feckless wretches.[2]

The focus of such people's lives was clearly on children's work, and teaching them the right attitudes to it. Jósef's straightforward account of his father is illuminating about attitudes toward children and their place in the community. They were essentially seen as small adults, individuals in the process of formation, who might go astray without close supervision. And work was the most effective means of achieving that. "Strange as it may seem," comments Jósef Björnsson in his book, "we children were always diffident with him [their father] after we were grown up, for we were all shy by nature." This was the price he paid for demanding hard work; members of the household avoided him, though without judging him: "It never happened that he spoke unnecessarily about himself, or something important to him, except to my mother—and even that was rarely."[3] Over and over again, statements of this kind provide insight into people's emotional lives and the interaction between members of the household. I believe that the atmosphere was generally of this nature. Children and adults alike were expected to do their duty: anything else was excessive, a waste of time, and showed disrespect for the home.

In Icelandic agrarian society, entertainment was closely bound up with work. The winter-eve gathering was, as discussed previously, the cornerstone of the household. This was the setting for woolwork and other crafts during the winter, along with the instruction of children and entertainment for adults; it symbolized the unity of household life.

Jósef Björnsson describes this well in his autobiography:

> In the home, work took priority over everything else. We got to work as soon as we awoke, and in the evening we worked until bedtime. The winter-eve gatherings were more formalized, and different from what they are today, for certain reasons, such as the status of farm workers. When the lamps were lit, everybody was by their bed with their work, except the cattleman, who did not come in until after 7. It was a matter of course that one person was exempted from work to read to the household. In those days, there was no private reading, there was no time for that. This arrangement was most efficient in terms of productivity, and the knowledge and cultural influence of the books was better utilized, as those who were not readers listened like the rest.[4]

Jósef's description clearly indicates the principle of the winter-eve gathering: it was intended to enhance productivity in the tasks carried out, though it was also believed to have a beneficial mental effect. "With the exception of newspapers, the Sagas of Icelanders, chivalric sagas and legendary sagas were what was mostly read," says Jósef in his discussion of the winter-eve gathering—combining work with education. He goes on to say: "I recall that the *Prose Edda* was much read. There was something mystical about it that I think was fitting for the mental life of the household."[5]

Accounts of the winter-eve gathering are much the same in the writings of autobiographers of the nineteenth and early twentieth centuries. This was where children received their education—whether formal instruction in preparation for confirmation or more informal learning from listening to their elders reading aloud. Almost all autobiographers devote considerable space to discussing the routine of the winter-eve gathering, and the learning derived from it. They often specify what was read and what reading material was available to them. They also address the impact of this education on their mental life and general well-being. All this discussion provides an unusually vivid insight into the mental lives of the peasantry in the nineteenth and twentieth centuries, especially the period 1870–1930, and it illustrates well what influenced their mental well-being.

It should be pointed out that the concept of *education* is used here in a broad sense, as the vast majority of Icelanders had no access to formal education until the early twentieth century. In the home, the family provided the instruction, which was mandated by law, that is, teaching their children to read and learn the catechism, and at the same time a more general education arising from adults' reading and storytelling for entertainment. Hence, I permit myself to refer to *education* in discussion of people's relationship with book culture as manifested in the winter-eve gathering.[6]

Matters of pedagogy are often addressed in autobiographies. Many authors discuss people's ideas about parenting, and how best to rear children. Closely related to this subject are relationships with parents and other important people in the autobiographer's life. Religion also is almost always discussed, in the context of confirmation—and often, in fact, at a much earlier age. The authors report, for instance, the saying of prayers, reading of devotional texts during the winter-eve gatherings, and the age at which children started to learn hymns and biblical verses. Also related to religious faith was discussion of folklore and the role it played in people's lives when the author was growing up.[7]

Autobiographers recount not only their experiences of divine authority but also their interactions with secular authorities. These are predominantly local councils and their leaders, sheriffs, and sometimes even renowned politicians of the time. Such accounts can be quite personal and on occasion they are placed within the broader political context of the time. Thus, autobiographies are often part of contemporary social discourse. And the author inevitably becomes a participant—for instance in the campaign for Iceland's self-determination.

Figure 22 Öxl, Snæfellsnes.

Autobiographies are truly a living testimony to a widespread interest in a range of social issues. The authors were rarely people who spoke out in public, but at the winter-eve gatherings they talked about the clergy, parliamentarians, and Iceland's relationship with its foreign rulers, for instance. Poets were praised, and vagabonds were always welcome for the news and stories they brought. Debate on social matters was live and was familiar to those who gathered in the rural *baðstofa*.

I have briefly touched on some of the major subjects addressed in autobiographies, but of course there are many more. Each autobiography encompasses a complex combination of the subjects addressed above. The common feature of the autobiographers is their participation in the improvisation which is the individual's life: the ongoing quest for a better life for themselves and their loved ones. It is this quest by each individual to find themselves that makes many autobiographies such a rich historical source. For it is precisely in this context—in the life of each person – that issues attain their greatest depth and weight.

Modes of Expression

If we attempt to analyze the significance of the influence from the sagas, discussed earlier in the book, on society and the writing of autobiographies, two matters in particular require consideration: first, how society and the environment influenced people's memories in general, and, second, how the sagas played into people's actual lived experience. Here, we must always bear in mind the general truth that in any text, form influences content. In this, autobiographies are no exception.[8] Language alone sets parameters and limitations on all experience, and descriptions and accounts of events are not the events themselves but textual recreations of those events. Every text follows certain rules that have nothing to do with the author's actual experience but arise from the structure of the language—the structure of the narrative—that governs a person's options for expression and, at times, controls it entirely. Accounts of events are thus to a real extent shaped by the form in which they are cast.

A further feature of autobiographies is that they are, in one sense or another, constrained within and marked by the framework set by the life course, which is in turn deeply rooted in the structure of society and receives its strength from the traditions of society—in this case, for example, literature such as the ancient sagas and the religious iconography of the church.

I have sought to draw attention to significant connections between the old Icelandic sagas and the autobiographical writings of Icelandic working men and women of the nineteenth and early twentieth centuries. These connections were, I believe, positive inasmuch as they deepened and broadened the mental world of people who lived and moved in what was in most ways a simple and unsophisticated society. They provided channels for ordinary people to raise themselves constructively above the daily round of everyday toil. But were there adverse sides to these connections? One of the features of the ancient sagas is how seldom the characters are permitted to give expression to feelings and emotions. The matter is discussed by literary critic Professor Torfi H. Tulinius when considering the one-dimensional nature of characterization in the Icelandic romances:

> In this respect the romances [composed in Iceland] differ from many of the translated courtly sagas, in which one finds comparatively lengthy descriptions of feelings and emotions. For some reason the authors and readers of romances in Iceland had no taste for this kind of thing, and it has been suggested that this was because there already existed a rich saga tradition which recounted first and foremost people's actions and left readers to speculate for themselves on the emotions that might lie behind them.[9]

The storytelling tradition that Torfi is describing, and whose origins lie in the narrative technique of the classical sagas, had a profound influence on people's modes of expression in the nineteenth century. We see this, for instance, in the uncomfortable reticence observable among many of the autobiographers when it came to expressing themselves on matters that touched their emotions. This applies particularly once authors have reached adulthood and left their childhood behind them. Fortunately, this reticence is by no means universal and it seems in many ways as if authors who suffered major hardship and adversity in their youths often succeeded better than others in breaking free of the constraints of the narrative technique. But it cannot be denied that the iron grip that the sagas exerted over many authors' views of life and reality compromises the candor of many of the autobiographies and reduces their value as sources.

One may, for example, note that few of the autobiographers devote much space to domestic life after they achieve the status of head of household: their attention in these so-called "productive years" was, in most cases, directed toward quite different matters, and their spouses, children, family, and emotional lives are passed over largely in silence. The crucial turning point—one which the autobiographers often discuss at considerable length as we mentioned earlier in the book—is the rite of confirmation. Its impact is often analyzed and described in detail in so far as it prefigures the future development of the person involved. This is particularly striking since, in the same autobiographies, marriage is almost invariably noted merely in passing. The reason appears obvious: men were not supposed to expose their feelings, but to bear their joys and sorrows in silence. In this respect, the narrative mode undeniably detracts from the value of the autobiography as a historical source and, what is worse, impedes the individual's personal expression even on day-to-day matters. It is important to be aware of these limitations, since it means that one has to seek other ways of approaching the subject. This may be done, for example, by deconstructing texts produced by people about themselves and reading their accounts in the context of their other experience of everyday life and how they talk about it.[10]

The ancient Icelandic sagas, we must conclude, exerted a powerful influence on the mental world of the largely uneducated members of the Icelandic peasantry who set about recording their life stories in writing in the nineteenth century and the earlier part of the twentieth century. This influence comes out, perhaps, as much in their outlook and personalities as in their narrative form. The centrality of the sagas in Icelandic culture makes its mark on how events are reported in autobiographies in, for instance, their authors' avoidance of the treatment of emotions—one of the most striking features of the saga style. As noted earlier, there is a circularity in this process: one part feeds into another, and historians and others who use autobiographies in their research need to be aware of this reciprocal interrelationship. The glorification of the sagas remains a potent force, especially on high days and holidays, in the society in which people produce their work, and colors their thinking exactly as it did that of the autobiographers!

Strands of Memory

In the end, one important question remains: Why were ordinary Icelanders so willing to tell their stories, especially in the nineteenth and twentieth centuries? What was it, in people's environment, that gave rise to the desire to sit down and tell their story? There are, of course, no easy answers to these questions. But I believe that we can approach the subject in a certain manner, which I shall explain here:

In trying to gain an insight into the development of Icelandic society in recent times, it is instructive to consider the country from the point of view of "cultural memory," that is, what people remembered from the past and how this colored their perceptions of themselves and the world they lived in. Looking at the nineteenth century, we can discern significant differences between conditions in Iceland and what we find in most of the rest of Europe. If we consider the three different forms of cultural memory—collective memory, historical memory, and individual memory—there are good reasons to believe that the first of these, collective memory, was exceptionally weak in Icelandic peasant society. As a result of the geographical conditions in the country, with almost no urban centers and settlement widely scattered on farms with considerable distances between them, it was difficult for groups to coalesce within sufficiently firm bonds for them to be able to share their memories and hold them in common. Even the group best placed to sustain its collective memory, namely the educated elite, was dispersed among the common people with no central focus. Any earlier links that ministers of the church or government officials might have forged during their schooling and education were extremely weak compared to their links with the agricultural community among whom they lived and whose thoughts and activities they shared. As a result, the collective memory, that is, the shared worldview and experience of a relatively small group of people as passed on from one generation to the next, was so tenuous that "extra space" opened up to be filled by the other forms of memory.

In consequence of this, people had much greater scope to create and shape their own individual memories than in most other parts of Europe. The strength of the individual memory manifests itself in a wide variety of ways in Icelandic society, but perhaps most notably in the massive outpouring of written material by ordinary working-class peasants in the eighteenth, nineteenth, and twentieth centuries. In these writings, people found an opportunity to create a world of ideas that had a considerable influence on how they coped with the situations they faced in their daily lives. The effects of this process fed through to the wider context of power and politics, and through this ordinary people were also able to influence the way that the historical memory was shaped and the form it took. The strength of the historical memory thus increased steadily through the period, especially when compared to the rather weak position it occupied in many other nineteenth-century societies before the formation of the modern state.

The wide scope open to individual Icelanders to shape their own memories was inextricably linked with the burgeoning of the historical memory, built upon people's interpretation of the country's ancient past. In the nineteenth century, both of these forms of memory were nourished by the rhetoric of the leaders of the independence movement with its compelling emotional appeal to the idea of Iceland as a sovereign democratic state. The literature of medieval Iceland, and above all the sagas, were consciously employed to create a national historical memory and a perception of the values that were felt worth fighting for. Written and manuscript culture took central place in the intellectual and political case for independence. The leader of the movement, Jón Sigurðsson, an archivist and historian by profession, applied his specialist knowledge to argue that Iceland had in fact never lawfully surrendered its national independence in medieval times, and thus the Norwegians and subsequently the Danes had no claim over the country. There was thus an intimate connection between social and political aspirations, individual memory—the fates of the saga characters projected into the lives of their nineteenth-century readers—and historical memory. Forming part of the creation of individual memory, the new historical memory became a part of everyone's lives, something every Icelander needed to assimilate and come to terms with. This perhaps goes some way to explaining why autobiographies and other personal writings became such a ubiquitous form of self-expression in Iceland compared to other parts of Europe.

The need for self-expression has varied according to society, class, and gender. In agrarian societies of the eighteenth, nineteenth, and twentieth centuries, where time moved slowly to the rhythm of the seasons, those who were growing up could get by on standardized images gleaned from the immediate environment, for example, from religion, literature, and human life. In nineteenth-century Iceland, we have clear evidence of young people from the working class turning with enthusiasm to the opportunities on offer to express what they thought about their lives and existence in written form, based on their own personal experience. Society was evidently changing. The heritage of the Enlightenment had trickled down to the lowest stratum of society. The ordinary people of Iceland, who were almost without exception able to read and in most cases also to write, especially the men, appear to have had a deep desire to embrace whatever knowledge they could find. We see this, for instance, in the importance that so many Icelanders of the time seem to have ascribed to weighing and measuring just about anything they could see or touch in their environments. Farm buildings, hay meadows, and sheep pens were assessed and measured and precise figures recorded for the milk yields of cows and ewes. All this was done in order to obtain a firmer grip on the uncertainties of life. The people of the nineteenth century were, in fact, beginning to discover, in ever-increasing measure, that it was possible to have an influence on their own existences through organized and systematic action.

In this, diaries became an important tool in the hands of motivated individuals' intent on facing up to the future. With time, ever more people came to use diaries as a means of reflecting on their position in the world. The authors approached their writing slowly and methodically with the clear intention of giving form to their own existence. The new Icelander was emerging, an individual grounded in the old culture but keen to take on the challenges of the future with an open mind.[11]

It is one thing to express one's ideas in the privacy of one's own diary, another to offer them for general circulation. The twentieth century was a time of increased specialization; society was becoming more varied and complex than it had ever been before. The self-expression of ordinary people, it was widely felt, required specialist support if it was to be considered relevant to others. There was a rich demand for such writings. Democracy required access to public opinion, that as many people as possible might be able to open their mouths and have their say on the issues of the day. The age of the published book had arrived, and the individual became something to be marketed for what they could contribute to the sense of national identity. As a result, the autobiographical form came to appeal to an ever-increasing number of writers and we begin to hear a richer variety of voices than before. Women, for example, started to bring their life stories to a wider reading public. In the vast majority of cases, the "production of memories" followed the prescribed nationalist formula that shaped people's attitudes to life through much of the twentieth century. In a sense, though, Icelandic culture had created greater freedom for people to shape their own worlds, private worlds which eventually became an important constituent in the shaping of the nation's historical memory.

In recent years, the world has seen what has been called a "culture of confession." This phenomenon supplanted what may be called the "culture of testimony," the mode of self-expression described above that dominated public expression in Iceland in the first half of the twentieth century. This culture of testimony was based first and foremost on accounts of events that had contributed to the general shaping of Icelandic society and that detailed the parts played by individual contributors in this process. This testimony served to reinforce the overall picture by presenting the lives of those who, directly or indirectly, had had input into the events that had shaped the current state of society. Thus, the autobiographies of Icelanders of the nineteenth century and the first half of the twentieth century are permeated with the testimony of people who took part in "building" the country, the newly free land that had thrown off the shackles of foreign domination. Each "victory," great or small, was rehearsed in detail, each step registered on the country's road to independence. This culture of testimony was a tool that proved extremely useful in promoting nationalistic perspectives and thus contributing to the unity of the nation.

In this sense, autobiographies written in the spirit of the culture of testimony can be seen as political writing. They were part of Icelanders' struggle for national independence, a device intended to boost the morale and self-confidence of a people setting out into the unknown that inevitably came with political autonomy. They contributed to shaping the country's historical memory. These sources, which I have used and quoted unsparingly throughout this book, were thus an element in the general renewal of society as a whole. Individual people felt impelled to step into the spotlight to describe how they had lived and worked and, by doing so, help to lay the foundation for a stronger and better society through their day-to-day actions and sense of responsibility.

With the advent of the new mode of expression, the culture of confession, came a change of perspective. People from all walks of life came forward in the present to tell their stories, but now unmotivated by the precepts of nationalism. The stories they had to tell were presented on their own terms, without any apparent connection to power interests that might call for such texts. The culture of confession did not, of course, operate *in vacuo*, completely isolated from the forces and values of society. Expression of this type had links to countless informal influences and institutions that operate within society, but it was difficult to control such expression and channel it in particular directions. This created a certain "fragmentation" within the cultural space that, in the final decades of the twentieth century, left society wide open to outside influences.

Figure 23 Snjóholt, Eiðaþinghá.

Subjective World

All written sources encompass subjective qualities, and it is unavoidable that a source will be marked by the author's character. For that reason, individual stories are not rejected simply because they are unconventional or are inconsistent with what is generally believed to be true. Here, I simply point out that it is important to assess, every time a book is opened, how the subjectivity of the writing affects the narrative and what motivated the author to write it.

The writing of egodocuments generally springs from a person's internal need. It is safe to say that the individual's battle with themself is a vital element in the life of almost every person. The manifestation and revelation of the self and attempts at confession in the context of the life course and the individual's place in the world, appear to be almost a necessity for those who have sought to shape their own self. Politicians, poets, authors, and other artists, for instance, are among those who are likely to experience a compelling desire to reveal themselves—probably more than most other groups in society. It is arguable that the "self" comes into existence only when others have reached a view about it, evaluated the strength of the confession and the revelation of the life as it appears in each individual's narrative. Daily interaction with others offers such opportunities for confession.

Revelation of the self is almost always imperfect, and never permanent, and it demands constant reevaluation. Even when a person is especially well equipped for a reckoning with themself, the fact remains that it may be hard to get the confessions down on paper. The reflection of ideas in text is a classic problem for all who seek to express themselves in writing. For that reason, most of the works discussed here are primarily accounts of an objective reality, in which the author avoids confession of any kind or discussion of their inner self. Yet, such works are concerned with the life course and the ups and downs the person has been through.

For much of the nineteenth and twentieth centuries, many people have sought to sum up and develop various ideas that have come to their mind. These mental connections are concerned with the author's *self*, and their relationship with objectified aspects of their environment—life and existence. When the end of the road is approaching, for many people it becomes a necessity to make a systematic summary of the reckonings carried out at regular intervals. Here, the childhood and teenage years often appear to be remembered with the greatest clarity. That is consistent with the argument put forward above, that people pass rapidly through the life stages during the first two decades of life, and that each transition from one life stage to the next requires a methodical reckoning. Young people tend to be preoccupied with grappling with what life entails—what choices it has to offer—and what their role should be. For that reason, the early years are often ingrained in the mind.

To write an autobiography is not unlike sitting down with the family album, turning the pages and remembering old times. Revisiting the past in this way may be seen not only as an enjoyable experience, but it may also have a significant

Figure 24 Litli-Gjábakki, Vestmannaeyjar.

psychological impact. The simple task of tying up loose ends toward the end of life can be a great relief, for in the end life seems to require each person to go through considerable inner conflict and turmoil. Hence, it is as if, by writing their story down, a person can achieve a certain reconciliation with the warring elements that have been in conflict in their mind—whether that strife has ended well or badly.

The above analysis has been mainly concerned with the early period of autobiographical writing in Iceland. The autobiographical form is primarily a twentieth-century phenomenon in Iceland, and in my analysis I have mainly cited authors born in the latter half of the nineteenth century and the first decades of the twentieth century. Their books were written from the 1910s to the 1970s and 1980s. I may be said to have examined the majority of the egodocuments published during that period. These extensive sources have given me the opportunity to approach people's everyday lives with more accuracy than most other historians, and from a different perspective. The value of autobiographical writings lies precisely in the fact that, by systematic use of them, an opportunity is created for examining the day-to-day lives of ordinary people in a new light.

Notes

Culture and History

1 I know of no published research dedicated to the variety, currency, and popularity of egodocuments in different countries and cultures; this is an area that still requires considerable research. An immensely useful database of Dutch egodocuments, including much material relating to autobiographies and similar sources, can be found on http://www.egodocument.net/egodocument/index.html. For an important contribution to international research in this area, see Rudolf Dekker, "Jacques Presser's Heritage: Egodocuments in the Study of History," *Memoria y Civilización* 5 (2002): 13–37. See also an important paper: Michael Mascuch, Rudolf Dekker, and Arianne Baggerman, "Egodocuments and History: A Short Account of the *Longue Durée*," *The Historian* 78, no. 1 (2016): 11–56.
2 See Leonieke Vermeer, "Stretching the Archives: Ego-documents and Life Writing Research in the Netherlands: State of the Art," *Low Countries Historical Review* 135, no. 1 (2020): 31–69.
3 For the various genres of life writing and egodocuments in Iceland, see my *Fortíðardraumar: Sjálfsbókmenntir á Íslandi*. Sýnisbók íslenskrar alþýðumenningar 9 (Reykjavík: Háskólaútgáfan in collaboration with the Center for Microhistorical Research, 2004)—(Dreams of Things Past); and also *Sjálfssögur: minni, minningar og saga*. Sýnisbók íslenskrar alþýðumenningar 11 (Reykjavík: Háskólaútgáfan in collaboration with the Center for Microhistorical Research, 2005)—(Metastories).
4 See here a new study on the development of diary writing in Iceland by Davíð Ólafsson, *Frá degi til dags. Dagbækur, almanök og veðurbækur 1720–1920*. Sýnisbók íslenskrar alþýðumenningar 27 (Reykjavík: Háskólaútgáfan, 2021)—(Day by Day).
5 These sources have been investigated in depth and used to great and varied effect by members of the Icelandic School of Microhistory: see for example, Sigurður Gylfi Magnússon, *Menntun, ást og sorg: Einsögurannsókn á íslensku sveitasamfélagi 19. og 20. aldar*. Sagnfræðirannsóknir 13 (Reykjavík: Sagnfræðistofnun Háskóla Íslands og Háskólaútgáfan, 1997)—(Education, Love and Grief); and Davíð Ólafsson, "Wordmongers: Post-Medieval Scribal Culture and the Case of Sighvatur Grímsson" (PhD diss., University of St Andrews, Scotland, 2008).
6 Hannes Þorsteinsson, "Fimmtíu ára afmæli Þjóðólfs," [Þjóðólfur's 50th anniversary] Fylgiblað no. 2, *Þjóðólfur*, November 5, 1898. There is good reason to believe that this is accurate information because the author had a reputation for being thorough and precise. He later sold his newspaper and became the head of the National Archives.

7 Sigurður Gylfi Magnússon, *Wasteland with Words: A Social History of Iceland* (London: Reaktion Books, 2010), 147–65 in a chapter called: "The Middle Ages and Beyond: A Cultural Foundation."
8 See, for example, Sigurður Gylfi Magnússon and István M. Szijártó, *What is Microhistory? Theory and Practice* (London: Routledge, 2013), 134–46. Also: Sigurður Gylfi Magnússon, *Kyrrlátur heimur: Örsögur og ljóð*. Teikningar eftir Pétur Bjarna Einarsson (Reykjavík: Miðstöð einsögurannsókna, 2015)—(Quiet World: Short Stories and Poetry).
9 See discussions in the following book of mine on diary writing: Sigurður Gylfi Magnússon, *Archive, Slow Ideology and Egodocuments as Microhistorical Autobiography: Potential History* (London: Routledge, 2022), 117–43.
10 Part of this chapter is based on discussions in the book *Wasteland with Words*, chapter one. I would like to thank the publisher for permission to use part of this material in the book.
11 See an interesting study on an inland settlement during the seventeenth century: Kristján Mímisson, "A Life in Stones: The Material Biography of a 17th Century Peasant from the Southern Highlands of Iceland" (PhD diss. in archaeology from University of Iceland, 2020).
12 For an overview of the island's history, see: Gunnar Karlsson, *Iceland's 1100 Years: The History of a Marginal Society* (London: Gardners Books, 2000). See also: Steinunn Kristjánsdóttir, *The Awakening of Christianity in Iceland. Discovery of a Timber Church and Graveyard at Þórarinsstadir in Seyðisfjörður* (Gothenburg: Gotarc, 2004); Orri Vésteinsson, *The Christianization of Iceland: Priests, Power and Social Change 1000–1300* (Oxford: Oxford University Press, 2000); Már Jónsson, *Arnas Magnæus Philologus (1663–1739)* (Viborg: University Press of Southern Denmark, 2012); Steinunn Kristjánsdóttir, *Monastic Iceland* (London: Routledge, 2022). Finally, Guðni Th. Jóhannesson, *The History of Iceland*. The Greenwood Histories of the Modern Nations (Santa Barbara: ABC-CLIO, 2013).
13 Sigurður Þórarinsson, "Population Changes in Iceland," *The Geographical Review* 3 (1961): 519–20; Pétur Pétursson, *Church and Social Change: A Study of the Secularization Process in Iceland, 1830–1930* (Vanersborg: Bokförlaget Plus Ultra, 1983), 22.
14 Sigurður Nordal, *Icelandic Culture*, trans. Vilhjálmur T. Bjarnar (Ithaca: Cornell University Library, 1990), 53.
15 See an interesting study that places Iceland in the larger context of the North Atlantic: Karen Oslund, *Iceland Imagined: Nature, Culture, and Storytelling in the North Atlantic* (Seattle: University of Washington Press, 2011). See also two review articles on this book: Guðmundur Hálfdanarson, *Journal of World History* 24, no. 2 (2013): 465–8; Sigurður Gylfi Magnússon, *Journal of Social History* 46, no. 2 (2012): 603–5.
16 See Harald Sigurðsson, *Ísland í skrifum erlendra manna um þjóðlíf og náttúru landsins*. Ritskrá. (Writings of Foreigners Relating to the Nature and People of Iceland. A Bibliography) (Reykjavík: Landsbókasafn Íslands: 1991).

17 Guðmundur Hálfdanarson, "Old Provinces, Modern Nations: Political Responses to State Integration in Late Nineteenth and Early Twentieth-Century Iceland and Brittany" (PhD diss., Cornell University, 1991), 40.
18 See, for example, Alfred W. Crosby, *The Columbian Exchange. Biological and Cultural Consequences of 1492* (Westport: Greenwood Press, 1972).
19 *Hagskinna: sögulegar hagtölur um Ísland*, eds. Guðmundur Jónsson and Magnús S. Magnússon (Reykjavík: Hagstofan, 1997), 52–3 (Icelandic Historical Statistics).
20 See discussions about natural disasters at the end of the eighteenth century called the Laki eruption in *Skaftáreldar 1783–1784. Ritgerðir og heimildir* (Reykjavík: Mál og menning, 1984). The book deals with the consequences including mortality and the subsequent famine, as described by eyewitnesses and officials. See also: Gísli Ágúst Gunnlaugsson, *Family and Household in Iceland 1801–1930: Studies in the Relationship Between Demographic and Socio-Economic Development, Social Legislation and Family and Household Structures* (Uppsala: Acta Universitatis Upsaliensis, 1988), 27–9.
21 Magnússon, *Menntun, ást og sorg*, 171–214. See also Ólöf Garðarsdóttir, *Saving the Child: Regional, Cultural and Social Aspects of the Infant Mortality Decline in Iceland, 1770–1920* (Umeå: Umeå University, 2002).
22 For a discussion of Icelandic emigration to North America, see Sigurður Gylfi Magnússon, "The Continuity of Everyday Life: Popular Culture in Iceland 1850–1940" (PhD diss., Carnegie Mellon University, 1993), 45–89; *Burt – og meir en bæjarleið: dagbækur og persónuleg skrif Vesturheimsfara á síðari hluta 19. aldar*, eds. Davíð Ólafsson and Sigurður Gylfi Magnússon. Sýnisbók íslenskrar alþýðumenningar, 5 (Reykjavík: Háskólaútgáfan, 2001)—(Away – Far Away). See also: Viðar Hreinsson, *Wakeful Nights Stephan G. Stephansson: Icelandic-Canadian Poet* (Calgary: Benson Ranch Inc., 2013); Laurie Kristine Bertram, *The Viking Immigrants. Icelandic North Americans* (Toronto: University of Toronto Press, 2020). Finally, two more studies: Helgi Skúli Kjartansson, "Icelandic Emigration," in *European Expansion and Migration. Essays on the International Migration from Afrika, Asia, and Europe*, eds. Emmer and M. Mörner (New York: Berg Publisher, 1992), 105–19; Guðmundur Hálfdanarson, "'Are you Leaving, My Dear Friend!' Iceland in the Time of Immigration to America," *Mormon Historical Studies* 17, no. 1–2 (2016): 243–61.
23 For these changes in Icelandic society, see Sigurður Gylfi Magnússon, "From Children's Point of View: Childhood in Nineteenth Century Iceland," *Journal of Social History* 29 (Winter 1995): 295–323.
24 Árni Daníel Júlíusson and Jónas Jónsson, *Landbúnaðarsaga Íslands*, II bindi (Reykjavík: Skrudda, 2013)—(Agricultural History of Iceland).
25 Björn Lárusson, *The Old Icelandic Land Registers* (Lund: Gleerup, 1967), 71–82. See also Gunnlaugsson, *Family and Household*, 32; Hjörleifur Stefánsson, *From Earth: Icelandic Turf Houses*, trans. Anna Yates (Reykjavík: Gullinsnið, 2019); Finnur

Jónasson, Sólveig Ólafsdóttir, and Sigurður Gylfi Magnússon, *Híbýli fátæktar. Húsnæði og veraldleg gæði fátæks fólks á 19. og fram á 20. öld*. Sýnisbók íslenskrar alþýðumenningar 24 (Reykjavík: Háskólaútgáfan, 2019)—(Homes of Poverty).

26 Ágústa Edwald Maxwell, "Household Material Culture in 19th-century Iceland: Contextualising Change in the Archaeological Record," *Post-Medieval Archaeology* 55, no. 1 (2021): 1–14; Ágústa Edwald Maxwell and Gavin Lucas, "The Archaeology of Z: Household Economies in Nineteenth-Century Iceland," *Historical Archaeology* 55, no. 2 (2021): 238–49.

27 Magnús S. Magnússon, *Iceland in Transition: Labor and Socio-Economic Change Before 1940* (Lund: Ekonomisk-historiska föreningen, 1985), 28. See also Gunnlaugsson, *Family and Household*, 32.

28 Gísli Ágúst Gunnlaugsson, *Ómagar og utangarðsfólk: fátækramál Reykjavíkur 1786–1907* (Reykjavík: Sögufélag, 1982)—(Private Paupers and People on the Periphery); Magnússon, *Menntun, ást og sorg*, 87–120. Jón Ólafur Ísberg and Sigurður Gylfi Magnússon, *Fátækt og fúlga. Þurfalingarnir 1902*. Sýnisbók íslenskrar alþýðumenningar 19 (Reykjavík: Háskólaútgáfan, 2016)—(Penury and Poor Relief).

29 Hafsteinn Sigurbjarnarson, *Ævisaga Hafsteins Sigurbjarnarsonar Reykholti í Höfðakaupstað. Skráð af honum sjálfum* (Reykjavík: Leiftur, 1974), 116—(Biography of Hafsteinn Sigubjarnarson).

30 Magnússon, *Iceland in Transition*, 32.

31 See an overview given by Sveinn Agnarsson on the economy of Iceland in the modern period: "Icelandic Economic History: Fishing, Farming and Modernization," *Revue d'histoire Nordique* 20, no. 1 (2015): 83–108.

32 Gunnlaugsson, *Family and Household*, 33.

33 Gunnlaugsson, *Family and Household*, 33–4.

34 Hrefna Róbertsdóttir, *Wool and Society. Manufacturing Policy, Economic Thought and Local Production in 18th-Century Iceland*. Centrum för Danmarksstudier 21 (Göteborg: Makadam, 2008).

35 See Finnur Magnússon, *The Hidden Class: Culture and Class in a Maritime Setting – Iceland 1880–1942* (Aarhus: Aarhus University Press, 1990).

36 Magnússon, *Iceland in Transition*, 52.

37 See Gavin Lucas, "The Widespread Adoption of Pottery in Iceland 1850–1950," in *Þriðja íslenska söguþingið 18.–21. maí 2006*, eds. Benedikt Eyþórsson and Hrafnkell Lárusson (Reykjavík: Sagnfræðingafélag Íslands, 2007), 62–8.

38 *The Icelandic Adventures of Pike Ward*, ed. K. J. Findley (Exeter: Amphora Press, 2018).

39 Gísli Gunnarsson, *Monopoly Trade and Economic Stagnation: Studies in the Foreign Trade of Iceland, 1602–1787* (Lund: Ekonomisk-Historiska föreningen, 1983).

40 Guðmundur Hálfdanarson, "Private Spaces and Private Lives: Privacy, Intimacy, and Culture in Icelandic 19th-Century Rural Homes," in *Power and Culture: New Perspectives on Spatiality in European History*, eds. Pieter François, Taina Syrjämaa, and Henri Terho (Písa: Edizioni Plus, 2008), 109–24.

41 Guðmundur Jónsson, "Changes in Food Consumption in Iceland ca. 1770–1940," in *Kultur och konsumtion I Norden 1750–1950*, eds. Johan Söderberg and Lars Magnusson (Helsinki: Finska historiska samfundet, 1997), 37–60.
42 Gunnlaugsson, *Family and Household*, 128–53. See also: Gísli Ágúst Gunnlaugsson, "Um fjölskyldurannsóknir og íslensku fjölskylduna 1801–1930," *Saga* 24 (1986): 7–43 (On Family Research and the Icelandic Family).
43 Már Jónsson, "Securing inheritance. Probate Proceedings in the Nordic Countries 1600–1800," *Sjuttonhundratal. Nordic Yearbook for Eighteenth-Century Studies* 13 (2016): 7–30.
44 Gunnlaugsson, *Family and Household*, 112.
45 Gísli Ágúst Gunnlaugsson and Ólöf Garðarsdóttir, "Transition into Widowhood: A Life Course Perspective on the Household Position of Icelandic Widows at the Beginning of the Twentieth Century," *Continuity and Change* 11, no. 3 (1996): 435–58.
46 Pétursson, *Church and Social Change*, 52.
47 Guðný Hallgrímsdóttir, *Tale of a Fool? A Microhistorical Study of an 18th Century Peasant Woman*. Microhistories (London: Routledge, 2019).
48 Sigurður Gylfi Magnússon, *Emotional Experience and Microhistory: A Life Story of a Destitute Pauper Poet in the 19th Century*. Microhistories (London: Routledge, 2021).
49 Gunnlaugsson, *Family and Household*, 64.
50 Gísli Ágúst Gunnlaugsson, "'Everyone's been Good to Me, Especially the Dogs': Foster-Children and Young Paupers in Nineteenth-Century Southern Iceland," *Journal of Social History* 27, no. 2 (1993): 341–58.
51 Gísli Gunnarsson, *Sex Ratio, the Infant Mortality and Adjoining Social Response in Pre-Transitional Iceland* (Lund: Ekonomisk-historiska institutionen, 1983).
52 Jón Jónsson, *Á mörkum mennskunnar. Viðhorf til förufólks í sögum og samfélagi*. Sýnisbók íslenskrar alþýðumenningar 23 (Reykjavík: Háskólaútgáfan, 2018)— (On the brink of humanity). See also: Eva Þórdís Ebenezersdóttir and Sólveig Ólafsdóttir, "From Life With a Different Body to Recreated Folklore of Accentuated Difference: Sigríður Benediktsdóttir versus Stutta-Sigga," in *Understanding Disability Throughout History: Interdisciplinary Perspectives in Iceland from Settlement to 1936*, eds. Hanna Björg Sigurjónsdóttir and James Rice (London: Routledge, 2022), 76–94.
53 Gunnlaugsson, *Family and Household*, 95.
54 Gunnlaugsson, *Family and Household*, 127.

Chapter 1

1 Magnússon, *Fortíðardraumar*; Magnússon, *Sjálfssögur*. This first sub-chapter, however, is drawn mostly from an article that I wrote a few years ago:

"Microhistory, Biography and Ego-documents in Historical Writing," *Revue d'histoire Nordique* 20 (2016): 133–53. I would like to thank the publisher for permission to use part of this article in the book.

2 Þorsteinn Helgason, *Minnng og saga í ljósi Tyrkjránsins* (Reykjavík: Hugvísindastofnun, 2013)—(*Memory and History in the Light of the Turkish Raid*).

3 *Reisubók séra Ólafs Egilssonar*, ed. Sverrir Kristjánsson (Reykjavík: Almenna bókafélagið, 1969)—(*Travel Book of the Rev Ólafur Egilsson*). See also the same book in an English translation: *The Travels of Reverend Ólafur Egilsson. The Story of the Barbary Corair Raid on Iceland in 1627*, revised edition, trans. Karl Smári Hreinsson and Adam Nichols (Keflavík: Saga Akademía ehf, 2019); Jón Ólafsson, *Reisubók Jóns Ólafssonar Indíafara: Samin af honum sjálfum* (1661), ed. Völundur Óskarsson (Reykjavík: Mál og menning, 1992)—(*Travel Book of Jón Ólafsson the India-Traveler*); "Reisusaga Ásgeirs Sigurðssonar" (Travel Story of Ásgeir Sigurðsson).

4 Guðbrandur Jónsson, "Formáli," (Foreword) in *Reisubók séra Ólafs Egilssonar*, ed. Sverrir Kristjánsson (Reykjavík: Almenna bokafélagið, 1969), xi.

5 Jón Steingrímsson, *Ævisaga síra Jóns Steingrímssonar eftir hann sjálfan*, ed. Guðbrandur Jónsson, 2nd ed. (Reykjavík: Skaftfellingafélagið, 1945)—(*Autobiography of the Rev Jón Steingrímsson*); *Sjálfsævisaga síra Þorsteins Péturssonar á Staðarbakka*, ed. Haraldur Sigurðsson (Reykjavík: Hlaðbúð, 1947)—(*Autobiography of the Rev Þorsteinn Pétursson*).

6 Haraldur Sigurðsson, "Inngangur," in *Sjálfsævisaga síra Þorsteins Péturssonar á Staðarbakka*, ed. Haraldur Sigurðsson (Reykjavík: Hlaðbúð, 1947), xv—(Introduction).

7 Guðbrandur Jónsson, "Formáli," in Jón Steingrímsson, *Ævisaga síra Jóns Steingrímssonar eftir hann sjálfan* (Reykjavík: Skaftfellingafélagið, 1945), ix—(Foreword).

8 Jónsson, "Formáli," ix–x.

9 See Matthías Viðar Sæmundsson, "Bókmenntir um sjálfið," in *Íslensk bókmenntasaga*, vol. 3, ed. Halldór Guðmundsson (Reykjavík: Mál og menning, 1996), 112–43—(Literature of the Self).

10 Sæmundsson, "Bókmenntir um sjálfið," 123.

11 Magnússon, *Wasteland with Words*, 147–65.

12 For the development of writing implements and ink in Iceland, see Ólafur Halldórsson's paper "Skrifaðar bækur," in *Íslensk þjóðmenning, Vol. VI: Munnmenntir og bókmenning*, ed. Frosti F. Jóhannesson (Reykjavík: Þjóðsaga, 1989), 77–9—(Written Books).

13 Sigurður Gylfi Magnússon and Davíð Ólafsson, *Minor Knowledge and Microhistory. Manuscript Culture in the Nineteenth Century* (London: Routledge, 2017).

14 Sigurður Gylfi Magnússon, "Living by the Book: Form, Text, and Life Experience in Iceland," in *White Field, Black Seeds: Nordic Literacy Practices in the Long*

Nineteenth-Century, eds. Matthew James Driscoll and Anna Kuismin (Helsinki: Finnish Literature Society, 2013), 53-62.
15 Magnússon, *Menntun, ást og sorg*, 113-20; Hálfdanarson, "Private Spaces and Private Lives," 109-124.
16 Robert Darnton, "What Is the History of Books? Revisited," *Modern Intellectual History* 4, no. 3 (2007): 495-508.
17 Darnton, "What Is the History of Books? Revisited," 504.
18 Darnton, "What Is the History of Books? Revisited," 504-5.
19 Harold Love, *The Culture and Commerce of Texts: Scribal Publication in Seventeenth Century England* (Amherst: University of Massachusetts Press, 1998), 177; Harold Love, *Scribal Publication in Seventeenth Century England* (Oxford: Oxford University Press, 1993).
20 Love, *The Culture and Commerce of Texts*, 180.
21 Jason Scott-Warren, "Reconstructing Manuscript Networks: The Textual Transactions of Sir Stephan Powle," in *Communities in Early Modern England. Network, Place, Rhetoric*, eds. Alexandra Shepard and Phil Withington (Manchester: Manchester University Press, 2000), 19.
22 Magnússon, *Menntun, ást og sorg*.
23 *Einsagan - ólíkar leiðir. Átta ritgerðir og eitt myndlistarverk*, eds. Sigurður Gylfi Magnússon and Erla Hulda Halldórsdóttir (Reykjavík: Háskólaútgáfan, 1998)—(Microhistory: Different Paths). See also Erla Hulda Halldórsdóttir, *Nútímans konur: Menntun kvenna og mótun kyngervis á Íslandi 1850-1903* (Reykjavík: University of Iceland Press, 2011)—(Women of Modernity: Women's Education and the Construction of Gender in Iceland).
24 Magnússon, "From Children's Point of View," 295-323.
25 Ólafsson, "Wordmangers."
26 Ólafsson, *Frá degi til dags*.
27 *Kraftbirtingarhljómur Guðdómsins: Dagbók, sjálfsævisaga, bréf og kvæði Magnúsar Hj. Magnússonar skáldsins á Þröm*, ed. Sigurður Gylfi Magnússon. Sýnisbók íslenskrar alþýðumenningar 2 (Reykjavík: Háskólaútgáfan, 1998)—(The Sound of Divine Revelation); Magnússon, *Emotional Experience and Microhistory*.
28 Sigurður Gylfi Magnússon and Davíð Ólafsson, "Barefoot Historians: Education in Iceland in the Modern Period," in *Writing Peasant: Studies on Peasant Literacy in Early Modern Northern Europe*, eds. Klaus-Joachim Lorenzen-Schmidt, and Bjørn Poulsen (Kerteminde: Landbohistorisk Selskab, 2002), 175-209; Sigurður Gylfi Magnússon and Davíð Ólafsson, "Minor Knowledge: Microhistory, Scribal Communities, and the Importance of Institutional Structures," *Quaderni Storici* 47, no. 140 (2) (2012): 495-524.
29 For examples of new trends in archival research, see *Archive Stories. Facts, Fictions, and the Writing of History*, ed. Antoinette Burton (Durham: Duke University Press, 2005); Magnússon, *Archive, Slow Ideology and Egodocuments as Microhistorical Autobiography*.

30 This matter has been widely discussed in works dealing with historical methodology: see, for example, Norman J. Wilson, *History in Crisis? Recent Directions in Historiography* (Upper Saddle River: Prentice Hall PTR, 1999).

31 Matthew J. Driscoll, *The Unwashed Children of Eve: The Production, Dissemination and Reception of Popular Literature in Post-Reformation Iceland* (Enfield Lock: Hisarlik Press, 1997); Matthew J. Driscoll, "The Oral, the Written, and the In-Between: Textual Instability in the Post-Reformation Lygisaga," in *Medieval Insular Literature between the Oral and the Written* II, Script Oralia, XCIX, ed. Hildegard L. C. Tristram (Tübingen: Gunter Narr Verlag, 1997), 193–220. Magnússon and Ólafsson, *Minor Knowledge and Microhistory.*

32 Ólafsson, *Frá degi til dags.*

33 Publications arising from this project include G. L. Justice and N. Tinker, *Women's Writing and the Circulation of Ideas: Manuscript Publication in England 1550–1800* (Cambridge: Cambridge University Press, 2002); V. E. Burke and J. Gibson, *Early Modern Women's Manuscript Writing. Selected Essays of the Trinity/Trent Colloquium* (Hampshire and Burlington: Ashgate Publishing, Ltd., 2004); *Early Modern Women's Manuscript Poetry*, eds. Jill Seal Millman and Gillian Wright (Manchester: Manchester University Press, 2005). For further information on the Perdita Project, see www.warwick.ac.uk/english/perdita/html/).

34 Guðný Hallgrímsdóttir, *Sagan af Guðrúnu Ketilsdóttur. Einsögurannsókn á ævi 18. aldar vinnukonu.* Sýnisbók íslenskrar alþýðumenningar 16 (Reykjavík: Háskólaútgáfan, 2013)—(The Story of Guðrún Ketilsdóttir).

35 On the use of personal sources in Iceland, see Magnússon, *Fortíðardraumar*; and Magnússon, *Sjálfssögur*. These monographs are based on the results of research into all the written remains that might be classified as egodocuments in Iceland from the start of the print publication of such material in the second half of the nineteenth century up to the year 2004.

36 George G. Iggers, *Historiography in the Twentieth Century. From Scientific Objectivity to the Postmodern Challenge* (Hanover: Wesleyan University Press, 1997), 112–13.

37 Sigurður Gylfi Magnússon, "Einvæðing sögunnar," in *Molar og mygla. Um einsögu og glataðan tíma* (*Pieces and Molds. On Microhistory and Lost Time*), eds. Ólafur Rastrick and Valdimar Hafstein. Atvik 5 (Reykjavík: Bjartur, 2000), 100–41; see other papers by the same author: Sigurður Gylfi Magnússon, "Social History as 'Sites of Memory'? The Institutionalization of History: Microhistory and the Grand Narrative," *Journal of Social History*, Special issue 39, no. 3 (2006): 891–913. The paper from 2003 in *Journal of Social History* was republished by Routledge in vol. 4, *Cultural History*, of an anthology of historical criticism, *Historiography: Critical Concepts in Historical Studies*, I-V, ed. R. M. Burns (London: Routledge, 2006), 222–60.

38 The general ideas advanced in the *Journal of Social History* articles from 2003 and 2006 attracted powerful responses from the American historians Peter N. Stearns

and Harvey J. Graff in a volume of articles published in Iceland under the title *Sögustríð. Greinar og frásagnir um hugmyndafræði* (*The History War. Essays and Narratives on Ideology*) (Reykjavík: The Center of Microhistorical Research, 2007): see Peter N. Stearns, "Debates About Social History and Its Scope," in *Sögustríð. Greinar og frásagnir um hugmyndafræði* (*The History War. Essays and Narratives on Ideology*) (Reykjavík: The Center of Microhistorical Research, 2007), 17–21; Harvey J. Graff, "History's War of the Wor(l)ds," in *Sögustríð. Greinar og frásagnir um hugmyndafræði* (*The History War. Essays and Narratives on Ideology*) (Reykjavík: The Center of Microhistorical Research, 2007), 475–81.

39 Charles E. Orser Jr., "Introduction: Singularization of History and Archaeological Farming," *International Journal of Historical Archaeology* 20 (2016): 175–81; Kristján Mímisson, "Building Identities: The Architecture of the Persona," *International Journal of Historical Archaeology* 20 (2016): 207–27. See also two recent doctoral dissertations where the concept of the singularization of history is used in a very innovative way: Anna Heiða Baldusdóttir, "Hlutir úr fortíð: Eigur fólks og safnkostur frá 19. öld" (Things from the Past: Peoples Possessions and Museum Collection from the 19th Century). (PhD diss., at the Faculty of Philosophy, History and Archaeology, University of Iceland, 2022); Sólveig Ólafsdóttir, "Vald og vanmáttur: Eitt hundrað og ein/saga á jaðri samfélagsins 1770–1936" (Power and Inability: 101 Microstories of Marginalized Individuals 1770–1936). (PhD diss., at the Faculty of Philosophy, History and Archaeology, University of Iceland, 2022). Finally, see an interesting discussion about microhistory and ethics (including an argument about the singularization of history) by Marnie Huges-Warrington, *Big and Little Histories. Sizing up Ethics in Historiography* (London: Routledge, 2022), 102–17.

40 For an excellent example of this kind of discourse between differing "groups" or "areas," see Louise White, *Speaking with Vampires. Rumor and History in Colonial Africa* (California: University of California Press, 2000).

41 Magnússon and Ólafsson, "Barefoot Historians," 175–209; Gylfi Magnússon and Ólafsson, "Minor Knowledge," 495–524.

42 A good account of this historiographical development is found in Iggers, *Historiography in the Twentieth Century*.

43 Magnússon and Szijártó, *What Is Microhistory?* 121–3.

44 As an example of the trend toward greater synthesis in social history in the latter part of the twentieth century, see Charles Tilly, *Big Structures, Large Processes, Huge Comparisons* (New York: Russell Sage Foundation, 1984). Peter N. Stearns also made calls in many of his writings at the time for more synthesis in social-historical research and attempted to show the importance of this for the discipline as a whole; see, for example, Peter N. Stearns, "Social History and History: A Progress Report," *Journal of Social History* 19 (Winter 1985): 319–34. The question of synthesis in history generated a lively debate in the 1980s and 1990s. Important contributions

include Thomas A. Bender, "Wholes and Parts: The Need for Synthesis in American History," *Journal of American History* 73 (June 1986): 120–35. For reactions to Bender's paper, see David Thelen, Nell Irvin Painter, Richard Wightman Fox, Roy Rosenzweig, and Thomas Bender, "A Round Table: Synthesis in American History," *Journal of American History* 74 (June 1987): 107–30; and Eric H. Monkkonen, "The Dangers of Synthesis," *American Historical Review* 91 (December 1986): 1146–57. See also Thomas Bender, "'Venturesome and Cautious': American History in the 1990s," *Journal of American History* 81 (December 1994): 992–1003; and George M. Fredrickson, "Commentary on Thomas Bender's Call for Synthesis in American History," in *Reconstructing American Literary and Historical Studies*, eds. Günther Lenz, Harmut Keil, and Sabine Bröck-Sallah (New York: Palgrave Macmillan, 1990), 74–81.

45 I refer here to my discussion in *Wasteland*: in the introduction I discuss a discovery I made about my subject, some time after publication. See Magnússon, *Wasteland with Words*, 7–14.

46 Carlo Ginzburg, "Clues: Roots of an Evidential Paradigm," in Carlo Ginzburg, *Clues, Myths, and the Historical Method*, trans. John and Anne Tedeschi (Baltimore: Johns Hopkins University Press, 1989), 96–125.

47 Magnússon and Szijártó, *What Is Microhistory?* 134–7.

48 See further discussions in Sigurður Gylfi Magnússon, "Tales of the Unexpected: The 'Textual Environment', Ego-Documents and a Nineteenth-Century Icelandic Love Story – An Approach in Microhistory," *Cultural and Social History* 12, no. 1 (2015): 77–94.

49 White, *Speaking with Vampires*, 3–86.

50 See a few good examples of studies that have used all kinds of different sources, among others egodocuments, and may all be labeled microhistories: Alenxandra Parma Cook and Noble David Cook, *Good Faith and Truthful Ignorance. A Case of Transatlantic Bigamy* (Durham: Duke University Press, 1991); Cynthia B. Herrup, *A House in Gross Disorder. Sex, Law, and the 2nd Earl of Castlehaven* (New York: Oxford Univeristy Press, 1999); Richard L. Kagan, *Lucrecia's Dreams. Politics and Prophecy in Sixteenth-Century Spain* (Berkeley: University of California Press, 1995); Ruth MacKay, *The Baker Who Pretended to Be King of Portugal* (Chicago: University of Chicago Press, 2012); Douglas Smith, *The Pearl. A True Tale of Forbidden Love in Catherine the Great's Russia* (New Haven: Yale Univeristy Press, 2008); Nicholas Terpastra, *Lost Girls. Sex and Death in Renaissance Florence* (Baltimore: Johns Hopkins Univeristy Press, 2012); Craig Harline and Eddy Put, *A Bishop's Tale. Aathia Hovius Among His Flock in Seventeenth-Century Flanders* (New Haven: Yale Univeristy Press, 2000); Elaine Forman Crane, *Killed Strangely. The Death of Rebecca Cornell* (Ithaca: Cornell University Press, 2002); Craig Harline, *The Burdens of Sister Margaret. Inside a Seventeenth-Century Convent.* Abridged Edition (New Haven: Yale University Press, 2000); P. Renée Baernstein, *A*

Convent Tale. A Century of Sisterhood in Spanish Milan (London: Routledge, 2002); Tim Hitchcock and Robert Shoemaker, *Tales from the Hanging Court* (London: Bloomsbury Academic, 2006); Paul Kléber Monod, *The Murder of Mr. Grebell. Madness and Civility in an English Town* (New Haven: Yale Univeristy Press, 2003); Thomas Robisheaux, *The Last Witch of Langenburg. Murder in a German Village* (New York: W.W. Norton & Company, 2009); Donna Merwick, *Death of a Notary. Conquest and Change in Colonial New York* (Ithaca: Cornell University Press, 1999); John Ruston Pagan, *Anne Ortwood's Bastard. Sex and Law in Early Virgina* (New York: Oxford University Press, 2003); Bryan Givens, *Judging Maria De Macedo. A Female Visionary and the Inquisition in Early Modern Portugal* (Baton Rouge: Louisiana State University Press, 2011); Júnia Ferreira Furtado, *Chica Da Silva. A Brazilian Slave of the Eighteenth Century* (Cambridge: Cambridge University Press, 2009); Jay M. Smith, *Monsters of the Gévaudan. The Making of a Beast* (Cambridge, MA: Harvard University Press, 2011); David L. Ransel, *A Russian Merchant's Tale. The Life and Adventures of Ivan Alekseevich Tolchënov, Based on His Diary* (Indiana: Indiana University Press, 2009).

51 See new theoretical discussions on microhistory in the following works from the turn of the century and up to recent times: Karl Appuhn, "Microhistory," in *The Encyclopaedia of European Social History* I, ed. Peter N. Stearns (New York, 2001), 105–12; *Small Worlds. Method, Meaning and Narrative in Microhistory*, eds. James F. Brooks, Christopher R. N. DeCorse, and John Walton (Santa Fe: School of Advanced Research Press, 2008); Richard D. Brown, "Microhistory and the Post-Modern Challenge," *Journal of the Early Republic* 23, no. 1 (2003): 1–20; *Between Sociology and History. Essays on Microhistory, Collective Action, and Nation-Building*, Anna-Maija Castrén, Karkku Lonkila, and Matti Peltonen (Helsinki: Finnish Literature Society, 2004); Magnússon, *Wasteland with Words*; Matti Peltonen, "Clues, Margins and Monads. The Micro-Macro Link in Historical Research," *History and Theory* 40 (2001): 347–59; István M. Szijártó, "Four Arguments for Microhistory," *Rethinking History* 6, no. 2 (2002): 209–15; *Microhistory and the Picaresque Novel. A First Exploration into Commensurable Perspectives*, eds. Binne de Haan and Kostantin Mierau (London: Cambridge Scholars Publishing, 2014); Carlo Ginzburg, "Microhistory and World History," in *The Cambridge World History*, eds. Jerry H. Bentley, Sanjay Subrahmanyam, and Merry E. Wiesner-Hanks (London: Cambridge University Press, 2015), 446–73; Brad S. Gregory, "Is Small Beautiful? Microhistory and the Writing of Everyday Life," Review essay in *History and Theory* 38, no. 1(1999): 100–10; Magnússon, "Tales of the Unexpected," 77–94; Sigurður Gylfi Magnússon, "Views into the Fragments: An Approach from a Microhistorical Perspective," *International Journal of Historical Archaeology* 20 (2016): 182–206; Sigurður Gylfi Magnússon, "The Love Game as Expressed in Ego-Documents: The Culture of Emotions in Late Nineteenth Century Iceland," *Journal of Social History* 50, no. 1 (2016): 102–19;

Lara Putnam, "To Study the Fragments/Whole: Microhistory and the Atlantic World," *Journal of Social History* 39, no. 3 (2006): 615–30; Zoltán Boldizsár Simon, "Microhistory: In General," *Journal of Social History* 49, no. 1 (2015): 237–48; Francesca Trivellato, "Is There a Future for Italian Microhistory in the Age of Global History?" *California Italian Studies* 2, no. 1 (2011). http://escholarship.org/uc/item/0z94n9hq; Francesca Trivellato, "Microhistoria/Microhistorie/Microhistory," *French Politics, Culture and Society* 33, no. 1 (2015): 122–34; Sigurður Gylfi Magnússon, "Far-reaching Microhistory: The Use of Microhistorical Perspective in a Globalized World," *Rethinking History* 21, no. 3 (2017): 312–41.

52 Mascuch, Dekker, and Baggerman, "Egodocuments and History," 24.
53 Magnússon, "Social History as 'Sites of Memory'?" 905–8.
54 Rudolf Dekker, *Family, Culture and Society in the Diary of Constantijn Huygens Jr, Secretary to Stadholder-King William of Orange*. Egodocument and History Series 5 (Leiden: Brill, 2013).
55 Nicolae Alexandru Virastau, *Early Modern French Autobiography*. Egodocuments and History Series 12 (Leiden: Brill, 2021).
56 See, for example, Arianne Baggerman and Rudolf M. Dekker, *Child of the Enlightenment. Revolutionary Europe Reflected in Boyhood Diary*. Egodocument and History Series 1 (Leiden: Brill, 2008); Jeroen Blaak, *Literacy in Everyday Life: Reading adnd Writing in Early Modern Dutch Diaries*. Egodocuments and History Series 2 (Leiden: Brill, 2009); *Contolling Time and Shaping the Self: Developments in Autobiographical Writing sinces the Sixteenth Century*, eds. Arianne Baggerman, Rudolf M. Dekker, and Michael James Mascuch. Egodocuments and History Series 3 (Leiden: Brill, 2011); *Mapping the 'I': Research on Self-Narratives in Germany Switzerland*, eds. Caudia Ulbrich, Kaspar von Greyerz, and Lorenz Heiligensetzer. Egodocuments and History Series 8 (Leiden: Brill, 2014).

Chapter 2

1 See, for example,, Giovanni Levi, "The Use of Biography," in *Theoretical Discussions of Biography: Approaches from History Microhistory, and Life Writing*, eds. Hans Renders and Binne de Haan (Lewiston: The Edwin Mellen Press, 2013), 89–111; Sabina Loriga, "The Role of the Individual in History: Biographical and Historical Writing in the Nineteenth and the Twentieth Century," in *Theoretical Discussions of Biography: Approaches from History Microhistory, and Life Writing*, eds. Hans Renders and Binne de Haan (Lewiston: The Edwin Mellen Press, 2013), 113–41.
2 John W. Blassingame, *The Slave Community. Plantation Life in the Antebellum South* (New York: Oxford University Press, 1979); David Vincent, *Bread, Knowledge and*

Freedom: A Study of Nineteenth-Century Working-Class Autobiography (London: Routledge, 1981); *Destiny Obscure: Autobiographies of Childhood, Education and Family from the 1820s to the 1920s*, ed. John Burnett (London: Penguin Books, 1982); *The Annals of Labour: Autobiographies of British Working-Class People 1820–1920*, ed. John Burnett (Bloomington: Indiana University Press, 1974); Richard Coe, *When the Grass was Taller. Autobiography and the Experience of Childhood* (New Haven: Yale University Press, 1984).

3 Eugene D. Genovese, *Roll, Jordan, Roll. The World the Slaves Made* (New York: Vintage Books. A Division of Random House, 1972).

4 E. P. Thompson, *The Making of the English Working Class* (London: Vintage Books, 1963). A similar approach is seen in Herbert G. Gutman, *Work, Culture and Society in Industrializing America. Essays in American Working-Class and Social History* (New York: Vintage Books, 1977 [1966]).

5 Another example of work that has influenced this field of study is Alan Macfarlane, *The Family Life of Ralph Josselin. A Seventeenth-Century Clergyman* (New York: W.W. Norton & Company, 1970).

6 Guðmundur Hálfdanarson, "Börn – höfuðstóll fátæklingsins?" (Children – Poor People's Capital?), *Saga* 24 (1986): 121–46.

7 Hálfdanarson, "Börn – höfuðstóll fátæklingsins?" 123.

8 Loftur Guttormsson, *Bernska, ungdómur og uppeldi á einveldisöld. Tilraun til félagslegrar og lýðfræðilegrar greiningar*. Ritsafn Sagnfræðistofnunar 10 (Reykjavík: Sagnfræðistofnun, 1983). English translation, without revision, published in 2017 by the Institute of History at the University of Iceland as *Childhood, Youth and Upbringing in the Age of Absolutism. An Exercise in Socio-Demographic Analysis.* University of Iceland Historical Series, eds. Anna Agnarsdóttir and Ólöf Garðarsdóttir (Reykjavík: Iceland University Press, 2017).

9 Guttormsson, *Bernska, ungdómur og uppeldi á einveldisöld*, 163. This meant in effect that under the Edict on Domestic Discipline of 1748 everyone in a household was subject to the master's authority: children, workers, and other outsiders with a connection to the family.

10 Magnússon, "The Continuity of Everyday Life." See also Sigurður Gylfi Magnússon, "Siðferðilegar fyrirmyndir á 19. öld" (Moral Models in the Nineteenth Century), *Ný Saga* 7 (1995): 57–72; Magnússon, "From Children's Point of View," 295–323.

11 John Modell, *Into One's Own: From Youth to Adulthood in United States, 1920–1975* (California: University of California Press, 1989), 25.

12 Marlis Buchmann, *The Script of Life in Modern Society: Entry into Adulthood in a Changing World* (Chicago: University of Chicago Press, 1989), 2.

13 In her study, Tamara K. Hareven sums up how historians have generally used the life course as an analytical tool: "The life-course framework thus has a multiple utility for historians. First, it offers a comprehensive, integrative approach that steers one to interpret individual and family transitions as part of a continuous interactive

process, even if they are observed only at one point in time. Second, it helps one view an individual transition as part of a cluster of other concurrent transitions, and as part of a sequence of transitions affecting each other. Finally, it treats a cohort not only as belonging to the specific period of study, but also as located in earlier times, its experience shaped by different historical forces." Tamara K. Hareven, "Introduction: The Histocial Study of the Life Course," in *Transition: The Family and the Life Course in Historical Perspective*, ed. Tamara K. Hareven (New York: Academic Press, 1978), 8.

14 See all the essays in the collection *Einsagan – ólíkar leiðir*.
15 Halldórsdóttir, *Nútímans konur*.
16 Erla Hulda Halldórsdóttir, "Fragments of Lives—The Use of Private Letters in Historical Research," *NORA. Nordic Journal of Women's Studies* 15, no. 1 (2008): 35–49.
17 See, for example, Magnússon, *Iceland in Transition*; Anna Agnarsdóttir, *Sir Joseph Banks, Iceland and the North Atlantic 1772-1820. Journals, Letters and Documents* (London: The Hakluyt Society and Routledge, 2016).
18 Graff, *Conflicting Paths: Growing Up in America* (Cambridge, MA: Harvard University Press, 1997), 1–25; Sigurður Gylfi Magnússon, "(Review) Conflicting Paths. Growing Up in America. By Harvey J. Graff," *Journal of Social History* 30 (Spring 1997): 733–5.
19 Sigurður Gylfi Magnússon, "Kynjasögur á 19. og 20. öld? Hlutverkaskipan í íslensku samfélagi" ("Modern Fairy Tales? Gender Roles in Icelandic Society"), *Saga* XXXV (Spring 1997): 164.
20 "Daglegt líf í dreifbýli og þéttbýli á 20. öld" (Daily Life in Rural and Urban Communities in the 20th Century).
21 Mary Jo Maynes, "The Contours of Childhood: Demography, Strategy, and Mythology of Childhood in French and German Lower-Class Autobiographies," in *The European Experience of Declining Fertility, 1850–1970. The Quiet Revolution*, eds. John R. Gillis, Louise A. Tilly, and David Levine (Cambridge, MA: Blackwell, 1992), 101–24. See also Mary Jo Maynes, *Taking the Hard Road. Life Course in French and German Workers' Autobiographies in the Era of Industrialization* (Chapel Hill: The University of North Carolina Press, 1995); Casper, *Constructing American Lives*.
22 Bjarne Stoklund, "On Interpreting Peasant Diaries: Material Life and Collective Consciousness," *Ethnologia Europea* 2 (1979–1980): 191–206. Another good approach of this kind is by Ben Eklof, "Peasant Sloth Reconsidered: Strategies of Education and Leaving in Rural Russia Before the Revolution," *Journal of Social History* 14 (1981): 355–85.
23 See Linda A. Pollock, *Forgotten Children: Parent–Child Relations from 1500 to 1900* (Cambridge: Cambridge University Press, 1983); Edward Shorter, *The Making of the Modern Family* (New York: Basic Books, 1975). In an issue of the journal

Continuity and Change devoted to the history of childhood, Brigitte H. E. Niestroj wrote an excellent article on childhood studies in Germany. She notes in a section on autobiographies that they are a much more sizable source than one might expect in Germany (several thousand for the eighteenth and nineteenth centuries). She also goes into some detail about how they have been used and the resulting major findings. See Brigitte H. E. Niestroj, "Some Recent German Literature on Socialization and Childhood in Past Times," *Continuity and Change* 4 (1989): 351–4.

24 See, for example, J. Dollard, *Criteria for the Life History* (New Haven: Yale University Press, 1935); H. S. Becker, "Introduction," in *Sociological Methods*, ed. N. K. Denzin (Chicago: Aldine, 1970); Paul Thompson, *The Voice of the Past. Oral History* (Oxford: Oxford University Press, 1978).

25 See, for example, a good discussion about how the life-history approach deals differently with phenomena like social mobility as contrasted with traditional quantitative studies: Daniel Bertaux, "From The Life-History Approach to the Transformation of Sociological Practice," in *Biography and Society. The Life History Approach in the Social Sciences*, ed. Daniel Bertaux (Beverly Hills: Saga, 1981), 31–40. See also in the same book: Thompson, "Life Histories and the Analysis of Social Change," 289–306.

26 See, for example, *Studies in Autobiography*, ed. James Olney (London: Oxford University Press, 1988); *Autobiography: Essays Theoretical and Critical*, ed. James Olney (Princeton: Princeton University Press, 1980); John N. Morris, *Version of the Self: Studies in English Autobiography from John Bunyan to John Stuart Mill* (New York: Basic Books, 1966).

27 Magnússon, "From Children's Point of View," 295–323.

28 See, for example, *Rewriting the Self. Histories from the Renaissance to the Present*, ed. Roy Porter (London: Routledge, 1997).

29 See, for example, Mark Freeman, *Rewriting the Self. History, Memory and Narrative* (London: Routledge, 1993); Sidonie Smith, *A Poetics of Women's Autobiography. Marginality and the Fictions of Self-Representation* (Bloomington: Indiana University Press, 1987).

30 See a detailed discussion of the evolution of social history at this period in Georg G. Iggers, *Historiography in the Twentieth Century*. I have also discussed this period in Magnússon, "*The Singularization of History*: Social History and Microhistory within the Postmodern State of Knowledge," *Journal of Social History* 36 (Spring 2003): 701–35.

31 On the evolution of social history in the United States, see Alice Kessler-Harris, *Social History*. The New American History (Philadelphia: Temple University Press, 1990). The position of social history at different periods has given rise to considerable debate. See for example, the following papers from the last two decades of the twentieth century: Peter N. Stearns, "Toward a Wider Vision: Trends

in Social History," in *The Past Before Us. Contemporary Historical Writing in the United States*, ed. Michael Kammen (Ithaca: Cornell University Press, 1980), 205–30; Stearns, "Social History and History," 319–34; Konrad H. Jarausch, "German Social History—American Style," *Journal of Social History* 19 (Winter 1985): 349–59. The US *Journal of Social History* has a regular feature called *Social History Update*, where interesting papers on aspects of social history have been published. See, for example, Lynne M. Adrian, "Social History Update: An American Studies Contribution to Social History," *Journal of Social History* 23 (Summer 1990): 875–85; Peter N. Stearns, "Social History Update: Encountering Postmodernism," *Journal of Social History* 24 (Winter 1990): 449–52. As a matter of interest, the tenth anniversary issue of the *Journal of Social History* included a discussion of social history. See *Journal of Social History* (Winter 1976): 10th Anniversary Issue. Social History Today . . . and Tomorrow? A number of scholars from different countries write about the position of social history in their own countries, when the discipline had moved beyond its period of infancy. Finally, see many articles in the extensive *Encyclopedia of European Social History. From 1350 to 2000*. Volume 1–6. Editor-in-chief Peter N. Stearns (New York: Charles Scribner's Sons, 2001). The French school of history which was a major influence on the practice of history in the twentieth century is the subject of Roger Chartier's *Cultural History: Between Practice and Representations*, trans. Lydia G. Cochrane (Cambridge: Polity in association with Blackwell, 1988).

32 French scholar Philippe Lejeune has written an essential book on this subject, published in an English translation as *On Autobiography*, ed. Paul John Eakin, trans. Katherine Leary (Minneapolis: University of Minnesota, 1989). The content of the book had been published in France in the 1970s. Note the introductory chapter by Paul John Eakin, in which he draws attention to the importance of the book for research on autobiography, and makes connections with other developments in this scholarly field. See also a new book on the subject matter by Virastau, *Early Modern French Autobiography*. Finally, a few important studies on autobiographies: James Amelang, *The Flight of Icarus: Artisan Autobiography in Early Modern Europe* (Stanford: Stanford University Press, 1998); James Amelang, "Popular Autobiography in Early Modern Europe: Many Questions, a Few Answers," *Memoria y civilización* 5 (2002): 101–18; Andrea Frisch, *The Invention of the Eyewitness* (Chapel Hill: The University of North Carolina Press, 2004); Peter Burke, *Eyewitnessing: The Uses of Images as Historical Evidence* (London: Reaktion Books, 2001); Barry Reay, *Watching Hannah: Sexuality, Horror and Bodily De-formation in Victorian England* (London: Reaktion Books, 2002); Adam Smyth, *Autobiography in Early Modern England* (Cambridge: Cambridge University Press, 2010).

33 Maynes, *Taking the Hard Road*, 1–3.

34 See, for example, books such as *The French Worker. Autobiographies from the Early Industrial Era*, ed. Mark Traugott (Berkeley: University of California Press, 1993).

Also books cited above: *Annals of Labor*; Vincent, *Bread, Knowledge and Freedom*; *Destiny Obscure*.

35 See, for example, the following: Maynes, "The Contours of Childhood"; Mary Jo Maynes, "Adolescent Sexuality and Social Identity in French and German Lower-Class Autobiography," *Journal of Family History* 17 (1992): 397–418; Mary Jo Maynes, "Autobiography and Class Formation in Nineteenth-Century Europe: Methodological Considerations," *Social Science History* 16 (1992): 517–37.

36 Maynes, *Taking the Hard Road*, 2.

37 Maynes, "Autobiography and Class Formation," 522–3.

38 Maynes, *Taking the Hard Road*, 4.

39 This is well addressed by Susanna Egan in her *Patterns of Experience in Autobiography* (Chapel Hill: University of North Carolina, 1984).

40 The same view is seen in Mark Traugott's introduction to *The French Worker*, 1–43.

41 Traugott, *The French Worker*, 27–37.

42 Maynes, *Taking the Hard Road*, 5.

43 Maynes, "Autobiography and Class Formation," 523. She refers here to Luisa Passerini and her paper "Women's Personal Narratives: Myths, Experiences, and Emotions," in *Interpreting Women's Lives*, eds. Personal Narrative Group (Bloomington: Indiana University Press, 1989), 197.

44 See Harvey J. Graff's retrospective article on the association's twenty-fifth anniversary in 2000, when he was its president: Harvey J. Graff, "The Shock of the 'New' (Histories). Social Science Histories and Historical Literacies," *Social Science History* 24, no. 4 (Winter 2001): 484–533.

45 Maynes, *Taking the Hard Road*, 9.

46 "Álitsgerð um hæfi umsækjanda um lektorsstöðu í sagnfræði við Háskóla Íslands," Háskóli Íslands, rektorsskrifstofa 12. mars 1997. (Opinion). Note that the italics are mine. The issue of representation is discussed in the following article: Loriga, "The Role of the Individual in History: Biographical and Historical Writing in the Nineteenth and the Twentieth Century," 136–7.

47 "Álitsgerð dómnefndar um hæfi umsækjenda um lektorsstöðu í sagnfræði við heimspekideild Háskóla Íslands. Mars 1994," Háskóli Íslands, rektorsskrifstofa 20. mars 1994.

48 I also remind the reader of Harvey J. Graff's *Conflicting Paths*, which was discussed earlier in the book. In a sense, Graff applies innovative methods in the use of egodocuments, and strives to throw off the trammels of the strictly defined demographic tradition which was so influential in the latter part of the twentieth century.

49 Traugott, "Introduction," in *The French Worker*, 27–8.

50 Traugott, "Introduction," 30.

51 Traugott, "Introduction," 37.

52 Britt Liljewall, "'Self-written Lives' or Why did Peasants Write Autobiographies?" in *Writing Peasants. Studies on Peasant Literacy in Early Modern Northern*

Europe, eds. Klaus-Joachim Lorenzen-Schmidt and Bjørn Poulsen (Kerteminde: Landbohistorisk Selskab, 2002), 213.

53 Mary Jo Maynes, Jennifer L. Pierce, and Barbara Laslett, *Telling Stories. The Use of Personal Narratives in the Social Science and History* (Ithaca: Cornell University Press, 2008).

54 Maynes, Pierce, and Laslett, *Telling Stories*, 3–4.

Chapter 3

1 This is evident in a wide-ranging paper on the evolution of egodocuments: Mascuch, Dekker, and Baggerman, "Egodocuments and History," 11–56.
2 For an excellent discussion of the original aims of social history, see Miguel A. Cabrera, "The Linguistic Approach or Return to Subjectivism? In Search of an Alternative to Social History," trans. Marie McMahon, *Social History* 24 (January 1999): 75.
3 Hálfdanarson, "Börn – höfuðstóll fátæklingsins?" 123.
4 Chartier, *Cultural History*, 29. This volume is a collection of articles by Chartier, mostly written in the early 1980s. See my discussion of the relationship between ideological history and statistical analysis in the following paper in *Skírnir* 177 (2003): "Að stíga tvisvar í sama strauminn. Til varnar sagnfræði. Síðari grein." (To Step Twice in the Same Stream. In Defense of History), 132–42.
5 For a more detailed discussion of the new, challenging approaches to traditional social history, see Jürgen Pieters, "New Historicism: Postmodern Historiography between Narrativism and Heterology," *History and Theory* 39 (February 2000): 21–38; C. Behan McCullagh, "Bias in Historical Description, Interpretation, and Explanation," *History and Theory* 39 (February 2000): 39–66; and Ignacio Olábarri, "'New' New History: A *Longue Durée* Structure," *History and Theory* 34 (1995): 1–29. In 1989, the *American Historical Review* devoted an entire issue to these new challenges in history in their AHR Forum; notable contributions included David Harlan, "Intellectual History and the Return of Literature," *American Historical Review* 94 (June 1989): 581–609; David Hollinger, "The Return of the Prodigal: The Persistence of Historical Knowing," *American Historical Review* 94 (June 1989): 610–21; David Harlan, "Reply to David Hollinger," *American Historical Review* 94 (June 1989): 622–6; Allan Megill, "Recounting the Past: Description, Explanation, and Narrative in Historiography," *American Historical Review* 94 (June 1989): 627–53; Theodore S. Hamerow, "The Bureaucratization of History," *American Historical Review* 94 (June 1989): 654–60; Gertrude Himmelfarb, "Some Reflections on the New History," *American Historical Review* 94 (June 1989): 661–70; Lawrence W. Levine, "The Unpredictable Past: Reflections on Recent American Historiography,"

American Historical Review 94 (June 1989): 671–9; Joan Wallach Scott, "History in Crisis? The Others' Side of the Story," *American Historical Review* 94 (June 1989): 680–92; John E. Toews, "Perspectives on 'The Old History and the New': A Comment," *American Historical Review* 94 (June 1989): 693–8.

6 This matter is addressed in my *Fortíðardraumar*, 192–8.

7 Just to cite a few scholarly works on the use of the autobiography at the end of the twentieth century, see Timothy Dow Adams, *Light Writing and Life Writing: Photography in Autobiography* (Chapel Hill: University of North Carolina Press, 1999); Leigh Gilmore, "The Mark of Autobiography: Postmodernism, Autobiography, and Genre," in *Autobiography and Postmodernism*, eds. Kathleen Ashley, Leigh Gilmore, and Gerald Peters (Amherst: University of Massachusetts Press, 1994), 3–18; Janice Haaken, *Pillar of Salt: Gender, Memory, and the Perils of Looking Back* (New Brunswick: Rutgers University Press, 1998); Philippe Lejeune, *On Autobiography*; *Postcolonialism and Autobiography*, eds. Alfred Hornung and Ernst-Peter Ruhe (Amsterdam: Brill, 1998); Sidonie Smith, "Memory, Narrative, and the Discourses of Identity in *Abeng* and *No Telephone to Haven*," in *Postcolonialism and Autobiography*, eds. Alfred Hornung and Ernst-Peter Ruhe (Amsterdam: Brill, 1998), 37–59; *Women, Autobiography, Theory: A Reader*, eds. Sidonie Smith and Julia Watson (Madison: University of Wisconsin Press, 1998); *Getting a Life: Everyday Use of Autobiography*, eds. Sidonie Smith and Julia Watson (Minneapolis: University of Minnesota Press, 1996); Carolyn Steedman, *Past Tenses: Essays on Writing, Autobiography and History* (London: Rivers Oram Press, 1992); Hertha D. Wong, "Plains Indian Names and 'the Autobiographical Act'," in *Autobiography and Postmodernism*, eds. Kathleen Ashley, Leigh Gilmore, and Gerald Peters (Amherst: University of Massachusetts Press, 1994), 212–39; Sau-ling Cynthia Wong, "Autobiography as Guided Chinatown Tour? Maxime Hong Kingston's The Woman Warrior and the Chinese-American Autobiographical Controversy," in *Multicultural Autobiography: American Lives*, ed. James Robert Payne (Knoxville: University of Tennessee Press, 1992), 248–79.

8 I wish to cite here an interesting paper on the state of historical demography and quantitative methods in general in the late 1980s. It clearly expounds similar perspectives to mine in my own work. See Eric A. Johnson, "Reflections on an Old 'New History': Quantitative Social Science History in Postmodern Middle Age," *Central European History* 22 (1989): 408–26.

9 This point is addressed by microhistorian Guido Ruggiero in "The Strange Death of Margarita Marcellini: *Male*, Signs, and the Everyday World of Pre-Modern Medicine," *American Historical Review* 106 (2001): 1146. He makes the argument that critics of microhistory have tended to be skeptical of the value of historical research based on a single, specific case. That criticism can, in his view, be easily refuted by explaining that while most microhistorical research is based on a single subject, it is generally supported by much more extensive research.

10 Davíð Ólafsson discusses the quest for truth in his paper: "Fræðin minni" (Minor Scholarship). He also considers the emphases of scholars who have focused on this field. See Davíð Ólafsson, "Fræðin minni. Einsaga, póstmódernismi og íslensk sagnfræði," *Molar og mygla. Um einsögu og glataðan tíma*. Atvik 5, eds. Ólafur Rastrick and Valdimar Hafstein (Reykjavík: Bjartur, 2000), 55–99.
11 André Maurois, *Aspects of Biography*, trans. S. C. Roberts (New York: Cambridge University Press, 1929), 133.
12 Mascuch, Dekker, and Baggerman, "Egodocuments and History," 16.
13 Mascuch, Dekker, and Baggerman, "Egodocuments and History," 16.
14 Maurois, *Aspects of Biography*, 137.
15 Maurois, *Aspects of Biography*, 137–8.
16 Hálfdanarson, "Börn – höfuðstóll fátæklingsins?" 123.
17 Guttormsson, *Bernska, ungdómur og uppeldi á einveldisöld*, 149. Jón Guðnason expresses similar views in his paper on oral sources. See Jón Guðnason, "Um munnlegar heimildir" (On Oral Sources), 11.
18 Guttormsson, *Bernska, ungdómur og uppeldi á einveldisöld*, 149.
19 Guttormsson, *Bernska, ungdómur og uppeldi á einveldisöld*, 149.
20 Evidence for this claim comes from two directions. On the one hand, we have writings published in the 1980s such as Michael Kammen, ed. for the American Historical Association, *The Past Before Us: Contemporary Historical Writing in the United States* (Ithaca: Cornell University Press, 1980); and *Reliving the Past: The Worlds of Social History*, ed. Oliver Zunz (Chapel Hill: University of North Carolina Press, 1985). On the other, the tasks and preoccupations of social historians are clearly reflected in general reference works on social history, such as Peter N. Stearns, ed., *Encyclopedia of Social History* (New York: Garland Publishing, Inc., 1994).
21 This subject was addressed in my *Fortíðardraumar*, 192–8.
22 John A. Garraty, *The Nature of Biography* (New York: Michigan State University Press, 1958), 182.
23 Few have addressed the subject of the importance of narrative better than historian Hayden White: *Metahistory. The Historical Imagination in Nineteenth-Century Europe* (Baltimore: The Johns Hopkins University Press, 1973).
24 One of the best-known critics of this psychological methodology is the renowned social scientist Robyn Dawes, whose writings include: *House of Cards: Psychology and Psychotherapy Built on Myth* (New York: Free Press, 1996). See also: *Sexual Abuse Recalled: Treating Trauma in the Era of the Recovered Memory Debate*, ed. Judith L. Alpert (Northvale: Aronsos, Jason Inc, 1995); Sandi Ashley, *The Missing Voice: Writings by Mothers of Incest Victims* (Dubuque: Kendall Hunt Pub Co, 1992); John Briere, *Child Abuse Trauma: Theory and Treatment of the Lasting Effects* (Newbury Park: Sage Publishing, 1992); *Trauma: Explorations on Memory*, ed. Cathy Caruth (Baltimore: Johns Hopkins University Press, 1995); Shoshana

Felman and Dori Laub, *Testimony: Crises of Witnessing* (New York: Routledge, 1992); Jennifer J. Freyd, *Betrayal Trauma: The Logic of Forgetting Childhood Abuse* (Cambridge, MA: Harvard University Press, 1996); Elizabeth F. Loftus and Katherine Ketcham, *The Myth of Repressed Memory: False Memories and Allegations of Sexual Abuse* (New York: St. Martins Griffin, 1994); Elizabeth F. Loftus, *Witness for the Defense: The Accused, the Eyewitness, and the Expert Who Puts Memory on Trial* (New York: St. Martins Griffin, 1994).

25 Michael S. Roth, *The Ironist's Cage. Memory, Trauma, and the Construction of History* (New York: Columbia University Press, 1995); Dominick LaCapra, *Writing History, Writing Trauma* (Baltimore: The Johns Hopkins University Press, 2001).

26 See, for example, Carlo Ginzburg, "Just One Witness," in *Probing the Limits of Representation: Nazism and the "Final Solution,"* ed. Saul Friedlander (Cambridge, MA: Harvard University Press, 1992).

27 Maurois, *Aspects of Biography*, 152–65.

28 Maurois, *Aspects of Biography*, 146–7.

29 See, for example, White's discussion of this matter: he succeeded in drawing historians' attention to the courses followed by our language and expression: White, *Metahistory*.

30 See a most enlightening discussion on memory function from various perspectives in the writings of Susan A. Crane, such as "*AHR Forum*: Writing the Individual Back into Collective Memory," *American Historical Review* 102 (December 1997): 1372–85. See also Susan A. Crane, "(Not) Writing History: Rethinking the Intersections of Personal History and Collective Memory with Hans von Aufsess," *History and Memory* 8 (Spring/Summer 1996): 5–29; Susan A. Crane, "Memory, History, and Distortion in the Museum," *History and Theory*, Theme Issue "Producing the Past," 36 (1997): 44–63. Crane also edited the interesting book: *Museums and Memory*, ed. Susan A. Crane (Stanford: Stanford University Press, 2000).

31 A work that addresses scholarly experiments with taking the Theory of Relativity seriously, and welcomes the potential they offer, is Alun Munslow, *Deconstructing History* (London: Routledge, 1997).

32 The role of fiction in scholarship has been widely addressed. See, for example, Natalie Z. Davis, *Fiction in the Archives: Pardon Tales and Their Tellers in Sixteenth-Century France* (Stanford: Stanford University Press, 1987); Simon Schama, *Dead Certainties. (Unwarranted Speculations)* (New York: Vintage Books, 1992); Eunice Lipton, *Alias Olympia: A Woman's Search for Manet's Notorious Model and Her Own Desire* (Ithaca: Cornell University Press, 1992).

33 A vast number of studies have been made of autobiography in the context of literary studies. The common factor of this research is that it focuses on the form and the path of the narrative, while paying less attention to historical questions, such as whether the autobiography accurately reflects people's everyday life. In this field, the structure of the autobiography as a work of literature receives the most attention.

See, for example, Olney, ed., *Studies in Autobiography*; Olney, ed., *Autobiography*; Morris, *Version of the Self*.

34 Maurois, *Aspects of Biography*, 149.

35 Out of the many postmodernist writings that have influenced the work of historians, see, for example, *The Postmodern History Reader*, ed. Keith Jenkins (London: Routledge, 1997); Keith Jenkins, *Re-Thinking History* (London: Routledge, 1991); White, *Metahistory*.

36 Georg Misch, *A History of Autobiography in Antiquity* I (London: Harvard University Press, 1950), 12.

37 Misch, *A History of Autobiography in Antiquity* I, 12.

38 Misch, *A History of Autobiography in Antiquity* I, 12.

39 Several books and papers address or apply modernization theory. See, for example, Cyril E. Black et al., *The Modernization of Japan and Russia* (New York: Free Press, 1975); Marion J. Levy Jr., *Modernization and the Structure of Societies* (Princeton: Princeton University Press, 1966); *The Modernization of China*, ed. Gilbert Rozman (New York: Free Press, 1980); Raymond Grew, "More on Modernization," *Journal of Social History* 14 (1980): 179–87; Alex Inkeles and David H. Smith, *Becoming Modern: Individual Change in Six Developing Countries* (London: Harvard University Press, 1975); Peter N. Stearns, "Modernization and Social History: Some Suggestions, and a Muted Cheer," *Journal of Social History* 14 (Winter 1980): 189–209. See also rather forceful criticism of the theory by Dean C. Tipps, "Modernization Theory and the Comparative Study of Societies: A Critical Perspective," *Comparative Studies in Society and History* (Summer 1973): 199–222; Peter N. Stearns, "Modernization," in *Encyclopedia of European Social History. From 1350 to 2000* (New York: Charles Scribner's Sons, 2001), 3–12.

40 Two publications are cited here as good examples of studies of these societies: Franklin Mendels, "Proto-Industrialization: The First Phase of the Industrialization Process," *Journal of Economic History* XXXI (1972): 241–61; Maths Isacson and Lars Magnusson, *Proto-Industrialisation in Scandinavia. Craft Skills in the Industrial Revolution* (New York: St. Martin's Press, 1987). See also a review of the latter by Sigurður Gylfi Magnússon in *Journal of Social History* (Winter 1988): 396–8.

41 I discuss these priorities in research in the United States in the late 1980s in my paper: "*The Singularization of History:* Social History and Microhistory within the Postmodern State of Knowledge," 701–35.

42 I discuss all the life stages, especially those concerned with childhood and adolescence, and how they influenced individuals' attitude to life, *inter alia* in "From Children's Point of View," 295–323.

43 Bernharð Stefánsson, *Endurminningar* I (Reykjavík: Kvöldvökuútgáfan, 1961), 28.

44 Andrés Kristjánsson, *Vopnaviðskipti og vinakynni. Ævifrásögn Hannesar Pálssonar* (Reykjavík: Örn og Örlygur, 1979), 29.

45 Finnur Jónsson, *Þjóðhættir og ævisögur frá 19. öld* (Akureyri: Bókaútgáfa Pálma H. Jónssonar, 1945), 13–14.
46 See Guðmundur Jónsson, *Vinnuhjú á 19. öld* (Servants in the 19th century) (Reykjavík: Sagnfræðistofnun Háskóla Íslands, 1982). Vilhelm Vilhelmsson, *Sjálfstætt fólk: Vistarbandið og íslenskt samfélag á 19. öld* (Reykjavík: Sögufélag, 2017)—(Independent People).
47 Regarding the significance of the life stages and a detailed discussion of them, see Magnússon, "The Continuity of Everyday Life."
48 This may be seen, for instance, in many diaries that continue into the diarist's old age. I have studied, for example, the diary of Finnbogi Bernódusson (1892–1980, *Lbs* 891–949 fol.), and it was most interesting to read his writings in light of the way his life changed after he lost his wife in old age. Alone, he had to deal with difficult challenges on entirely new terms. A field of study should also be mentioned here, which attracted growing interest in the 1980s and 1990s, focusing on the elderly and their position. See, for example, Thomas R. Cole, *Journey of Life. A Cultural History of Aging in America* (New York: Cambridge University Press, 1992); Peter N. Stearns, *Old Age in European Society: The Case of France* (New York: Holmes & Meier Publishers, 1976).
49 Tryggvi Emilsson, *Fátækt fólk. Æviminningar* I (Poor People)—(Reykjavík: Mál og menning, 1976), 68–9.
50 See discussion on life-stage study: *Transitions: The Family and the Life Course in Historical Perspective*, ed. Tamara K. Hareven (New York: Academic Press, 1978). Some information on the use of this research technique in studies that are not demographic in nature is found in Magnússon, "Alþýðumenning á Íslandi 1850–1940," 265–71.
51 Tryggvi Jónsson, *Árblik og aftanskin. Nokkrir ævipættir* (Dawn and Dusk. Autobiographical sketches) (Akureyri: Norðri, 1946), 27.
52 Ágúst Jósefsson, *Minningar og svipmyndir úr Reykjavík* (*Memories and Scenes from Reykjavík*) (Reykjavík: Leiftur, 1959), 52.
53 Friðgeir H. Berg, *Að heiman og heim. Endurminningar Vestur-Íslendings* (*Away and Home Again. Memoirs of an Icelandic Canadian*) (Reykjavík: Leiftur, 1968), 35.
54 Gunnar Benediktsson, *Stiklað á stóru. Frá bernsku til brauðleysis* (*The Long and the Short*) (Reykjavík: Örn og Örlygur, 1976), 14.

Chapter 4

1 Matthías Jochumsson, *Sögukaflar af sjálfum mér* (Reykjavík: Þorsteinn Gíslason, 1922), 57–8.
2 Recently, the history of smell has come under consideration by many historians. The subject matter is not totally unknown, but for the last few years the history of smell has been booming, and exciting studies of smell's history have been published. See

an interesting conversation between William Tullett, Inger Leemans, Hsuan Hsu, Stephanie Weismann, Cecilia Bembibre, Melanie A. Kiechle, Duane Jethro, Anna Chen, Xuelei Huang, Jorge Otero-Pailos, and Mark Bradley, "Smell, History, and Heritage," *American Historical Review*, AHR History Lab, 127, no. 1 (March 2022): 261–310.

3 Jochumsson, *Sögukaflar af sjálfum mér*, 37–8.
4 *Bræður af Ströndum* (*Brothers from Strandir*), 152. Quotation from Níels' diary, which he kept for forty years.
5 Berg, *Að heiman og heim*, 11–12.
6 Vincent, *Bread, Knowledge, and Freedom*, 7.
7 Hannes J. Magnússon, *Hetjur hversdagslífsins. Nokkrar þjóðlífsmyndir frá upphafi 20. aldarinnar* (*Heroes of Everyday Life*) (Akureyri: Norðri, 1953), 7.
8 Magnússon, *Hetjur hversdagslífsins*, 7.
9 Jóhanna Kristjónsdóttir, *Perlur og steinar. Árin með Jökli* (*Pearls and Stones*) (Reykjavík: Almenna bókafélagið, 1993), 279.
10 In 1994, I compiled a scholarly questionnaire for the Museum of Iceland Ethnological Collection based on the principles of the life course. The respondents were encouraged to apply their answers to the whole life course. See Sigurður Gylfi Magnússon, "Daglegt líf í dreifbýli og þéttbýli á 20. öld," Spurningaskrá 86. Þjóðháttadeild Þjóðminjasafns Íslands, 1994.
11 *Destiny Obscure*, 11.
12 Magnús Magnússon, *Syndugur maður segir frá. Minningar og mannlýsingar* (*Testimony of a Sinner*) (Reykjavík: Leiftur, 1969), 5; Magnús Bl. Jónsson, *Endurminningar. Bernska og námsár* I (*Memoirs*) (Reykjavík: Ljóðhús, 1980), 13–14.
13 Natalie Zemon Davis, *The Return of Martin Guerre* (Cambridge, MA: Harvard University Press, 1983).
14 Martin Kohlin, "Biography: Account, Text, Method," in *Biography and Society. The Life History Approach in the Social Sciences*, ed. Daniel Bertaux (Beverly Hill: Saga, 1981), 70.
15 Garraty, *The Nature of Biography*, 184.
16 Magnússon, "Einvæðing sögunnar," 100–41.
17 See Graff, *Conflicting Paths*; Magnússon, "The Continuity of Everyday Life."
18 Jóhannes Birkiland, *Harmsaga æfi minnar. Hvers vegna ég varð auðnuleysingi*, 2nd edition (revised) (Reykjavík: Published by the author, 1948).
19 It is worth pointing out that some people have tended to belittle the autobiography, on the grounds that autobiographers reveal how egocentric they are. Davíð Oddsson, who was prime minister of Iceland for twelve years, said in a major personal interview about himself and his writings that he had no intention of writing an autobiography: "I have absolutely no interest in writing my life story. I find most other subjects interesting. You have to be so extraordinarily self-centered to do so (...) and I feel that all politicians' autobiographies should be called: *A Self-Satisfied Man Tells His Story*. And I would be no better than the rest." "Áhugamaður

um fólk. Skáldið Davíð Oddsson í einkaviðtali við DV-Magasín" (Passionate about people. The poet Davíð Oddsson in an exclusive interview with DV-Magasín), *DV-Magasín*, December 5, issue 13, year 1, 2002.

20 Various scholars have expressed their views on the subject. See, for example, John Garraty, Georg Misch, David Vincent, and John Burnett. This list is, however, based primarily on my detailed research on Icelandic egodocuments, mostly published in the first seven to eight decades of the twentieth century.

21 Jean-Jacques Rousseau, *Confessions*, trans. Angela Scholar (London: Oxford University Press, 2000). The book was first published in the 1790s, after the author's death. See also St. Augustine's *Confessions of a Sinner* (London: Penguin, 1995).

22 Many books in this category could be mentioned, but here only a few examples are given: Magnús H. Árnason, *Ljúfa vor. Bernskuminningar og eyfirskir þættir* (*A Lovely Spring*) (Akureyri: Prentsmiðja Björns Jónssonar, 1961); Sæmundur Dúason, *Einu sinni var I. Æviminningar* (*Once Upon a Time. Memoirs*) (Akureyri: Prentverk Odds Björnssonar, 1966); Snorri Sigfússon, *Ferðin frá Brekku. Minningar* I (*The Journey from Brekka*) (Reykjavík: Iðunn, 1968); Ólafur Jónsson, *Á tveimur jafnfljótum. Minningaþættir* I (*Shanks' Pony*) (Reykjavík: Leiftur, 1971); Þórarinn Helgason, *Leikir og störf. Bernskuminningar úr Landbroti* (*Play and Work*) (Reykjavík: AB, 1976).

23 Hannes Þorsteinsson, *Endurminningar og hugleiðingar um hitt og þetta er á dagana hefur drifið* (Reykjavík: Almenna bókafélagið, 1962), 55.

24 See, for example, the autobiography of opera singer Eggert Stefánsson: *Lífið og ég* I-IV (*Life and Me*) (Reykjavík: Ísafoldaprentsmiðja, 1950–1957); Jóhannes Birkiland, *Harmsaga ævi minnar* (*The Tragedy of My Life*); Steindór Steindórsson, *Sól ég sá. Sjálfsævisaga Steindórs Steindórssonar frá Hlöðum* I (*The Sun I Saw*) (Reykjavík: Örn og Örlygur, 1982). The author of the last of these was deemed to judge his contemporaries especially harshly, generally in order to glorify himself.

25 See, for example, a highly unusual book by Jakob M. Bjarnason, *Söguleg sjóferð* (*A Historic Sea Voyage*) (Reykjavík: Höfundur, 1950).

26 Benediktsson, *Stiklað á stóru*, 8.

27 Birkiland, *Harmsaga ævi minnar*, 5.

28 Birkiland, *Harmsaga ævi minnar*, 285.

29 See further discussion of Jóhannes and his autobiography in an essay by Þorsteinn Antonsson, "Utangarðsskáldið Jóhannes Birkiland," *Skírnir* 159 (1985): 225–58.

30 Birkiland, *Harmsaga ævi minnar*, 315.

Chapter 5

1 Egodocuments, like autobiographies, are hugely popular among Icelandic readers, often featuring among the bestsellers each year. Icelanders have been said to have this literary form, and personal history in general, "on the brain."

2 Magnússon, *Menntun, ást og sorg*, 265–86; Jón Karl Helgason, *Hetjan og höfundurinn. Brot úr menningarsögu* (*The Hero and the Author*) (Reykjavík: Mál og menning, 1998).
3 Einarsson, *Ævisaga Helga Einarssonar fra Neranesi í Stafholtstungum í Myrasyslu, Islandi: skrifa af honum sjálfum, byrja vi Lake St. Martin, April 3, 1920* (Reykjavík: Ísafoldarprentsmiðja, 1954), 9.
4 Magnússon, "Siðferðilegar fyrirmyndir á 19. Öld," 57–72; Magnússon, "From Children's Point of View," 295–323; Vésteinn Ólason, "Bóksögur" (Book Histories), in *Íslensk þjóðmenning* VI. *Munnmenntir og bókmenning*, ed. Frosti F. Jóhannesson (Reykjavík: Þjóðsaga, 1989), 196–217.
5 Berg, *Að heiman og heim*, 11–12.
6 Jochumsson, *Sögukaflar af sjálfum mér*, 3–4.
7 Jochumsson, *Sögukaflar af sjálfum mér*, 4–5.
8 Jochumsson, *Sögukaflar af sjálfum mér*, 6.
9 For some time, ethnologist Jón Jónsson has been researching the role of vagabonds in Icelandic life. See his *Á mörkum mennskunar* (*On the Brink of Humanity*): *Sögur af förufólki í íslenska sveitasamfélaginu*. Sýnisbók íslenskrar alþýðumenningar 23 (Reykjavík: Háskólaútgáfan, 2018). What is it that makes someone unusual, that distinguishes a person from their peers, most of whom society considers "normal" (a phenomenon that does not actually exist, of course)? That is the question at the center of *Tales of Peculiar People*. The book attempts to understand what is behind the idea of "normal" and considers deviations from so-called normal behavior or customs. When it comes to defining who belongs to the majority—and at the same time, by default, who is relegated to the minority—the idea of "otherness" is key. See the following book: Anna Heiða Baldursdóttir, Atli Þór Kristinsson, Daníel Guðmundur Daníelsson, Marín Árnadóttir, Sólveig Ólafsdóttir, and Sigurður Gylfi Magnússon, *Þættir af sérkennilegu fólki. Menning fátæktar* (*Tales of Peculiar People: The Culture of Poverty*). Sýnisbók íslenskrar alþýðumenningar 28 (Reykjavík: Háskólaútgáfan, 2021).
10 Jósef Björnsson, *Æskustöðvar* (Reykjavík: Ísafold, 1954), 104–5.
11 Björnsson, *Æskustöðvar*, 85.
12 Björnsson, *Æskustöðvar*, 84–5.
13 Jónas Jónasson, *Íslenskir þjóðhættir* (*Icelandic Folkways*), 2nd ed. (Reykjavík: Jóna og Halldóra Rafnar, 1945), 3–9; Magnús Gíslason, *Kvällsvaka. En isländsk kulturtradition belyst genom studier i bondebefolkningens vardagsliv och miljö under senare hälften av 1800-talet och början av 1900-talet* (*The Winter-Eve Gathering*). Studia Ethnologica Upsaliensia 2 (Uppsalir: Acta Universitatis Upsaliensis, 1977); Hjalti Hugason, "Kristnir trúarhættir" (Christian religious traditions), in *Íslensk þjóðmenning* V. *Trúarhættir*, ed. Frosti F. Jóhannsson (Reykjavík: Þjóðsaga, 1988), 75–339.
14 Magnús Helgason, *Skólaræður og önnur erindi. Uppeldis- og heimilishættir í Birtingarholti fyrir 70 árum* (Reykjavík: Samband íslenskra barnakennara, 1934), 2.

15 Helgason, *Skólaræður og önnur erindi*, 4.
16 Magnússon, "The Continuity of Everyday Life"; Magnússon, "Alþýðumenning á Íslandi 1850–1940," 277–8.
17 In this context, see Ólafur F. Hjartar's overview of book publication in Iceland: "Íslenzk bókaútgáfa 1887–1966" (Icelandic book publishing), *Árbók Landsbókasafns Íslands* 24 (1967): 137–41; Ólafur Halldórsson, "Skrifaðar bækur" (Written books), *Íslensk þjóðmenning* VI, 57–89; Steingrímur Jónsson, "Prentaðar bækur" (Printed books), *Íslensk þjóðmenning* VI, 91–115.
18 Jochumsson, *Sögukaflar af sjálfum mér*, 47.
19 Björnsson, *Æskustöðvar*, 120–1.
20 Magnússon, "From Children's Point of View."
21 See Davíð Ólafsson's discussion of the status of peasant culture in the following papers: Davíð Ólafsson, "Scribal communities in Iceland: The case of Sighvatur Grímsson," in *White Field, Black Seeds: Nordic Literacy Practices in the Long Nineteenth Century*, eds. Anna Kuismin and Matthew J. Driscoll (Helsinki: Finnish Literature Society, 2013), 40–9; Davíð Ólafsson and Ólafur Rastrick, "Current Trends in Icelandic Cultural History: Practices, Products and Perspectives," *Revue d'Histoire Nordique* 20 (2016)d: 155–82.
22 Sigurður Gylfi Magnússon, "The Life is Never Over: Biography as a Microhistorical Approach," in *The Biographical Turn. Lives in History*, eds. Hans Renders, Binne de Haan, and Jonne Harmsma (London: Routledge, 2017), 42–52; Sigurður Gylfi Magnússon, "The Icelandic Biography and Egodocuments in Historical Writing," in *Different Lives. Global Perspectives on Biography in Public Cultures and Societies*. Biography Studies, eds. Hans Renders and David Veltman, in collaboration with Madelon Nanninga-Franssen (Leiden: Brill, 2020), 165–81; Sigurður Gylfi Magnússon, "The Backside of the Biography: Microhistory as a Research Tool," in *Fear of Theory*. Biography Studies, eds. Hans Renders and David Veltman (Leiden: Brill, 2021), 89–102.
23 Bergsteinn Jónsson, "Íslenzkar ævisögur. Hugleiðingar í tilefni af sjálfsævisögu Halldórs E. Sigurðssonar" (Icelandic biographies), *Saga* 25 (1987): 205–8.
24 Guðmundur Hálfdanarson has discussed Icelandic biographies in: "Biskupasögur hinar nýju. Um ævisögur fjögurra stjórnmálamanna" (Biographies of four politicians), *Saga* 31 (1993): 169–90. See new trends in the writing of biographies: *The Biographical Turn. Lives in History*.
25 This is a conclusion reached by many studies.
26 See the discussion in *Microhistory and the Lost People of Europe*, eds. Edward Muir and Guido Ruggiero, trans. Eren Branch (Baltimore: Johns Hopkins University, 1991).
27 This is discussed in detail in Magnússon and Ólafsson, *Minor Knowledge and Microhistory*.
28 Magnússon and Ólafsson, *Minor Knowledge and Microhistory*. See also: *Mirrors of Virtue. Manuscript and Print in Late Pre-modern Iceland*, eds. Margrét Eggertsdóttir

and Matthew James Driscoll (Copenhagen: Museum Tusculanum Press, 2017). See a review essay of this book by Sigurður Gylfi Magnússon, "What takes Place, When Nothing Happens? The Importance of Late Modern Manuscript Culture," *Scripta Islandica* 69 (2018): 149–76.

29 I shall return to this issue later in the book, exploring the reasons for academic apathy and referring to various historians and other scholars who have made use of these resources.

30 Vilhjálmur Þ. Gíslason, "Formálsorð," in *Brautryðjendur. Þrjár sjálfsævisögur. Páll Melsted, Tryggvi Gunnarson, Jón Ólafsson,* [Foreword. Pioneers. Three Autobiographies] ed. Vilhjálmur Þ. Gíslason (Reykjavíkd: Bókfellsútgáfan, 1950), ix.

31 Carlo Ginzburg, "Microhistory: Two or Three Things that I know about It," *Critical Inquiry* 20 (Autumn 1993): 10–35. I first wrote about the methods of microhistory in my book *Menntun, ást og sorg*. See also Sigurður Gylfi Magnússon, "Félagssagan fyrr og nú" (Social History, then and now), in *Einsagan – ólíkar leiðir. Átta ritgerðir og eitt myndlistarverk,* eds. Erla Hulda Halldórsdóttir and Sigurður Gylfi Magnússon (Reykjavík: University of Iceland Press, 1998), 17–50. See also the latest version of the discussion on microhistory: Magnússon and Szijártó, *What is Microhistory?*. See also: Sigurður Gylfi Magnússon, "Microhistory," in *The Routledge Handbook of Research Methods in the Study of Religion,* second edition, eds. Steven Engler and Michael Stausberg (London: Routledge, 2022), 365–74.

32 Ginzburg, "Microhistory: Two or Three Things that I know about It," 22–3.

33 Ginzburg, "Microhistory: Two or Three Things that I know about It," 23.

34 Examples are seen in the Icelandic periodical *Skák* (Chess), which publishes features on the chess-playing careers of individuals, and specific games, in a regular feature, "Íslenskir skákmeistarar" (Icelandic chess champions). See, for example, a piece on Bragi Halldórsson in *Skák* 52, no. 3 (2001): 257–80.

35 This small number of women autobiographers can be compensated for by use of ethnological questionnaires, for which women make up a majority of respondents. In addition, some autobiographical fragments and essays by women have been published in the press.

36 This trend was discussed in detail at the end of *Sjálfssögur*, as was the question of how the autobiographical form has offered opportunities for women's self-expression. I shall return to that subject later in this book.

37 The 60+ not accounted for in the totals could not be categorized due to lack of adequate information.

38 Magnússon, "The Continuity of Everyday Life," 22–3.

39 For the various genres of life writing and egodocuments in Iceland, see my *Fortíðardraumar*; and also *Sjálfssögur*. It is important to note that I make a distinction between "life writing" and "egodocuments"; the former marked by its publication process, but the latter a wider concept covering a diverse quality of written material, which contains personal expressions in any shape or form.

40 See the book *Fortíðardraumar*, 352–8.
41 I know of no published research dedicated to the variety, currency, and popularity of egodocuments in different countries and cultures; this is an area that still requires considerable research. An immensely useful database of Dutch egodocuments, including much material relating to autobiographies and similar sources, can be found on http://www.egodocument.net/egodocument/index.html. For an important contribution to research in this area, see Dekker, "Jacques Presser's Heritage: Egodocuments in the Study of History," 13–37.
42 See Erla Hulda Halldórsdóttir, "Fragments of Lives – The Use of Private Letters in Historical Research," *NORA – Nordic Journal of Feminist and Gender Research* 15, no. 1 (2008): 35–49.
43 These sources have been investigated in depth and used to wide and varied effect by members of the Icelandic school of microhistory: see, for example, Magnússon, "From Children's Point of View," 295–323; Ólafsson, "Wordmongers"; and Magnússon and Ólafsson, "Minor Knowledge," 495–524. For the status of children within this society and its literary production see also Hálfdanarson, "Börn – höfuðstóll fátæklingsins?" 121–46; and Guttormsson, *Bernska, ungdómur og uppeldi á einveldisöld*.
44 Ólafsson, "Wordmongers," 110. The accounts for all counties (sýslur) have been published, one by one, over the last fifty years, see, for example, *Mýra- og Borgarfjarðarsýslur: Sýslu- og sóknalýsingar Hins íslenska bókmenntafélags 1839–1873*, eds. Guðrún Ása Grímsdóttir and Björk Ingimundardóttir (Reykjavík: Sögufélag and Örnefnastofnun Íslands, 2005). See also: Ögmundur Helgason, "Skriftarkunnátta í Skagafjarðarprófastsdæmi um 1840," *Skagfirðingabók* 12 (1983): 110–20.
45 Loftur Guttormsson, "The Development of Popular Religious Literacy in the Seventeenth and Eighteenth Centuries," *Scandinavian Journal of History* 15, no. 1 (1990): 15–35. See also: Erla Hulda Halldórsdóttir, "Af bréfaskriftum kvenna á 19. öld" (Women's letter-writing in the 19th century), in *Alþýðumenning á Íslandi 1830–1930: Ritað mál, menntun og félagshreyfingar*. Sagnfræðirannsóknir 18, eds. Loftur Guttormsson and Ingi Sigurðsson (Reykjavík: Háskólaútgáfan, 2003), 247–68; Erla Hulda Halldórsdóttir, "'Don't You Forget Your Always Loving Sister': Writing as a Social and Cultural Capital," in *Vernacular Literacies – Past, Present and Future*, eds. Ann-Catrine Edlund, Lars-Erik Edlund, and Susanne Haugen (Umeå: Umeå University and Royal Skyttean Society, 2014), 181–92.
46 Björnsson, *Æskustöðvar*, 32.
47 Björnsson, *Æskustöðvar*, 33.
48 See Sigurður Gylfi Magnússon and Davíð Ólafsson, "In the Name of Barefoot Historians: In-Between Spaces within the Icelandic Educational System," in *Education beyond Europe. Models and Traditions before Modernities*, eds. Cristiano Casalini, Edward Choi, and Ayenachew A. Woldegiyorgis (Leiden: Brill, 2021).

49 See a good example of this way of doing history in Ólafsdóttir, "Vald og vanmáttur: Eitt hundrað og ein/saga á jaðri samfélagsins 1770–1936."
50 Guðrún Valgerður Stefánsdóttir, *Bíbí í Berlín. Sjálfsævisaga Bjargeyjar Kristjánsdóttur*. Sýnisbók íslenskrar alþýðumenningar 29 (Reykjavík: Háskólaútgáfan, 2022). Forthcoming is a book that will be published by Routledge in 2024 called: *Disability Studies Meets Microhistory: The Secret Life of Bíbí in Berlín*, written by Sigurður Gylfi Magnússon, Sólveig Ólafsdóttir, and Guðrún Valgerður Stefánsdóttir. See also: Guðrún Valgerður Stefánsdóttir and Sólveig Ólafsdóttir, "The Peculiar Attitude of the People: The Life and Social Conditions of One 'Feebleminded' Girl in the Early 20th Century," in *Understanding Disability Throughout History: Interdisciplinary Perspectives in Iceland from Settlement to 1936* (London: Routledge, 2022), 58–75.

Chapter 6

1 See, for example, Magnússon and Ólafsson, "Barefoot Historians," 175–209. This chapter is partly based on the following article: Magnússon, "Living by the Book," 53–62. I would like to express my thanks to the publisher for permission to use part of this article in the book.
2 Magnússon, "The Continuity of Everyday Life."
3 Magnússon, *Wasteland with Words*, 85–98.
4 I know of no published research dedicated to the currency and popularity of egodocuments in different countries and cultures; this is an area that still requires considerable research. Again, there is, however, an immensely useful Dutch database of egodocuments, including large amounts of material related to autobiographies and similar sources, available on http://www.egodocument.net/egodocument/index.html.
5 I have addressed this in an essay, "Alþýðumenning á Íslandi 1850–1940," and in my doctoral thesis, "The Continuity of Everyday Life."
6 Reference may be made here, for instance, to the debate that arose from the publication of Jóhanna Kristjónsdóttir's autobiography, *Perlur og steinar*. See further discussion below.
7 Þorkell Bjarnason, "Fyrir 40 árum" (40 Years Ago), *Tímarit hins íslenzka bókmenntafélags* 13 (1892): 170–258; Ólafur Sigurðsson, "Fyrir 40 árum" (40 years ago), *Tímarit hins íslenzka bókmenntafélags* 15 (1894): 198–246. Þorkell responded the following year to Ólafur's essay: Þorkell Bjarnason, "Fyrir 40 árum" (40 years ago), *Tímarit hins íslenzka bókmenntafélags* 16 (1895): 204–29.
8 Sigurðsson, "Fyrir 40 árum," 199–200.
9 Sigurðsson, "Fyrir 40 árum," 200.

10 See a discussion of this viewpoint in Magnússon, *Menntun, ást og sorg*, 87–120.
11 Þorkell Bjarnason, "Fyrir 40 árum," *Þjóðólfur*, October 5, 1894, 186.
12 Magnússon, *Syndugur maður segir frá*, 5. See also Jónsson, *Endurminningar*, 13; Lárus J. Rist, *Synda eða stökkva. Endurminningar (To Swim or to Jump)* (Akureyri: Sigurjón Rist, 1947), 7.
13 Sigurður Ingjaldsson, *Æfisaga Sigurðar Ingjaldssonar frá Balaskarði. Rituð af honum sjálfum*. Önnur útgáfa (A Biography) (Reykjavík: Bókfellsútgáfan, 1957), 8.
14 Kristjónsdóttir, *Perlur og steinar*.
15 Guðrún Sigríður Jakobsdóttir, Jón Einar Jakobsson, Svava Jakobsdóttir, and Þór Jakobsson, "Andmæli gegn óhróðri" (A Rebuttal of Slander), *Morgunblaðið*, January 13, 1994.
16 Jakobsdóttir et al. "Andmæli gegn óhróðri."
17 Jakobsdóttir et al. "Andmæli gegn óhróðri."
18 Einar Falur Ingólfsson, "Að skjóta sér ekki til hlés" (Confrontation), *Morgunblaðið*, December 10, 1993.
19 Ingólfsson, "Að skjóta sér ekki til hlés."
20 Jónsson, *Á tveimur jafnfljótum*, 9.
21 Árnason, *Ljúfa vor*, 6.
22 On occasion, specific books will be cited, but it should be borne in mind that most of the autobiographies to which this chapter refers were written in the first half of the twentieth century, and hence their authors were born in the late nineteenth to early twentieth centuries.
23 Ingólfur Margeirsson, *Sálumessa syndara. Ævi og eftirþankar Esra S. Péturssonar geðlæknis og sálkönnuðar* (Reykjavík, 1997)—(*A Sinner's Requiem*).
24 Ingólfur Margeirsson, *Sálumessa syndara*, "Formáli höfundar," pages unnumbered.
25 See case no. 252/1998 in the supreme court, "Ákæruvaldið gegn Ingólfi Erni Margeirssyni." See website of the Supreme Court of Iceland: www.haestirettur.is.
26 Matthías Viðar Sæmundsson, "Esra Pétursson og rithöfundarnir," *DV*, 11 May 1998.
27 Ingólfur Margeirsson, "Hin sálfræðilega ævisaga" (The psychoanalytic biography), *Lesbók Morgunblaðsins*, November 4, 1995.
28 The reader is asked to bear this in mind when reading the citations from Ingólfur's article below.
29 The verdict of the Reykjavík district court is stated in the supreme court verdict no. 252/1998 "Ákæruvaldið gegn Ingólfi Erni Margeirssyni." Note that the *italics* are mine.
30 Ingólfur Margeirsson, *Lífsjátning. Endurminningar Guðmundu Elíasdóttur söngkonu* (Reykjavík: Iðunn, 1981). The book may be said, with some truth, to be a first-class work of memoirs.
31 "Held áfram að vera til," *Fréttablaðið*, April 4, 2004.

32　*Interpreting Women's Lives. Feminist Theory and Personal Narratives*, ed. the Personal Narratives Group (Bloomington: Indiana University Press, 1989), 3. The volume contains many interesting articles, the fruits of a working group over many years.

33　*Interpreting Women's Lives*, 4.

34　Davis, *The Return of Martin Guerre*. Sigurður Gylfi Magnússon and István Szijártó, *What is Microhistory?* 103–18.

35　Guðný Hallgrímsdóttir's thesis was the result of several years' research on the manuscript collection of the National and University Library of Iceland. Her findings are found in "Hulda: Sjálfstjáning kvenna á 18. og 19. Öld" (Women's self-expression in the 18th and 19th centuries), (MA diss., History Department of the University of Iceland 2009).

36　See Guðrún Ingólfsdóttir, *Á hverju liggja ekki vorar göfugu kellíngar. Bókmenning íslenskra kvenna frá miðöldum fram á 18. öld.* (*Women's Literary Culture from the Middle Ages to the 18th Century*) Sýnisbók íslenskrar alþýðumenningar 20 (Reykjavík: Háskólaútgáfan, 2016).

37　Publications arising from this project include George L. Justice and Nathan Tinker, *Women's Writing and the Circulation of Ideas: Manuscript Publication in England 1550–1800* (Cambridge: Cambridge University Press, 2010); and Victoria E. Burke and Jonathan Gibson, *Early Modern Women's Manuscript Writing. Selected Essays of the Trinity/Trent Colloquium* (Hampshire and Burlington: Ashgate Pub Ltd., 2004).

38　For the influence of new ideas in scholarship on how we view autobiographies, see, for example, Sidonie Smith and Julia Watson, "Introduction: Situating Subjectivity in Women's Autobiographical Practices," in *Women, Autobiography, Theory: A Reader*, eds. Sidonie Smith and Julia Watson (New York: University of Wisconsin Press, 1998), 3–52.

39　Jakobína Sigurðardóttir, *Í barndómi* (Reykjavík: Mál og menning, 1994).

40　Þorleifur Bjarnason, *Hornstrendingabók* I–III (Reykjavík: Örn og Örlygur, 1983).

41　Heather O'Donoghue, *Old Norse-Icelandic Literature: A Short Introduction* (Oxford: Oxford, 2004), 22–3. The sagas of Icelanders are translated in Viðar Hreinsson, ed., *The Complete Sagas of Icelanders*, 5 vols. (Reykjavík: Leifur Eiríksson, 1997).

42　The importance of the sagas on the mental and emotional development of young people in Iceland is treated in greater depth in Sigurður Gylfi Magnússon, "Siðferðilegar fyrirmyndir á 19. Öld," 57–72. See also Magnússon and Ólafsson, "Barefoot Historians." The sagas of Icelanders are translated in Viðar Hreinsson, ed., *The Complete Sagas of Icelanders*. This edition also includes the short stories in saga style known as *þættir* ("tales").

43　Magnússon, "From Children's Point of View," 295–323.

44　Magnússon, "Siðferðilegar fyrirmyndir á 19. Öld," 57–72.

45　Ólason, "Bóksögur," 216. Gender roles and the problems associated with treating "men" and "women" as totally discrete categories are discussed in Magnússon,

"Kynjasögur á 19. og 20. öld," 137–77. A far more profitable approach would seem to be to assume that every individual is endowed with both masculine and feminine characteristics to which they turn under differing circumstances.

46 *Rímur* are rhymed narrative poems, usually on ancient themes, for example, from the sagas or classical literature. They differ from ballads (*sagnadansar*) in being composed in more highly wrought meters and language and, ostensibly at least, usually reflecting heroic or literary values rather than popular peasant ones. They remained the dominant form of Icelandic verse from the Middle Ages until the nineteenth century.

47 Dúason, *Einu sinni var*, 69.

48 Dúason, *Einu sinni var*, 69.

49 Dúason, *Einu sinni var*, 69.

50 Árnason, *Ljúfa vor*, 29–30.

51 Árnason, *Ljúfa vor*, 30.

52 Sigurbjarnarson, *Ævisaga Hafsteins Sigurbjarnarsonar*, 100.

53 Holger Kjær 1: 5–6: Ethnological Collection [Þjóðháttasafn] of the National Museum of Iceland. See reference in Helgason, *Hetjan og höfundurinn*, 32. The passage quoted by Jón Karl comes from papers held by the Ethnological Collection of the National Museum of Iceland, specifically from Holger Kjær's research carried out in 1930 into upbringing and education in rural Icelandic society. Kjær collected a considerable body of material, concentrating on people born in the middle years of the nineteenth century. The citations that follow are also taken from Jón Karl's book. This particular quotation was used as an illustration and discussed in a lecture given by Viðar Hreinsson at Snorrastofa at Reykholt in Borgarfjörður under the title "Bókmenntir í öskustó: hugleiðingar um kolbíta fornsagnanna og bókelska almúgamenn" (Literature in the ash pit: animadversions on the coal-biter in the sagas and proletarian bookworms). Jón Karl wrote another book on the use of the sagas in modern times. See Jón Karl Helgason, *Echoes of Valhalla. The Afterlife of the Eddas and Sagas* (London: Reaktion Books, 2017).

54 Viðar Hreinsson, "Bókmenntir í öskustó". See Kristín Sigfúsdóttir, *Rit Kristínar Sigfúsdóttur: I (Writings of Kristín Sigfúsdóttir*, Vol. 1) (Reykjavík: Ísafoldarprentsmiðja, 1949), 95. The quotation comes from the section of the book titled "Í föðurgarði: bernskuminningar" (In my father's home: childhood memories).

55 For an illuminating analysis of the various courses open to young farmers' sons on entering into life and the consequences these could have for their futures, see Palle Ove Christiansen, "Culture and Contrasts in a Northern European Village: Lifestyles among Manorial Peasants in 18th-Century Denmark," *Journal of Social History* 29, no. 2 (1995): 275–94.

56 See, for example, the lecture "Bókmenntir í öskustó" cited above. Viðar Hreinsson delivered a lecture on similar subjects at the Sagnaþing í héraði (Local History

Conference) in 1997 under the title "Vandræðaunglingar í sveit" (Juvenile delinquents in rural areas).
57 Helgi Haraldsson, "Höfundur Njálu" (The Author of Njáls saga), *Tíminn*, 9 April 1948.
58 Kristín Geirsdóttir, "Fáein alþýðleg orð" (A Few Words in Everyday Language), *Skírnir* 153 (1979): 6.
59 Kristín Geirsdóttir, "Hugleiðing um fornsögur" (Thoughts about the sagas), *Skírnir* 164 (1990): 34–55; Kristín Geirsdóttir, "Hvað er sannleikur?" (What is truth?), *Skírnir* 169 (1995): 399–422.
60 The story is found in the *Book of Settlements* (Landnámabók), ch. 51. Stanzas in Old Norse skaldic meters are customarily referenced by their first line, as here; the intricacies of skaldic syntax make it pointless to attempt a translation.
61 Geirsdóttir, "Hvað er sannleikur?" 400–1.
62 Geirsdóttir, "Hvað er sannleikur?" 401.
63 Davíð Ólafsson, "Vernacular Literacy Practices in Nineteenth-Century Icelandic Scribal Culture," in *Att läsa och att skriva: Två vågor av vardagligt skriftbruk i Norden 1800–2000*. Nordliga studier, 3, ed. Anna-Catrine Edlund (Umeå: Umeå Universitet og Kungl. Skytteanska Samfundet, 2012), 65–85; Ólafsson, "Scribal Communities in Iceland," 40–9.

Chapter 7

1 Kristján Sigurðsson, *Þegar veðri slotar* ([place of publication unspecified], 1954), 16.
2 Sigurðsson, *Þegar veðri slotar*, 35.
3 Björn Jóhannsson, *Frá Valdastöðum til Veturhúsa. Brot úr endurminningum* (*Valdastaðir to Veturhús. Fragments of Memoir*) (Reykjavík: Fróði, 1964), 25.
4 Matthías Jochumsson, *Sögukaflar af sjálfum mér* (*Short Tales of Myself*), 57.
5 Jochumsson, *Sögukaflar af sjálfum mér*, 44–5.
6 Elías Halldórsson, *Heiðinginn. Minningar og skuggsjá* (*The Heathen*) (Reykjavík: Höfundur, 1956), 15.
7 See Garðarsdóttir, *Saving the Child*.
8 I discuss this in detail in my book *Menntun, ást og sorg* (*Education, Love and Grief*), 165–214.
9 Indriði Einarsson, *Sjeð og lifað. Endurminningar* (*Seen and Lived*) (Reykjavík: Bókaverslun Sigfúsar Eymundssonar, 1936), 40. I have addressed this subject and others relating to mortality in my doctoral thesis and in some essays. See, for example, Magnússon, "Alþýðumenning á Íslandi 1850–1940," 265–320. Sigurður Gylfi Magnússon, "'Dauðinn er lækur, en lífið er strá.' Líf og dauði á nítjándu öld" (Death is a river and life is a blade of grass), in *Eitt sinn skal hver deyja. Dauðinn*

í íslenskum veruleika, ed. Sigurjón Baldur Hafsteinsson (Reykjavík: Mokka Press, 1996), 128–42.
10 Jón Kr. Lárusson, Ævisaga Breiðfirðings. Endurminningar (A Biography of a Breiðafjörður Man) (Reykjavík: Ísafold, 1949), 7.
11 Guðrún Guðmundsdóttir, Minningar úr Hornafirði (Memoirs from Hornafjörður) (Reykjavík: Hið íslenska bókmenntafélag, 1975), 51–2.
12 Guðmundsdóttir, Minningar úr Hornafirði, 53.
13 Málfríður Einarsdóttir, Samastaður í tilverunni (A Place in Existence) (Reykjavík: Ljóðhús, 1977), 46.
14 Sigurður Jón Guðmundsson, Til sjós og lands. Minningar frá liðnum árum (At Sea and On Land) (Reykjavík: Letur, 1978), 15.
15 Guðmundsson, Til sjós og lands, 16.
16 Jónsson, Árblik og aftanskin. Nokkrir æviþættir (Daybreak and Evening Light), 20. See also Sigfússon, Ferðin frá Brekku. Minningar I (The Journey from Brekka), 51–2.
17 Dúason, Einu sinni var, 28.
18 Dúason, Einu sinni var, 29.
19 Valdimar J. Eylands, Úr Víðidal til Vesturheims: Minningar dr. Valdimars J. Eylands prests í Vesturheimi, skráð af honum sjálfum (From Víðidalur to the New World) (Reykjavík: Bókhlaðan, 1981), 15. Valdimar states that in his misery he turned increasingly to the Icelandic sagas for comfort.
20 Lárus J. Rist, Synda eða stökkva. Endurminningar (To Swim or Sink) (Akureyri: Sigurjón Rist, 1947), 17.
21 Jón H. Þorbergsson, Ævidagar (Days of a Life) (Akureyri: Bókaforlag Odds Björnssonar, 1964), 14.
22 Jónas Þórbergsson, Bréf til sonar míns. Horft um öxl. Æviminningar I (A Letter to My Son) (Hafnafjörður: Skuggsjá, 1966), 28–33.
23 Þórbergsson, Bréf til sonar míns, 33.
24 Arnljótur Ólafsson, "Um mannfjölda á Íslandi," in Skýrslur um landshagi 1 (About Population in Iceland) (Copenhagen: Hið íslenska bókmenntafélag, 1858), 387. A similar opinion is also expressed by a physician toward the end of the nineteenth century, who actually asks mothers who had lost their children if they would take a close look at their own behavior and evaluate whether they could not be blamed for the death of their children. In his mind, it was not a conscious act but rather ignorance. See Jónas Jónassen, Barnfóstran: Fyrirsögn handa alþýðu um rjetta meðferð á ungbörnum (The Nanny) (Reykjavík: Ísafoldarprentsmiðja, 1888), 5.
25 See discussions on emotional communities and the history of emotions in the following studies: Barbara H. Rosenwein, "Worrying about Emotions in History," American Historical Review 107 (June 2002): 842–3; Peter N. Stearns and Carol Z. Stearns, "Emotionology: Clarifying the History of Emotions and Emotional Standards," American Historical Review 90 (1985): 813–36; An Emotional History

of the United States, eds. Peter N. Stearns and Jan Lewis (New York: New York Universtiy Press, 1998); Barbara H. Rosenwein, *Emotional Communities in the Early Middle Ages* (Ithaca: Cornell University Press, 2006).

26 Here, Ásmundur makes reference to *Sonatorrek* (Lament for My Sons), a classic of Icelandic verse from the *Saga of Egill Skallagrímsson*. Farmer-warrior-poet Egill was so stricken by the deaths of two sons that he took to his bed and refused to eat. Ultimately, his recovery was aided by the composition of his great poem to his lost sons. See Ásmundur Helgason, *Á sjó og landi. Endurminningar* (Reykjavík: Ísafold, 1949), 136.

27 Sigfús Magnússon, "Endurminningar Guðrúnar Björnsdóttur. Lýsing á aldaranda, þjóðháttum, siðum og venjum um og eftir miðja síðustu öld" (Memoirs of Guðrún Björnsdóttir), *Skuggsjá* 1(1944): 42.

28 Magnússon, "From Children's Point of View," 295–323.

29 See Einar Sigurbjörnsson's introduction to the development of children's catechism books and their content: *Helgakver. Lærdómsrit Bókmenntafélagsins*. Introduction by Einar Sigurbjörnsson (Reykjavík: Hið íslenska bókmenntafélaga, 2000), 9–63.

30 Sigurður Árnason, *Með straumnum. Nokkur æviminningar* (*With the Stream*) (Reykjavík: Bókaútgáfa Guðjóns Ó., 1950). 43.

31 Sveinn Víkingur, *Myndir daganna. I. Bernskuárin* (*Flashback of the Day*) (Akureyri: Kvöldvökuútgáfan, 1965), 188.

32 Gunnar Benediktsson, *Stiklað á stóru. Frá bernsku til brauðleysis* (*Highlights*) (Reykjavík: Örn og Örlygur, 1976), 13–14.

33 Sigurbjarnarson, *Ævisaga Hafsteins Sigurbjarnarsonar*, 116.

34 See Pétur Pétursson's excellent discussion of the subject in *Church and Social Change*. Also *Landsins útvöldu synir. Ritgerðir skólapilta Lærða skólans í íslenskum stíl 1846–1904* (*The Nation's Chosen Sons*), ed. Bragi Þorgrímur Ólafsson. Sýnisbók íslenskrar alþýðumenningar 7 (Reykjavík: Háskólaútgáfan, 2004).

35 Friðrik Hallgrímsson, *Margslungið mannlíf. Sjálfsævisaga* (*Complicated Human Life*) (Akureyri: Bókaforlag Odds Björnssonar, 1979), 16–17.

36 Guðmundur J. Einarsson, *Kalt er við Kórbak. Ævisaga og aldarfarslýsing* (*Cold It Is at Kórbak*) (Hafnafjörður: Skuggsjá, 1964), 10.

37 Þorbjörn Björnsson, *Skyggnzt um af heimahlaði* (*The View from the Home Farm*) ([place of publication unspecified], 1954), 57–8.

38 Björnsson, *Skyggnzt um af heimahlaði*, 59.

39 Sigurbjarnarson, *Ævisaga Hafsteins Sigurbjarnarsonar*, 73–4.

40 See a discussion of the public discourse on these matters: Magnússon, *Menntun, ást og sorg*, 87–113.

41 Þórir Bergsson, *Endurminningar* (*Memoirs*), eds. Hannes Pétursson and Kristmundur Bjarnason (Akureyri: BOB, 1984), b23.

42 See Hálfdanarson, "Old Provinces," 43.

43 Sigurður Nordal, "Literary Heritage," in *Iceland 1986*, eds. Jóhannes Nordal and Valdimar Kristinsson (Reykjavík: Central Bank of Iceland, 1987), 73.
44 Hannes J. Magnússon, *Hetjur hversdagslífsins. Nokkrar þjóðlífsmyndir frá upphafi 20. aldarinnar* (*Everyday Heroes*) (Akureyri: Norðri, 1953), 237.
45 See Jónas Jónasson, *Hofdala Jónas: sjálfsævisaga, frásögn, þættir, bundið mál* (*Jónas from Hofdalir*) (Akureyri: Bókaútgáfa Odds Björnssonar, 1979), 66–7.
46 See Dúason, *Einu sinni var*, 69.
47 Sigurður Árnason (b. 1877), *Með straumnum. Nokkrar æviminningar* (*With the Stream*) (Reykjavík: Bókaútgáfa Guðjóns Ó., 1950), 40.
48 Eylands, *Úr Víðidal til Vesturheims*, 17.
49 Eylands, *Úr Víðidal til Vesturheims*, 17.
50 Ólína Jónsdóttir, *Ég vitja þín æska. Minningar og stökur* (*I Visit You, My Youth*) (Akureyri: Norðri, 1946), 25.
51 Egil Johansson, "The History of Literacy in Sweden," in *Literacy and Social Developments in the West: A Reader*, ed. Harvey J. Graff (Cambridge: Cambridge University Press, 1980), 182.
52 Harvey J. Graff makes a point about this phenomenon: "Since the twelfth century, writers and poets had recorded the history of Iceland, and had given the people a national and historical consciousness rare, and probably unique, in the West." See Harvey J. Graff, *The Legacies of Literacy: Continuities and Contradictions in Western Culture and Society* (Bloomington: Indiana University Press, 1987), 227. See a new and exciting study on the meaning of literacy by Harvey Graff, *Searching for Literacy: The Social and Intellectual Orgins of Literacy Studies* (London: Palgrave Macmillan, 2022).
53 Guðmundur Jónsson, *Endurminningar Guðmundar frá Nesi, ritaðar af honum sjálfum* (Reykjavík: [publisher unknown], 1948), 11.
54 It is difficult to evaluate exactly how many copies of the *Parliamentary Gazette* were published in the nineteenth century, but according to some documents from the Parliamentary Archive there were somewhere between 600 and 1,000 copies annually. We know that it was sent to every community in the country, that is, to the local council leader, for free. Members of the parliament also received it for free. But it was also sold to subscribers. The most important thing is that it reached each community, because we know from our sources that people passed books around to other farms. See, for example, Árni Gíslason, *Gullkistan. Endurminningar Árna Gíslasonar um fiskveiðar við Ísafjarðardjúp árin 1880–1905* (*The Treasure Chest*) (Ísafjörður: Ísrún, 1944), 115. Hence, it is reasonable to assume that the *Parliamentary Gazette* was widely read. This information is based on an interview with Eiríkur Eiríksson, an archivist at the Parliamentary Archive, in 1989. See Alþt. 1845, 34. Also based on letters from the Speaker of the House both to the printing press and the agent who distributed the *Parliamentary Gazette*: Letter no. 2, 1845; Letter no. 14, 1847.

55 See Guðbjörg Jónsdóttir, *Minningar frá bernsku og æskuárum* (*Memories from Years of Childhood and Youth*) (Reykjavík: Prentsmiðjan Gutenberg, 1929), 42.
56 See, for example, Guðjón Jónsson, *Á bernskustöðvum* (*From the Place of My Birth*) (Reykjavík: Ísafold, 1946), 32; Dúason, *Einu sinni var*, 69.
57 Einar Jónsson, *Minningar* (Reykjavík: Bókfellsútgáfan, 1944), 83.
58 Einarsson, *Sjéð og lifað*, 41.
59 Viktoría Bjarnadóttir, *Vökustundir að vestan* (*Wakeful Nights in the West*) (Reykjavík: Ísafold, 1958), 62. See also Matthias Þórðarson, *Litið til baka. Endurminningar. Æskuárin. Fiskveiðar og önnur störf* I (*Looking Back*) (Reykjavík: Leiftur, 1946); Kristinn Guðlaugsson, *Bernskuminningar Kristins á Núpi* (*Childhood Memories*) (Reykjavík: Menn og minjar. Íslenskur fróðleikur og skemmtun IX, 1960), 85.

Face 2 Face with the General Public

1 Jón Gísli Högnason, *Vinir í varpa. Æskudagar* (*Friends in the Neighborhood*) (Akureyri: Bókaforlag Odds Björnssonar, 1980), 178.
2 Björnsson, *Æskustöðvar*, 15–16.
3 Björnsson, *Æskustöðvar*, 17.
4 Björnsson, *Æskustöðvar*, 104–5.
5 Björnsson, *Æskustöðvar*, 105.
6 Magnússon, *Menntun, ást og sorg*, 69–86.
7 See Jónas Jónasson's classic volume, *Íslenzkir þjóðhættir* (*Icelandic Folkways*), 2nd ed. (Reykjavík: Jónas og Halldór Rafnar, 1945).
8 The ideas argued here owe much to White's *Metahistory*. White's book, one of the seminal works of historical analysis, ranges across such matters as how the language of any text defines how its matter is presented, establishes systematic parameters for people's thinking, and directs it into specific modes of expression.
9 Torfi H. Tulinius, "Kynjasögur úr fortíð og framandi löndum: riddarasögur og fornaldarsögur" (Fantastical tales from long ago and far away: chivalric and legendary sagas), in *Íslensk bókmenntasaga* II, ed. Vésteinn Ólason (Reykjavík: Mál og menning: 1993), 226.
10 Magnússon, *Menntun, ást og sorg*, 45–68.
11 Ólafsson, *Frá degi til dags*.

Select Bibliography

Published works

Adams, Timothy Dow. *Telling Lies in Modern American Autobiography*. Chapel Hill: University of North Carolina Press, 1990.
Adams, Timothy Dow. *Light Writing and Life Writing: Photography in Autobiography*. Chapel Hill: University of North Carolina Press, 1999.
African American Autobiography: A Collection of Critical Essays, edited by William Andrews. Englewood Cliffs: Longman, 1993.
Agnarsdóttir, Anna. *Sir Joseph Banks, Iceland and the North Atlantic 1772–1820. Journals, Letters and Documents*. London: The Hakluyt Society and Routledge, 2016.
Agnarsson, Sveinn. "Icelandic Economic History: Fishing, Farming and Modernization." *Revue d'histoire Nordique* 20, no. 1 (2015): 83–108.
Amelang, James. *The Flight of Icarus: Artisan Autobiography in Early Modern Europe*. Stanford: Stanford University Press, 1998.
Anderson, Linda R. *Women and Autobiography in the Twentieth Century. Remembered Futures*. London: Prentice Hall, 1997.
Ankersmit, Frank. "Remembering the Holocaust: Mourning and Melancholia." In *Historical Perspectives on Memory*, edited by Anne Ollila, 91–113. Helsinki: Finnish Historical Society, 1999.
The Annals of Labour: Autobiographies of British Working-Class People 1820–1920, edited by John Burnett. Bloomington: Indiana University Press, 1974.
Appuhn, Karl. "Microhistory." In *Encyclopedia of European Social History. From 1350 to 2000*, vol. 1, edited by Peter N. Stearns, 105–12. New York: Charles Scribner's Sons, 2001.
Aurell, Jaume. "Making History by Contextualizing Oneself: Autobiography as Historiographical Intervention." *History and Theory* 54 (May 2015): 244–68.
Autobiography: Essays Theoretical and Critical, edited by James Olney. Princeton: Princeton University Press, 1980.
Autobiography by Women in German, edited by Merrid Puw Davies, Beth Linklater, and Gisela Shaw. Oxford: Peter Lang, 2000.
Bell, Rudolph M. and Judith C. Brown. "Renaissance Sexuality and the Florentine Archives: An Exchange." *Renaissance Quarterly* 40 (1987): 485–511.
Bertaux, Daniel. "From The Life-History Approach to the Transformation of Sociological Practice." In *Biography and Society. The Life History Approach in the Social Sciences*, edited by Daniel Bertaux, 31–40. Beverly Hills: Saga, 1981.

Bertens, Hans. *The Idea of the Postmodern*. London: Routledge, 1995.

Bertram, Laurie Kristine. *The Viking Immigrants. Icelandic North Americans*. Toronto: University of Toronto Press, 2020.

Between Sociology and History. Essays on Microhistory, Collective Action, and Nation-Building, edited by Anna-Maija Castrén, Karkku Lonkila, and Matti Peltonen. Helsinki: Finnish Literature Society, 2004.

The Biographical Turn. Lives in History, edited by Hans Renders, Binne de Haan, and Joanne Harmsma. London: Routledge, 2017.

Blassingame, John W. *The Slave Community. Plantation Life in the Antebellum South*. New York: Oxford University Press, 1972.

Broughton, Trev. *Men of Letters. Writing Lives: Masculinity and Literary Auto/biography in the Late Victorian Period*. London: Routledge, 1999.

Brown, Richard D. "Microhistory and the Post-Modern Challenge." *Journal of the Early Republic* 23 (2003): 1–20.

Buchmann, Marlis. *The Script of Life in Modern Society: Entry into Adulthood in a Changing World*. Chicago: University of Chicago Press, 1989.

Burke, Peter. *Eyewitnessing: The Uses of Images as Historical Evidence*. London: Reaktion Books, 2001.

Burke, Victoria E. and Jonathan Gibson. *Early Modern Women's Manuscript Writing. Selected Essays of the Trinity/Trent Colloquium*. Hampshire and Burlington: Ashgate Pub Ltd., 2004.

Cabrera, Miguel A. "The Linguistic Approach or Return to Subjectivism? In Search of an Alternative to Social History," translated by Marie McMahon, *Social History* 24, no. 1 (1999): 74–89.

Coe, Richard. *When the Grass was Taller. Autobiography and the Experience of Childhood*. New Haven: Yale University Press, 1984.

The Complete Sagas of Icelanders, 5 vols, edited by Viðar Hreinsson. Reykjavík: Leifur Eiríksson, 1997.

Confino, Alon. "*AHR Forum*: Collective Memory and Cultural History: Problems of Method." *American Historical Review* 102 (December 1997): 1386–403.

Connor, Steven. *Postmodernist Culture: An Introduction to Theories of the Contemporary*, 2nd ed. London: Wiley-Blackwell, 1997.

Contolling Time and Shaping the Self: Developments in Autobiographical Writing since the Sixteenth Century, edited by Arianne Baggerman, Rudolf M. Dekker, and Michael James Mascuch. Egodocuments and History Series 3. Leiden: Brill, 2011.

Coslett, Tess, Celia Lury, and Penny Summerfield. *Feminism and Autobiography. Texts, Theories, Methods*. London: Routledge, 2000.

Crane, Susan A. "*AHR Forum*: Writing the Individual Back into Collective Memory." *American Historical Review* 102 (December 1997): 1372–85.

Critical Junctions: Anthropology and History Beyond the Cultural Turn, edited by D. Kalb and H. Tak. London: Berghahn Books, 2005.

Darnton, Robert. *The Great Cat Massacre and Other Episodes in French Cultural History*. New York: Vintage Books. A Division of Random House, 1984.

Davis, Natalie Zemon. *The Return of Martin Guerre*. Cambridge, MA: Harvard University Press, 1983.

Davis, Natalie Zemon. *Fiction in the Archives: Pardon Tales and Their Tellers in Sixteenth-Century France*. Stanford: Stanford University Press, 1987.

Davis, Natalie Zemon. "On the Lame." *American Historical Review* 93 (1988): 572–603.

Davis, Natalie Zemon. "Who Owns History?" *Historical Perspectives on Memory*, edited by Anne Ollila, 19–34. Helsinki: SHS, 1999.

Dawes, Robyn. *House of Cards: Psychology and Psychotherapy Built on Myth*. New York: Free Press, 1996.

Dekker, Rudolf. "Jacques Presser's Heritage: Egodocuments in the Study of History." *Memoria y Civilización* 5 (2002): 13–37.

Destiny Obscure: Autobiographies of Childhood, Education and Family from the 1820s to the 1920s, edited by John Burnett. London: Penguin Books, 1982.

Dollard, J. *Criteria for the Life History*. New Haven: Yale University Press, 1935.

Domańska, Ewa. *Encounters. Philosophy of History after Postmodernism*. Charlottesville: University Press of Virginia, 1998.

Egan, Susanna. *Patterns of Experience in Autobiography*. Chapel Hill: The University of North Carolina Press, 1984.

Egan, Susanna. *Mirror Talk. Genres of Crisis in Contemporary Autobiography*. Chapel Hill: The University of North Carolina Press, 1999.

Egholm, Liv. "Peasant Diaries as a Microhistorical Investigation." In *Writing Peasants: Studies on Peasant Literacy in Early Modern Northern Europe*, edited by Klaus-Joachim Lorenzen-Schmidt and Bjørn Poulsen, 271–84. Århus: Landbohistorisk selskab, 2002.

Egmond, Florike and Peter Mason. *The Mammoth and the Mouse: Microhistory and Morphology*. Baltimore: Johns Hopkins University Press, 1997.

Eley, Geoff. "Labor History, Social History, *Alltagsgeschichte*: Experience, Culture, and the Politics of the Everyday. A New Direction for German Social History?" *Journal of Modern History* 61 (June 1989): 297–343.

Encyclopedia of European Social History. From 1350 to 2000, vols. 1–6, edited by Peter N. Stearns. New York: Charles Scribner's Sons, 2001.

Finlay, Robert. "The Refashioning of Martin Guerre." *The American Historical Review* 93 (1988): 553–71.

Freeman, Mark. *Rewriting the Self. History, Memory and Narrative*. London: Routledge, 1993.

The French Worker. Autobiographies from the Early Industrial Era, edited and translated by Mark Taugott. Berkeley: University of California Press, 1993.

Frisch, Andrea. *The Invention of the Eyewitness*. Chapel Hill: The University of North Carolina Press, 2004.

Fuery, Patrick and Nick Mansfield. *Cultural Studies and the New Humanities. Concepts and Controversies.* Melbourne: Oxford University Press, 1997.

Garðarsdóttir, Ólöf. *Saving the Child: Regional, Cultural and Social Aspects of the Infant Mortality Decline in Iceland, 1770–1920.* Umeå: Umeå University Press, 2002.

Garraty, John A. *The Nature of Biography.* New York: Michigan State University Press, 1957.

Gedi, Noa and Yigal Elam. "Collective Memory—What Is It?" *History and Memory* 8 (Spring/Summer 1996): 30–50.

Genovese, Eugene D. *Roll, Jordan, Roll. The World the Slaves Made.* New York: Vintage Books. A Division of Random House, 1972.

Getting a Life. Everyday Uses of Autobiography, edited by Sidonie Smith and Julia Watson. Minneapolis: University of Minnesota Press, 1996.

Gilmore, Leigh. "The Mark of Autobiography: Postmodernism, Autobiography, and Genre." In *Autobiography and Postmodernism,* edited by Kathleen Ashley, Leigh Gilmore, and Gerald Peters, 3–18. Amherst: University of Massachusetts Press, 1994.

Gilmore, Leigh. *The Limits of Autobiography. Trauma and Testimony.* Ithaca: Cornell University Press, 2001.

Ginzburg, Carlo. *The Cheese and the Worms: The Cosmos of a Sixteenth-Century Miller.* Baltimore: Johns Hopkins University Press, 1980.

Ginzburg, Carlo. "Clues: Roots of an Evidential Paradigm." In Carlo Ginzburg, *Clues, Myths, and the Historical Method,* translated by John and Anne Tedescbi, 96–125. Baltimore: Johns Hopkings University Press, 1989.

Ginzburg, Carlo. "Microhistory: Two or Three Things That I know about It." *Critical Inquiry* 20 (Autumn 1993): 10–35.

Ginzburg, Carlo. "Microhistory and World History." In *The Cambridge World History,* edited by Jerry H. Bentley, Sanjay Subrahmanyam, and Merry E. Wiesner-Hanks, 446–73. London: Cambridge University Press, 2015.

Ginzburg, Carlo and Carlo Poni. "The Name and the Game: Unequal Exchange and the Historical Marketplace." In *Microhistory and the Lost People of Europe,* edited by Edward Muir and Guido Ruggiero, translated by Eren Branch, 1–10. Baltimore: Johns Hopkins University Press, 1991.

Gíslason, Magnús. *Kvällsvaka. En isländsk kulturtradition belyst genom studier i bondebefolkningens vardagsliv och miljö under senare hälften av 1800-talet och början av 1900-talet.* Studia Ethnologica Upsaliensia 2. Uppsala: Uppsala Universitet, 1977.

Graff, Harvey J. *The Legacies of Literacy: Continuities and Contradictions in Western Culture and Society.* Bloomington: Indiana University Press, 1987.

Graff, Harvey J. *Conflicting Paths. Growing Up in America.* Cambridge, MA: Harvard University Press, 1995.

Graff, Harvey J. "The Shock of the 'New' (Histories). Social Science Histories and Historical Literacies." *Social Science History* 24, no. 4 (Winter 2001): 484–533.

Graff, Harvey J. "History's War of the Wor(l)ds." In *Sögustrið. Greinar og frásagnir um hugmyndafræði,* 475–81. Reykjavík: ReykjavíkurAkademían, 2007.

Graff, Harvey J. *Searching for Literacy: The Social and Intellectual Origins of Literacy Studies*. London: Palgrave Macmillan, 2022.

Gregory, Brad S. "Is Small Beautiful? Microhistory and the Writing of Everyday Life." Review essay in *History and Theory* 38, no. 1(1999): 100–10.

Guðmundsdóttir, Gunnþóra. *Borderlines: Autobiography and Fiction in Postmodern Life Writing*. New York: Rodopi, 2003.

Gunnlaugsson, Gísli Ágúst. *Family and Household in Iceland 1801–1930. Studies in the Relationship between Demographic and Socio-Economic Development, Social Legislation and Family and Household Structures*. Uppsala: Acta Universitatis Upsaliensis, 1988.

Guttormsson, Loftur. *Childhood, Youth and Upbringing in the Age of Absolutism. An Exercise in Socio-Demographic Analysis*. The University of Iceland Historical Series, edited by Anna Agnarsdóttir and Ólöf Garðarsdóttir. Reykjavík: Iceland University Press, 2017.

Hálfdanarson, Guðmundur. "Old Provinces, Modern Nations: Political Responses to State Integration in Late Nineteenth and Early Twentieth-Century Iceland and Brittany." Ph.D. diss., Cornell University, 1991.

Hálfdanarson, Guðmundur. "Private Spaces and Private Lives: Privacy, Intimacy, and Culture in Icelandic 19th-Century Rural Homes." In *Power and Culture: New Perspectives on Spatiality in European History*, edited by Pieter François, Taina Syrjämaa, and Henri Terho, 109–24. Pisa: Plus-Pisa University Press, 2008.

Halldórsdóttir, Erla Hulda. "Fragments of Lives—The Use of Private Letters in Historical Research." *NORA. Nordic Journal of Women's Studies* 15, no. 1 (2007): 35–49.

Halldórsdóttir, Erla Hulda. "'Don't You Forget Your Always Loving Sister': Writing as a Social and Cultural Capital." In *Vernacular Literacies—Past, Present and Future*, edited by Ann-Catrine Edlund, Lars-Erik Edlund, and Susanne Haugen, 181–92. Umeå: Umeå University and Royal Skyttean Society, 2014.

Hallgrímsdóttir, Guðný. *A Tale of a Fool? A Microhistory of an 18th-Century Peasant Woman*. London: Routledge, 2019.

Hareven, Tamara K. "Introduction: The Historical Study of the Life Course." In *Transition: The Family and the Life Course in Historical Perspective*, edited by Tamara K. Hareven, 1–16. New York: Academic Press, 1978.

Helgason, Jón Karl, *Echoes of Valhalla. The Afterlife of the Eddas and Sagas*. London: Reaktion Books, 2017.

Historiography: Critical Concepts in Historical Studies I–V, edited by Robert M. Burns. London, Routledge, 2006.

History from Crime, edited by Edward Muir and Guido Ruggiero, translation by Corrada Biazzo Curry, Margaret A. Gallucci, and Mary M. Gallucci. Baltimore: Johns Hopkins University Press, 1994.

Hoffer, Peter Charles. *Past Imperfect: Facts, Fictions, and Fraud in the Writing of American History*. New York: Public Affairs, 2004.

Hreinsson, Viðar. *Wakeful Nights Stephan G. Stephansson: Icelandic-Canadian Poet*. Calgary: Benson Ranch Inc., 2013.

Huges-Warrington, Marnie. *Big and Little Histories. Sizing up Ethics in Historiography*. London: Routledge, 2022.

The Icelandic Adventures of Pike Ward, edited by K. J. Findley. Exeter: Amphora Press, 2018.

Iggers, Georg G. *Historiography in the Twentieth Century. From Scientific Objectivity to the Postmodern Challenge*. Hanover: Wesleyan University Press, 1997.

Interpreting Women's Lives. Feminist Theory and Personal Narratives, edited by the Personal Narratives Group. Bloomington: Indiana University Press, 1989.

Jenkins, Keith. *Re-Thinking History*. London: Routledge, 1991.

Jóhannesson, Guðni Th. *The History of Iceland*. The Greenwood Histories of the Modern Nations. Santa Barbara: ABC-CLIO, 2013.

Jónsson, Már. *Arnas Magnæus Philologus (1663–1739)*. Viborg: University Press of Southern Denmark, 2012.

Justice, George L. and Nathan Tinker. *Women's Writing and the Circulation of Ideas: Manuscript Publication in England 1550–1800*. Cambridge: Cambridge University Press, 2010.

Karlsson, Gunnar. *Iceland's 1100 Years: The History of a Marginal Society*. London: Gardners Books, 2000.

Kohlin, Martin. "Biography: Account, Text, Method." In *Biography and Society. The Life History Approach in the Social Sciences*, edited by Daniel Bertaux, 61–75. Beverly Hills: Saga, 1981.

Kristjánsdóttir, Steinunn. *The Awakening of Christianity in Iceland. Discovery of a Timber Church and Graveyard at Þórarinsstadir in Seyðisfjörður*. Gothenburg: Gotarc, 2004.

Kristjánsdóttir, Steinunn. *Monastic Iceland*. London: Routledge, 2022.

Kuehn, Thomas. "Reading Microhistory: The Example of Giovanni and Lusanna." *Journal of Modern History* 61 (1989): 512–34.

Kuismin, Anne. "From Family Inscriptions to Autobiographical Novels: Motives of Writing in Grassroots Life Stories in 19th-Century Finland." In *White Field, Black Seeds: Nordic Literacy Practices in the Long Nineteenth-Century*, edited by Matthew James Driscoll and Anna Kuismin, 101–19. Helsinki: Finnish Literature Society, 2013.

Lebert, Stephan and Norbert Lebert. *My Father's Keeper. The Children of the Nazi Leaders—An Intimate History of Damage and Denial*, translated by Julian Evans. London: Abacus Book, 2002.

Lejeune, Philippe. *On Autobiography*, edited by Paul John Eakin and translated by Katherine Leary. Minneapolis: University of Minnesota Press, 1989.

Liljewall, Britt. "'Self-written Lives' or Why did Peasants Write Autobiographies?" In *Writing Peasants. Studies on Peasant Literacy in Early Modern Northern Europe*, edited by Klaus-Joachim Lorenzen-Schmidt and Bjørn Poulsen, 210–33. Kerteminde: Landbohistorisk Selskab, 2002.

Liljewall, Britt. "Recollections of Reading and Writing: Another Picture of Swedish Literacy." In *White Field, Black Seeds: Nordic Literacy Practices in the Long*

Nineteenth-Century, edited by Matthew James Driscoll and Anna Kuismin, 30–9. Helsinki: Finnish Literature Society, 2013.

Loriga, Sabina. "The Role of the Individual in History: Biographical and Historical Writing in the Nineteenth and the Twentieth Century." In *Theoretical Discussions of Biography: Approaches from History Microhistory, and Life Writing*, edited by Hans Renders and Binne de Haan, 113–41. Lewiston: The Edwin Mellen Press, 2013.

Love, Harold. *Scribal Publication in Seventeenth Century England*. Oxford: Oxford University Press, 1993.

Love, Harold. *The Culture and Commerce of Texts: Scribal Publication in Seventeenth Century England*. Amherst: University of Massachusetts Press, 1998.

Lüdtke, Alf. "Organizational Order or *Eigensinn*? Workers' Privacy and Workers' Politics in Imperial Germany." In *Rites of Power: Symbolism, Ritual, and Politics since the Middle Ages*, edited by Sean Wilentz, 303–33. Philadelphia: University of Pennsylvania Press, 1985.

Lüdtke, Alf. "Introduction: What is the History of Everyday Life and Who are its Practitioners?" In *The History of Everyday Life: Reconstructing Historical Experiences and Ways of Life*, edited by Alf Lüdtke and translated by William Templer. Princeton: Princeton University Press, 1995.

Lüdtke, Alf. "What Happened to the 'Fiery Red Glow'? Workers' Experiences and German Fascism." In *The History of Everyday Life: Reconstructing Historical Experiences and Ways of Life*, edited by Alf Lüdtke and translated by William Templer, 198–251. Princeton: Princeton University Press, 1995.

Magnússon, Finnur. *The Hidden Class: Culture and Class in a Maritime Setting—Iceland 1880–1942*. Aarhus: Aarhus University Press, 1990.

Magnússon, Magnús S. *Iceland in Transition. Labour and Socio-economic Change Before 1940*. Lund: Ekonomisk-historiska föreningen, 1985.

Magnússon, Sigurður Gylfi. "The Continuity of Everyday Life: Popular Culture in Iceland 1850–1940." Ph.D. diss., Carnegie Mellon University, USA, 1993.

Magnússon, Sigurður Gylfi. "From Children's Point of View: Childhood in Nineteenth Century Iceland." *Journal of Social History* 29 (Winter 1995): 295–323.

Magnússon, Sigurður Gylfi. "*The Singularization of History*: Social History and Microhistory within the Postmodern State of Knowledge." *Journal of Social History* 36 (Spring 2003): 701–35.

Magnússon, Sigurður Gylfi. "Social History as 'Sites of Memory'? The Institutionalization of History: Microhistory and the Grand Narrative." *Journal of Social History Special issue* 39, no. 3 (Spring 2006): 891–913.

Magnússon, Sigurður Gylfi. *Wasteland with Words. A Social History of Iceland*. London: Reaktion Books, 2010.

Magnússon, Sigurður Gylfi. "Gender: A Useful Category in Analysis of Ego-Documents? Memory, Historical Sources and Microhistory." *Scandinavian Journal of History* 38, no. 2 (2013): 202–22.

Magnússon, Sigurður Gylfi. "Living by the Book: Form, Text, and Life Experience in Iceland." In *White Field, Black Seeds: Nordic Literacy Practices in the Long Nineteenth-Century*, edited by James Driscoll and Anna Kuismin, 53–62. Helsinki: Finnish Literature Society, 2013.

Magnússon, Sigurður Gylfi. "Tales of the Unexpected: The 'Textual Environment', Ego-Documents and a Nineteenth-Century Icelandic Love Story—An Approach in Microhistory." *Cultural and Social History* 12, no. 1 (2015): 77–94.

Magnússon, Sigurður Gylfi. "The Love Game as Expressed in Ego-Documents: The Culture of Emotions in Late Nineteenth Century Iceland." *Journal of Social History* 50, no. 1 (2016): 102–19.

Magnússon, Sigurður Gylfi. "Microhistory, Biography and Ego-documents in Historical Writing." *Revue d'historire Nordique* 20 (2016): 133–53.

Magnússon, Sigurður Gylfi. "Views into the Fragments: An Approach from a Microhistorical Perspective." *International Journal of Historical Archaeology* 20 (2016): 182–206.

Magnússon, Sigurður Gylfi. "Far-reaching Microhistory: The Use of Microhistorical Perspective in a Globalized World." *Rethinking History* 21, no. 3 (2017): 312–41.

Magnússon, Sigurður Gylfi. *Emotional Experience and Microhistory: A Life Story of a Destitute Pauper Poet in the 19th Century*. Microhistories. London: Routledge, 2021.

Magnússon, Sigurður Gylfi. *Archive, Slow Ideology and Egodocuments as Microhistorical Autobiography: Potential History*. London: Routledge, 2022.

Magnússon, Sigurður Gylfi. "Microhistory." In *The Routledge Handbook of Research Methods in the Study of Religion*, Second edition, edited by Steven Engler and Michael Stausberg, 365–74. London: Routledge, 2022.

Magnússon, Sigurður Gylfi and Davíð Ólafsson. "Barefoot Historians: Education in Iceland in the Modern Period." In *Writing Peasant: Studies on Peasant Literacy in Early Modern Northern Europe*, edited by Klaus-Joachim Lorenzen-Schmidt and Bjørn Poulsen, 175–209. Kerteminde: Landbohistorisk Selskab, 2002.

Magnússon, Sigurður Gylfi and Davíð Ólafsson. "Minor Knowledge: Microhistory and the Importance of Institutional Structures." *Quaderni Storici* 47, no. 2 (2012): 495–524.

Magnússon, Sigurður Gylfi and Davíð Ólafsson. *Minor Knowledge and Microhistory. Manuscript Culture in the Nineteenth Century*. London: Routledge, 2017.

Magnússon, Sigurður Gylfi and Davíð Ólafsson. "In the Name of Barefoot Historians: In-Between Spaces within the Icelandic Educational System." In *Education beyond Europe. Models and Traditions before Modernities*, edited by Cristiano Casalini, Edward Choi, and Ayenachew A. Woldegiyorgis, 324–44. Leiden: Brill, 2021.

Magnússon, Sigurður Gylfi, Sólveig Ólafsdóttir, og Guðrún Valgerður Stefánsdóttir. *Disability Studies Meets Microhistory: The Secret Life of Bíbí in Berlín*. Forthcoming by Routledge, 2024.

Magnússon, Sigurður Gylfi and István M. Szijártó. *What is Microhistory? Theory and Practice*. London: Routledge, 2013.

Mapping the 'I': Research on Self-Narratives in Germany Switzerland. Egodocuments and History Series 8, edited by Caudia Ulbrich, Kaspar von Greyerz, and Lorenz Heiligensetzer. Leiden: Brill, 2014.

Martin, John. "[Review essay] Journeys to the World of the Dead: the Work of Carlo Ginzburg." *Journal of Social History* 25 (Spring 1992): 613–26.

Mascuch, Michael, Rudolf Dekker, and Arianne Baggerman. "Egodocuments and History: A Short Account of the *Longue Durée*." *The Historian* 78, no. 1 (2016): 11–56.

Maurois, André. *Aspects of Biography*, translated by S. C. Roberts. New York: Cambridge University Press, 1929.

Maxwell, Ágústa Edwald. "Household Material Culture in 19th-Century Iceland: Contextualising Change in the Archaeological Record." *Post-Medieval Archaeology* 55, nr. 1 (2021): 1–14.

Maxwell, Ágústa Edwald and Gavin Lucas. "The Archaeology of Z: Household Economies in Nineteenth-Century Iceland." *Historical Archaeology* 55, nr. 2 (2021): 238–49.

Maynes, Mary Jo. "Autobiography and Class Formation in Nineteenth-Century Europe: Methodological Considerations." *Social Science History* 16 (1992): 517–37.

Maynes, Mary Jo. "The Contours of Childhood: Demography, Strategy, and Mythology of Childhood in French and German Lower-Class Autobiographies." In *The European Experience of Declining Fertility, 1850–1970. The Quiet Revolution*, edited by John R. Gillis, Louise A. Tilly, and David Levine, 101–24. Cambridge: Blackwell, 1992.

Maynes, Mary Jo. *Taking the Hard Road. Life Course in French and German Workers' Autobiographies in the Era of Industrialization*. Chapel Hill: University of North Carolina, 1995.

Maynes, Mary Jo, Jennifer L. Pierce, and Barbara Laslett. *Telling Stories. The Use of Personal Narratives in the Social Science and History*. Ithaca: Cornell University Press, 2008.

Memory and History in the Twentieth-Century Australia, edited by Kate Darian-Smith and Paula Hamilton. Melbourne: Oxford University Press, 1994.

Microhistory and the Lost People of Europe, edited by Edward Muir and Guido Ruggiero, translated by Eren Branch. Baltimore: Johns Hopkins University Press, 1991.

Microhistory and the Picaresque Novel. A First Exploration into Commensurable Perspectives, edited by Binne de Haan and Kostantin Mierau. London: Cambridge Scholars Publishing, 2014.

Mímisson, Kristján, "A Life in Stones: The Material Biography of a 17th Century Peasant from the Southern Highlands of Iceland." Ph.D. diss., in archaeology from University of Iceland, 2020.

Mímisson, Kristján and Sigurður Gylfi Magnússon. "Singularizing the Past: The History and Archaeology of the Small and Ordinary." *Journal of Social Archaeology* 14, no. 2 (2014): 131–56.

Misch, Georg. *A History of Autobiography in Antiquity I*. London: Harvard University Press, 1950.

Modell, John. *Into One's Own: From Youth to Adulthood in United States, 1920–1975*. Berkeley: University of California Press, 1989.

Mohanty, Chandra. *Feminism Without Borders: Decolonizing Theory, Practicing Solidarity*. New York: Duke University Press Books, 2003.

Morris, John N. *Version of the Self: Studies in English Autobiography from John Bunyan to John Stuart Mill*. New York: Basic Books, 1966.

Muir, Edward. "Introduction: Observing Trifles." In *Microhistory and the Lost Peoples of Europe*, edited by Edward Muir and Guido Ruggiero, translated by Eren Branch, vii–xxviii. Baltimore: Johns Hopkins University Press, 1991.

Munslow, Alun. *Deconstructing History*. London: Routledge, 1997.

Niestroj, Brigitte H. E. "Some Recent German Literature on Socialization and Childhood in Past Times." *Continuity and Change* 4 (1989): 351–4.

Nordal, Sigurður. *Icelandic Culture*, translated by Vilhjálmur T. Bjarnar. Ithaca: Cornell University Library, 1990.

Representing Lives: Women and Auto/biography, edited by Alison Donell. Basingstoke: Palgrave Macmillan, 2000.

Rewriting the Self. Histories from the Renaissance to the Present, edited by Roy Porter. London: Routledge, 1997.

Róbertsdóttir, Hrefna. *Wool and Society. Manufacturing Policy, Economic Thought and Local Production in 18th-Century Iceland*. Centrum för Danmarksstudier 21. Göteborg: Makadam, 2008.

O'Donoghue, Heather. *Old Norse-Icelandic Literature: A Short Introduction*. Oxford: Oxford University Press, 2004.

Ólafsson, Davíð. "Wordmongers: Post-Medieval Scribal Culture and the Case of Sighvatur Grímsson." Ph.D. diss., University of St Andrews, Scotland, 2008.

Ólafsson, Davíð. "Vernacular Literacy Practices in Nineteenth-Century Icelandic Scribal Culture." In *Att läsa och att skriva: Två vågor av vardagligt skriftbruk i Norden 1800–2000*. Nordliga studier 3, edited by Ann-Catrine Edlund, 65–85. Umeå: Umeå Universitet og Kungl. Skytteanska Samfundet, 2012.

Ólafsson, Davíð. "Scribal Communities in Iceland: The Case of Sighvatur Grímsson." In *White Field, Black Seeds: Nordic Literacy Practices in the Long Nineteenth Century*, edited by Anna Kuismin and Matthew J. Driscoll, 40–9. Helsinki: Finnish Literature Society, 2013.

Ólafsson, Davíð and Ólafur Rastrick. "Current Trends in Icelandic Cultural History: Practices, Products and Perspectives." *Revue d'Histoire Nordique* 20 (2016): 155–82.

Olney, James. "(Auto) Biography." *Southern Review* 22 (1986): 428–41.

Oslund, Karen. *Iceland Imagined: Nature, Culture, and Storytelling in the North Atlantic*. Seattle: University of Washington Press, 2011.

Pallares-Burke, Maria Lúcia G. *The New History. Confessions and Conversations*. Cambridge: Polity Press, 2002.

Parati, Graziella. *Public History, Private Stories. Italian Women's Autobiographies.* Minneapolis: University of Minnesota Press, 1996.

Passerini, Luisa. "Women's Personal Narratives: Myths, Experiences, and Emotions." In *Interpretating Women's Lives*, edited by Personal Narrative Group, 262–88. Bloomington: Indiana University Press, 1989.

Peltonen, Matti. "Clues, Margins and Monads. The Micro-Macro Link in Historical Research." *History and Theory* 40 (2001): 347–59.

Peterson, Linda H. *Victorian Autobiography. The Tradition of Self-Interpretation.* New Haven: Yale University Press, 1986.

Pétursson, Pétur. *Church and Social Change: A Study of the Secularization Process in Iceland, 1830–1930.* Vanersborg: Bokförlaget Plus Ultra, 1983.

Pieters, Jürgen. "New Historicism: Postmodern Historiography between Narrativism and Heterology." *History and Theory* 39 (February 2000): 21–38.

Pollock, Linda A. *Forgotten Children: Parent-Child Relations from 1500 to 1900.* Cambridge: Cambridge University Press, 1983.

Ponsonby, Arthur. *English Diaries. A Review of English Diaries From the Sixteenth to the Twentieth Century With an Introduction on Diary Writing.* London: Methuen & Company, Limited, 1923.

The Postmodern History Reader, edited by Jenkins, Keith. London: Routledge, 1997.

Putnam, Lara. "To Study the Fragments/Whole: Microhistory and the Atlantic World." *Journal of Social History* 39, no. 3 (2006): 615–30.

Scott, Joan Wallach. "Gender: A Useful Category of Historical Analysis." *American Historical Review* 91, no. 5 (December 1986): 1053–75.

Scott, Joan Wallach. "History in Crisis? The Others' Side of the Story." *American Historical Review* 94 (June 1989): 680–92.

Scott, Joan Wallach. "The Evidence of Experience." *Critical Inquiry* 17, no. 4 (Summer 1991): 773–97.

Scott-Warren, Jason. "Reconstructing Manuscript Networks: The Textual Transactions of Sir Stephan Powle." In *Communities in Early Modern England. Network, Place, Rhetoric*, edited by Alexandra Shepard and Phil Withington, 18–37. Manchester: Manchester University Press, 2000.

Sex and Gender in Historical Perspective, translated by Margaret A. Gallucci with Mary M. Gallucci and Carole C. Gallucci. Baltimore: Johns Hopkins University Press, 1990.

Simon, Zoltán Boldizsár. "Microhistory: In General." *Journal of Social History* 49, no. 1 (2015): 237–48.

Small Worlds. Method, Meaning and Narrative in Microhistory, edited by James F. Brooks, Christopher R. N. DeCorse, and John Walton. Santa Fe: School of Advanced Research Press, 2008.

Smith, Sidonie. *A Poetics of Women's Autobiography. Marginality and the Fictions of Self-Representation.* Bloomington: Indiana University Press, 1987.

Smith, Sidonie and Julia Watson. "Introduction: Situating Subjectivity in Women's Autobiographical Practices." In *Women, Autobiography, Theory: A Reader*, edited by Sidonie Smith and Julia Watson, 3–52. New York: University of Wisconsin Press, 1998.

Smyth, Adam. *Autobiography in Early Modern England*. Cambridge: Cambridge University Press, 2010.

Stanley, Liz. "The Epistolarium: On Theorizing Letters and Correspondences." *Auto/Biography* 12 (2004): 201–35.

Steedman, Carolyn. *Past Tenses. Essays on Writing, Autobiography and History*. London: Rivers Oram Press, 1992.

Stefánsdóttir, Guðrún Valgerður, og Sólveig Ólafsdóttir. "The Peculiar Attitude of the People: The Life and Social Conditions of One 'Feebleminded' Girl in the Early 20th Century." In *Understanding Disability Throughout History: Interdisciplinary Perspectives in Iceland from Settlement to 1936*, edited by Hanna Björg Sigurjónsdóttir and James G. Rice, 58–75. London: Routledge, 2022.

Stefánsson, Hjörleifur. *From Earth: Icelandic Turf Houses*, translated by Anna Yates. Reykjavík: Gullinsnið, 2019.

Stoklund, Bjarne. "On Interpreting Peasant Diaries: Material Life and Collective Consciousness." *Ethnologia Europea* 2 (1979–1980): 191–206.

Studies in Autobiography, edited by James Olney. London: Oxford University Press, 1988.

Szijártó, István M. "Four Arguments for Microhistory." *Rethinking History* 6, no. 2 (2002): 209–15.

Thompson, Paul. *The Voice of the Past. Oral History*. Oxford: Oxford University Press, 1978.

Thompson, Paul. "Life Histories and the Analysis of Social Change." In *Biography and Society. The Life History Approach in the Social Sciences*, edited by Daniel Bertaux, 289–306. Beverly Hills: Saga, 1981.

Þórarinsson, Sigurður. "Population Changes in Iceland." *The Geographical Review* 3 (1961): 519–20.

Trivellato, Francesca. "Microhistoria/Microhistorie/Microhistory." *French Politics, Culture and Society* 33, no. 1 (2015): 122–34.

Tullett, William, Inger Leemans, Hsuan Hsu, Stephanie Weismann, Cecilia Bembibre, Melanie A. Kiechle, Duane Jethro, Anna Chen, Xuelei Huang, Jorge Otero-Pailos, and Mark Bradley. "Smell, History, and Heritage." *American Historical Review*, AHR History Lab, 127, no. 1 (March 2022): 261–310.

Vermeer, Leonieke. "Stretching the Archives: Ego-documents and Life Writing Research in the Netherlands: State of the Art." *Low Countries Historical Review* 135, no. 1 (2020): 31–69.

Vésteinsson, Orri. *The Christianization of Iceland: Priests, Power and Social Change 1000–1300*. Oxford: Oxford University Press, 2000.

Vincent, David. *Bread, Knowledge and Freedom: A Study of Nineteenth-Century Working-Class Autobiography*. London: Routledge, 1981.

Virastau, Nicolae Alexandru. *Early Modern French Autobiography*. Leiden: Brill, 2021.
Wong, Sau-ling Cynthia. "Autobiography as Guided Chinatown Tour? Maxime Hong Kingston's The Woman Warrior and the Chinese-American Autobiographical Controversy." In *Multicultural Autobiography: American Lives*, edited by James Robert Payne, 248–79. Knoxvill: University of Tennessee Press, 1992.

Index

Note: Page numbers followed by "n" refer to notes

Agnarsdóttir, Anna 49
archives
 cataloguing and analysis 34
 diaries and manuscripts 35
 manuscript culture of modern era 33–5
 medieval heritage 33
 miscatalogued and inaccessible 33–4
 Parliamentary Archive 231 n.54
 research 201 n.29
Ariès, Philippe 54
Árnason, Magnús H. 140, 150
Arnason, Sigurður 166
Ásmundsson, Grettir 154
Aspects of Biography (Maurois) 70
assessment methods 109
Á tveimur jafnfljótum (*Shanks' Pony*) (Jónsson) 139–40
autobiographical material 3, 44–5
 analysis 51, 64–5
 Icelandic culture in 129
 micro and macro approaches 109
 use of personal documents 52
autobiography, Icelandic egodocuments 113–24, 213 n.7, *see also* late Twentieth century, egodocuments in
 biographical turn 119
 cultural turn 118
 death 117
 Ginzburg's analysis on memory 122–3
 Jochumsson on recall of the past 114–15
 kvöldvaka or winter-eve gathering 116–17
 memory and personal experience 121, 123–124
 microhistorical research, features 122
 notions about life 99–100
 Parliamentarians, writing of 120
 peasantry 121
 perceptual sources 119
 technological advances 119
 telling a story or giving shape to readable text 113
 traumatic event in families 117
 vagabond with storytelling skill 115
 video recordings of family gatherings 119–20
 work, ideology of 116
 working-class people's direct testimony 118
 writing of (*see* writing of autobiography)
auto-fiction 3, 99, 119

baðstofa (communal living/sleeping loft) 105, 116–18, 152, 184
Baggerman, Arianne 42, 70
Banks, Sir Josephs 50
barefoot historians 32–3, 35, 36, 39
barndómi (*In Childhood*) (Sigurðardóttir) 147
Barthes, Roland 83
Benediktsson, Rev. Gunnar 86, 106, 167
Berg, Friðgeir H. 85, 91, 114
Bíbí in Berlín (Bjargey Kristjánsdóttir) 128–31
 childhood 129
 extensive autobiography 129–30
 life and experience of excluded woman 130–1
 methods of microhistory 128
 uniqueness 130
biographème 83
biographical tradition 25–43, 66
biography 27, 70, 97, 142–4
Birkiland, Jóhannes 99, 106–7, 126, 128
Bjarnadóttir, Viktoría 177
Bjarnason, Jósef 181

Bjarnason, Þorkell   135
Björnsdóttir, Guðrún   165
Björnsson, Jósef   116, 118, 127, 182
Blómsturvellir, Eyrabakka   108
book and sources   3–5, *see also* writing of autobiography
book history   29, 120
Bræðraborg, Seyðisfirði   93
Brautryðjendur (Pioneers) (Gíslason)   121
broad-brush approach   47
Buchmann, Marlis   48
Burnett, John   94

categories and subcategories   108
Chartier, Roger   67
childhood and death   158–65
   child-raising and status of children   158–9
   death, impact of   160–1, 164
   dream of future events   162–3
   helplessness and fear   163
   mental anguish, description of   159
   parental involvement   164–5
   religious belief and folklore   160
Church and Social Change (Pétursson)   18
classification system   101, 105, 107–8
class structure and economy   13–17
   act of 1887   15
   barter and money supply   16–17
   crown officials   14
   groups in agricultural society   14
   labor intensive agriculture   13
   landless poor   15
   landowning farmers   14
   legislation of social classes   13–14
   lodgers   14
   merchants   14
   paupers   14
   permission to settle   15
   seasonal fishing (*see* fishing)
   sub-tenants   14
   tenant farmers   14
   unattached wage earners   13
clergy   18, 126, 184
comparative truth   98–9
Conflicting Paths (Graff)   50, 67
considered censorship   72

conversational books   3, 46, 119–20, 125–6, 146
creative class approach   51
cultural environment in Iceland   45, 91–2
cultural history   31–2, 35, 53, 67, 119
cultural turn   64, 118
culture
   of confession   147–8
   Icelandic circumstances and   133–4
   Icelandic literary culture   28
   literacy   113, 120–1, 126–7, 132–3, 166, 174–6
   manuscript   33–5 (*see also* manuscript culture)
   peasant   36, 172, 221 n.21
   popular   125, 132
   scribal   28–31, 37, 120 (*see also* scribal culture)
   self in Icelandic culture   128
   of testimony   190

daily life   29, 55, 89, 91, 99, 118, 134, 149, 171, *see also* life course
Darnton, Robert   29
Davis, Nathalie Zemon   146
Dekker, Rudolf   42, 70
Design and Truth in Autobiography (Pascal)   55
Dithery, Wilhelm   77
Djúpavogi   177
Dúason, Sæmundur   150, 162

economy   17, 169, *see also* class structure and economy
education   18, 31, 36, 116–17, 119, 127, 174–5
   formal   37, 155, 174–5, 177
   informal   133, 174
   legally compulsory education system   130
   of peasantry   134
   work and (*see* work and education)
egodocuments   5, 195 n.1, 219 n.1
   creation of *self*   53
   life story approach   52
   life writing and   3
   narrative sources   54
   new focus on   52–5
   objective approach   54

personal documents in academic
    research 52
quantitative methods 53
reasons for writing of 100
sociohistorical changes 52–3
in Twentieth Century (*see also*
    late Twentieth century,
    egodocuments in)
  autobiographical material 44–5
  conversational books 46
  creative class approach 51
  evidence about the past 49
  grand narrative approach 47
  historical constructedness or
      historicity 51
  individuals' experience 51
  institutionalized life course 49
  integration 51
  life-course analysis 47–9
  linking of interactions 48–9
  Loftur's methods 47
  new focus on 52–5
  parenting methods and domestic
      discipline 46
  period traditional approach 51
  questionnaire 51
  redefined approach 51
  religious and spiritual
      dynamism 45
  rhythm of the moment 49
  semi autobiographies 46
  slaves 45
  traditional approach 51
  types of 47
Einarsson, Guðmundur J. 169
Einarsson, Helgi 113
Einarsson, Indriði 160, 176
Einu sinni var (*Once Upon a Time*)
    (Dúason) 150
Elias, Norbert 54
Elíasdóttir, Guðmunda 145
Emilsson, Tryggvi 82
emotions 172–8
  communities 165–6, 229 n.25
  education 175
  formal and informal education 174
  grief and care 165
  history of 65
  lack of emotional support 172

literary figures from the sagas 178
modernization process 175
moral authority 172
newspapers, importance of 177
politics, indirect participation in 176–7
Saga Age or brave stories of
    people 172
Scandinavian sagas 173
story-telling and poetry reciting 174
strategy for survival 173
work on farms 166
Enlightenment 46–7, 189
environment and egodocuments
  ancient sagas and living tradition (*see*
      sagas, ancient)
  approaches of autobiographers 136–41
  authors relationship with
      environment 132
  biography of Esra Pétursson
      controversy 141–3
  demand for truth 136–41
  evaluation of story 145
  Icelandic circumstances and
      culture 133–4
  Ingólfur's problems 143
  Jóhanna's portrayal of her parents-in-
      law 138
  literary motifs 152–7 (*see also*
      motifs)
  people and cultural landscape 134–6
  popular culture 132
  psychological longings 133
  responsibility of writers 141–5
  Sigurður's description 137
  unusual qualities 133
  use of autobiographical
      literature 153
  women 145–8
expression
  autobiographical
    effective use 67
    evidence 66–70
    life course (*see* life course)
    memories of past times 67–8
    memory and time (*see* memory)
    motivation for 68–9
    motives behind autobiographical
        writing 68–9

quantitative and qualitative
approaches 70
reliability of subject (*see* subject,
reliability of)
sources (*see* sources)
subjective sources 68
glorification of sagas 186–7
language 185
marriage 186
modes of 184–7
productive years 186
society and environment, influence
of 185
storytelling tradition 185–6
Eyland, Valdimar J. 163, 174

Falur, Einar 138–9
family 17–21
bonded service 18
children's education 18
distant relatives 20
Edict on Household Discipline,
1746 18
family sharing a single farm 21
foster children 19
hierarchical relationship, masters and
servants 18–19
high marriageable age 18–19
land acquisition 17–18
mean household size (MHS) 17
patriarchal household 18
private paupers 19
fiction 25, 44
in scholarship 215 n.32
fishing 8–9, 14–17
Fljótshlíð, farm in 86
Fortíðardraumar (*Dreams of Things
Past*) 28
Franklin, Benjamin 76
The French Worker (Traugott) 57, 61,
210 n.34
Freud, Sigmund 142
Friðgeir H. Berg 85, 91, 114
future after confirmation 166–71
attitude to work 168–9
experience of emotions 166
family life 169
next life stages, accounts of 169
orphans 167

process of achievements in life 170
productive years 171
structure of Icelandic society 171
teenage years, accounts of 168
Fyrir 40 árum (40 Years Ago) 135

Garraty, John A. 72, 95
Geirsdóttir, Kristín 155
genealogy 28, 97, 105
Genovese, Eugene D. 45
Ginzburg, Carlo 40, 121–3, 128
Gíslason, Vilhjálmur Þ. 121
Glaumbær, Skagafjörður 130
Glerárþorp, Akureyri 111
Graff, Harvey J. 50, 67, 98
grand narrative approach 33, 39, 46–7,
65, 145
Grettir's saga 150, 153–4
Grímsey 1, 179
Grímsson, Sighvatur 32
Grímsstaðir, Eyrabakka 64
Guðmundsdóttir, Guðrún 161
Guðmundsson, Sigurður Jón 162
Gunnlaugsson, Gísli Ágúst 11, 13, 14,
17–20
Guttormsson, Loftur 46, 71

Hálfdanarson, Guðmundur 7, 45, 67,
71, 172
Halldórsdóttir, Erla Huld 49
Halldórsson, Elías 160
Hallgrímsdóttir, Guðný 34, 146
Hallgrímsson, Friðrik 168
Haraldsson, Helgi 155
Helgason, Ásmundur 165
Helgason, Magnús 117
historical constructedness or
historicity 51
historical truth 97
historiography 70
history
book 29, 120
cultural 31–2, 35, 53, 67, 119
cultural turn in 118
life-history approach 209 n.29
microhistory 37
of smell 218 n.2
History of Autobiography in Antiquity
(Misch) 76

Högnason, Jón Gísli 181
Hólakot, Borgarfirði 77
Holocaust of 1930s and 1940s 74
Hornstrendingabók (*Book of the People of Hornstrandir*) (Bjarnason) 147
household, *see also* family
  baðstofa (communal living/sleeping loft) 116
  discussion of sagas 151
  Edict on Household Discipline 18
  farming 13
  foster children and distant relatives 19–20
  mean household size (MHS) 17
  patriarchal household 18
  possession of 15
  size 9
  standards of diligence 116
  status 14
  tasks 181
  winter-eve gathering 174
Hreinsson, Viðar 151, 153
Hvammstangi 54

Icelandic autobiography, *see* autobiography, Icelandic egodocuments
Icelandic Commonwealth 149
Icelandic emigration to North America 9, 197 n.22
Icelandic School of microhistory 1–43, 195 n.5, 223 n.43
Icelandic society 5, 10, 16, 36, 51, 109, 127, 132, 138, 157, 171, 187, 190, 227 n.53
industrialization 17, 78–9, 175
Industrial Revolution 7, 79
infant mortality 8, 160
infrastructure 37, 45, 135
Ingólfsson, Einar Falur 138
interpretation 38, 60, 63, 71, 76, 89, 124, 152, 172, 188
Interpreting Women's Lives 145–6
Íslensk bókmenntasaga (*History of Icelandic Literature*) 27
Italian School of Microhistory 31

Jakobsson, Jökull 92, 137
Jakobsson, Þór 139
Jochumsson, Matthías 88, 90, 114, 117, 159

Jóhannsson, Björn 159
Johansson, Egil 175
Jónasson, Jónas 173
Jónsdóttir, Guðbjörg 176
Jónsdóttir, Ólína 175
Jónsson, Bergsteinn 120
Jónsson, Einar 176
Jónsson, Finnur 80
Jónsson, Guðbrandur 25–7
Jónsson, Guðmundur 176
Jónsson, Halldór 31–2
Jónsson, Níels 31–2, 90
Jónsson, Tryggvi 84
Jósefsson, Ágúst 85
Journal of Social History 42

Keflavík, Hegranes 136
Keldumýrar á Síðu 20
Kjær, Holger 151
Kohlin, Martin 95, 97
Kristjánsdóttir, Bjargey 129
Kristjónsdóttir, Jóhanna 92, 137–8, 141
kvöldvaka (winter-eve gathering), *see* winter-eve gathering, principle of

Landnámabók (*Book of Settlements*) 28
Lárusson, Jón Kr. 160
Laslett, Barbara 63
late Twentieth century, egodocuments in 55–65
  class conflict 55–6
  committee, University of Iceland 59–61
  comparison with outside sources 58
  credibility of autobiography 57
  cultural turn 64
  demographic research 59, 61
  devotional autobiographies 55–65
  exploitation and injustice 55
  France, working-class autobiography 61–2
  historiographical issues 64
  Maynes, historical approach of 61–5
  official statistics 62
  personal narratives 55
  quantitative research model 56, 62
  strategy of selection 62
  subjective measure of human behavior 58

systematic analysis of
  autobiographies 57
working-class autobiographies 58
letters 3–4, 117, 126
  personal letters 119
  use of letters in historical
    scholarship 49
life course 79–87, 207 n.13
  analysis 47–9
  biographème 83
  challenges 83
  childhood and death (*see* childhood
    and death)
  confirmation ceremony 84–5
  from confirmation to marriage 80–1
  emotional communities 165–6 (*see
    also* emotions)
  emotional experiences 86–7
  family life 82
  formal elements of 83
  formal institution 83
  future (*see* future after confirmation)
  historical demography 79
  Icelandic agrarian society 80
  life-course analysis model 79
  from marriage and to death 82
  stocktaking 84
  transitions 82–3
  work, role of 80
life-history approach 209 n.29
life stages 47–8, 50, 61, 80–4, 87–9, 92,
    158, 163, 169–71, 192, 216 n.42,
    see also life course
life stories 143, 186, 189
  approach 52
  reasons for writing 100
Liljewall, Britt 63
literacy culture 113, 120–1, 126–7,
    132–3, 166, 174–6
literature 27–9, 52–3, 113–25, 132, 141–
    2, 147, 149–50, 153, 157, 172–8,
    185, 188, 215 n.33, 227 n.46
Litli-Gjábakki, Vestmannaeyjar 192
Ljúfa vor (*A Lovely Spring*)
    (Árnason) 140
local community
  assessed farms (*lögbýli*) 10
  collective control of government by
    farmers 13

commune 10–11
dependent farms 11
expansion in the farming
    community 11
independent farms 10
large space of pasturing 12
personal independence 12
poor relief 12
poor relief and its administration 11–12
sveitalimur 12
Love, Harold 30
Lutheran Reformation 19

Magnúsdóttir, Monika 3
Magnússon, Hannes J. 92, 173
Magnússon, Magnús S. 16, 137
The Making of the English Working Class
    (Thompson) 45
manuscript culture 33–5
Margeirsson, Ingólfur 141–4
Mascuch, Michael 42, 70
Maurois, André 70, 74–5
Maynes, Mary Jo 52–3, 55, 57–60, 63–4
memory 187–91
  collective memory 187
  and concept of time 77–9, 215 n.30
    change 78
    industrialization 79
    issues, using egodocuments 78
    proto-industry 78–9
    reliability of memory 77
  cultural memory 187
  culture of testimony 190
  Enlightenment, heritage of 189
  historical memory 187–8
  individual memory 187–8
  self-expression in Iceland 188–9
  studies 65
Menntun, ást og sorg (*Education, Love, and
    Grief*) 32
metamorphosis 86
metastories 101, 103
methods of microhistory 32, 34, 37, 41,
    49, 65–6, 118, 122–4, 128, 146,
    222 n.31
microhistory development and
    egodocuments 31–3, 205 n.51
  barefoot historians, activities 36–7
  context of local knowledge 33

historical study within local
    setting 35
Icelandic manuscript collections 32
in-between spaces, method 36
informal institution of scribal
    culture 37
microhistorians 31
minor knowledge 32, 37
Sighvatur's diaries 32
singularization of history 36
Miðgrund, Skagafirði 31
Mímisson, Kristján 36
Minor Catechism (Luther) 18, 166, 174–5
minor knowledge 30, 32, 37, 223 n.43
Misch, Georg 76, 150
Modell, John 48
Modern Intellectual History 29
modernization process 175, 215 n.39
motifs
    big personality traits 154
    coal-biter motif in
        autobiographies 153–4, 157
    feeling for the material 156
    folktale motif 154
    Golden Age, glossy image of 154
    great hero, image of 154
    heroic motifs 154
    influence of sagas 153
    literary motifs 152–7
    male Cinderella motif 153
    narrative methods 153
    religious or mythological
        material 148–9
    saga heroes/scholars 154
    sagas power 156
    self-image of rural Icelanders 155
    story of Jacob and Esau 153

narrative sources 45, 47, 54, 62, 66, 69, 79, 128
National Museum of Iceland 4, 51, 126, 227 n.53
natural disasters 8, 197 n.20
The Nature of Biography (Garraty) 72
Nazi genocide 74
negative elements 108
newspapers and periodicals 4
Njáls saga 155

non-traditional education 37, 95, 119, 133, 174, 183, 190, see also education
Nordal, Guðrún 155–6
Nordal, Sigurður 172–3
Nottingham Trent University 34, 147

objective approach 54
Ólafsson, Arnljótur 164
Ólafsson, Davíð 30, 32, 34, 36, 127
Ólafur, Reverend 25
Ólason, Vésteinn 149–50
Ormarsstaðir, Fellum 156
Orser, Charles, Jr. 36
Öxl, Snæfellsnes 184

Pálsson, Tryggvi 162
Parliamentary Archive 231 n.54
Pascal, Roy 55
Passerini, Luisa 58
Pastor, Fire 26–7, 84–5
peasant culture 36, 172, 221 n.21
people and cultural landscape,
    Iceland 6–10, 134–6
    autonomy, notions of 135–6
    capitalist modes of agriculture 7
    Danish crown, subjects of 6
    emigration to North America 9
    epidemics, earthquakes, and
        eruptions 8
    equivalence in environment and
        life 134
    farming 10
    fishing (*see* fishing)
    isolation 7
    kingdom of Norway 6
    labor-intensive business 9
    laws on bonded service 10
    marriage, age of 8
    memoir, decisive response to 135
    mode of production 9–10
    rural with farmsteads 7
    system of tied service 9
    working year, division of 9
Perdita Project: Early Modern Women's
    Manuscript Compilations 34, 146
Perlur og steinar (*Pearls and Stones*)
    (Kristjónsdóttir) 137

personal documents in academic
    research 52
personal narratives 55, 57, 64, 145
personal sources 56, 59, 146, 202 n.35
Pétursson, Esra 141–2, 144
Pétursson, Pétur 18
Pétursson, Rev. Þorsteinn 26
Pierce, Jennifer L. 63
Pietism 47
poets 88, 90, 92, 114, 134, 137, 143,
    150–1, 154, 169, 173–4, 176–7,
    184, 191
political autobiography 101
Pollock, Linda A. 52
popular culture 4–5, 34, 37, 47, 113, 119,
    125–6, 132
population 4, 6–13, 16–17, 19, 30,
    59–60, 62, 79, 97, 113, 134, 164
poverty 5, 11, 20, 82, 101, 103, 105, 135,
    152, 167, 169, 173
proto-industry 78–9

quantitative methods 52–3, 61, 67, 124,
    213 n.8

Raufarhöfn 42, 164
redefined approach 51
Reisubók Jóns Indíafara (Jónsson) 25
Reykir, Ölfusi 23
rímur 116, 150, 227 n.46
Rist, Lárus J. 163
Roll, Jordan, Roll (Genovese) 45
Rousseau, Jean-Jacques 102

Sæmundsson, Matthías Viðar 27, 142
saga literature 28, 113, 153
sagas, ancient 148–52, 226 n.42
    ancient literature, influence of 150,
        152
    attitudes to education 151
    farming communities 149
    Icelandic Commonwealth 149
    and living tradition 148–52
    Saga Age, Icelanders of 148
    sagas of Icelanders 148
    story-reading tradition 149
    themes and motifs 148
    winter-eve gatherings on the
        farm 151

St. Andrews University 32
scholarship 5, 33–5, 42, 49, 59, 66,
    70, 120, 128, 146–7, 215 n.32,
    226 n.36
Scott-Warren, Jason 31
scribal culture 29–31, 120
    manuscript community 31
    manuscript network 31
    manuscript transmission 30–1
    role of minor knowledge 30
    scribal communities 30
*Scribal Publication in Early-Modern
    Europe* (Love) 30
The Script of Life in Modern Society
    (Buchmann) 48
Second World War 55, 104–5
self, formation of
    autobiographies as sources 89
    childhood 89
    cultural environment in Iceland 92
    environmental and cultural
        circumstances 89
    in Icelandic culture 128
    in Icelandic historical context 25–9
        campaign for self-
            determination 26
        educated Icelanders 29
        genealogy 28
        literary culture 28
        literary genre 27
        manuscripts, preservation 26, 28
        paper 28
        peasantry 28
        prehistory of egodocuments 28
        saga literature 28–9
        scribal culture 28–9
        Turkish Raid 25
        vice 26
    personality, shaping from materials
        supplied by memory 89
    personal testimony 93
    relating events and life 89–90
    relationship with time 92
    self-confrontation 91
    stocktaking 92
    subjectivity of 93–9
        comparative truth 98–9
        historical truth 97
        personal testimony 93

self-creation or refashioning of
    self 95
self-images in egodocuments 94
social truth 97–8
subjective quality of
    autobiographies 94–5
subjective truth 95–7
semi autobiographies 3, 45–6, 101,
    125–6, 141, 143–6
Shorter, Edward 52
Short Tales of Myself (Jochumsson) 88
Sighvatur Grímsson, case of 32
Sigurbjarnarson, Hafsteinn 12, 151,
    167–8, 170
Sigurðardóttir, Jakobína 147
Sigurðsson, Jón 26, 188
Sigurðsson, Kristján 158
Sigurðsson, Ólafur 135
A Sinner's Requiem (Esra) 143–4
Skagafjörður 123
Skallagrímsson, Egill 154
Skírnir (Kristín) 155
slaves 25, 44–5, 176
Snjóholt, Eiðaþinghá 191
social history 53–4, 66, 94, 118, 124,
    209 n.30
social issues 184, *see also* work and
    education
Social Science Historical Association 59
Social Science History 56, 58
social truth 58, 97–8
society 5–6
sources 75–7, 204 n.50
    abstraction 38–9
    auto-delusion 76
    comparative approaches 41
    contextualization 38–9
    discourses of individual groups 39
    egodocuments for historical
        scholarship 42
    evidential paradigm, Ginzburg's 40
    examples 41
    generalization 38–9
    grand narrative 39
    Icelandic egodocuments 195 n.5
        categories of sources 125
        database 124, 126
        firsthand sources as
            egodocuments 126
        lack of women's
            autobiographies 125, 127
        personal writing and real-life
            experience, relationship 126
        popular culture in Iceland 1850–
            1940 125
        self in Icelandic culture 128
        semi-autobiographies 126
        source group and source
            bank 128
        350+ autobiographies 125
        women's general self-
            expression 125
    interplay of events, narrative and
        analysis 40
    life and works of "barefoot
        historians" 39
    limitations of language 75
    Luise White's writing 40–1
    mentalités, the history of
        mentalities 42
    microhistory 37
    models 76
    singularization of history 37, 39
    style 76
    textual environment 40
    time 75
    work outward and inward 38
Speaking with Vampires (White) 40
Stefánsson, Bernharð 80
Steingrímsson, Rev. Jón 26–7
Stephansson, Stephan G. 154
Stoklund, Bjarne 52
storytelling 115, 174, 185–6
subject, reliability of 70–5
    children's memories 71–2
    considered censorship 72–3
    linguistic limitations 73
    Maurois' description of memory 74–5
    recovered memories of events 73
    scientific reliability of sources 72
    systematic censorship of
        memory 70–1
subjective truth 95–7
subjective world 191–3
subjectivity 94, *see also* self, formation of
Syndugur maður segir frá (*Testimony of a
    Sinner*) (Magnússon) 137
Sýnisbók íslenskrar alþýðumenningar 34

Taking the Hard Road (Maynes)   55
Tale of Þorvaldur the Far-Traveled   153
Telling Stories (Maynes)   63
Þegar veðri slotar (*When the Weather Dies Down*) (Sigurðsson)   158
Þjóðólfur (periodical)   105–6, 135
Thompson, E. P.   45
Þórbergsson, Jón   164
Þorsteinsson, Hannes   105–6
traditional approach   51
traditional social history   212 n.5, *see also* social history
Traugott, Mark   57, 61–2
travel book   25, 27, 46, 104
truth
   comparative (*see* comparative truth)
   demand for   136–41
   historical (*see* historical truth)
   social (*see* social truth)
   subjective (*see* subjective truth)
Tulinius, Torfi H.   185
Twelve-Step Program pioneered by Alcoholics Anonymous   102

Úlfstaðir, Landeyjum   6
University of Iceland   27, 34, 45–6, 49, 59–60, 120, 142
unpublished autobiographies   104–5

vagabonds   115, 134, 184, 220 n.9
Vallakot, Grímsey   68
Víkingur, Sveinn   166
Vincent, David   91–2
Virastau, Nicolae Alexandru   42
von Ranke, Leopold   53

Warwick University   34, 147
weather report   90
"What Is the History of Books?" (Darnton)   29
White, Luise   40
winter-eve gathering, principle of   29, 116, 132, 134, 137, 149, 151, 173 4, 176, 182–4
women   145–8, *see also* Bíbí in Berlín (Bjargey Kristjánsdóttir)
   culture of confession   147–8
   general self-expression   125
   interviews   146
   lack of autobiographies   125, 127
   material in archives unascribed or under the male names   146
   methods of microhistory   146
   story of Martin Guerre   146
work and education   80, 178, 181–4
   campaign for Iceland's self-determination   183
   concept of education   183
   debate on social matters   184
   entertainment   182–3
   fathers, role of   181–2
   pedagogy   183
   religion   183
working class   44–5, 52, 55, 58–9, 61–2, 118, 136, 188
writing of autobiography   99–109
   assessment methods   109
   book
      of confession   102
      with global perspective   103
      of heritage conservation   103
      of justification   101, 105–6
      of life course   102
      of life experience   103–4
      of nostalgia   102
      of propaganda   101–2
      of reckoning   102
      of self-glorification   103
      of tales   102
   categories and subcategories   108
   classification system   107–8
   incentive behind the writing   100
   metastories   101
   negative elements   108
   political autobiography   101
   reasons for writing of egodocuments   100
   reflection of author's notions about life   99–100
   travel books   104
   unpublished autobiographies   104–5

www.ingramcontent.com/pod-product-compliance
Lightning Source LLC
Chambersburg PA
CBHW071818300426
44116CB00009B/1355